W9-BTJ-874

Emotion Concepts

Zoltán Kövecses

Emotion Concepts

Springer-Verlag
New York Berlin Heidelberg
London Paris Tokyo Hong Kong

Zoltán Kövecses
Department of English
Eötvös Loránd University
1052 Budapest
Hungary

Note: Chapter 4, "Anger," was coauthored with George Lakoff, and Chapter 10, "The Concept of Emotion: Further Metaphors," with Jim Averill.

Library of Congress Cataloging-in-Publication Data
Kövecses, Zoltán.
Emotion concepts/Zoltán Kövecses.
p. cm.
ISBN 0-387-97115-7 (alk. paper)
1. Emotions. I. Title.
BF531.K68 1989
152.4—dc20 89-36504

Printed on acid-free paper.

Typeset by TCSystems, Inc., Shippensburg, Pennsylvania.
Printed and bound by Edwards Brothers, Inc., Ann Arbor, Michigan.
Printed in the United States of America.

9 8 7 6 5 4 3 2 1

ISBN-0-387-97115-7 Springer-Verlag New York Berlin Heidelberg
ISBN 3-540-97115-7 Springer-Verlag Berlin Heidelberg New York

Acknowledgments

It is only appropriate tc begin with expressing my greatest appreciation to my collaborators in this project: George Lakoff and Jim Averill. If it turns out that the two best chapters, or the only good chapters in the book are those that I have done jointly with them, this will no doubt be due to the fact that they have collaborated with me on these chapters. I consider myself very fortunate to have had the opportunity to work with them.

I gratefully acknowledge the help and intellectual generosity of all the people who have read the manuscript in whole or in part. The thoughtful comments, suggestions, and critical remarks made by Jim Averill, Carolyn Mervis, Sy Epstein, Susan Fiske, Sy Berger, Wolfgang Stroebe, László T. András, Susan Gal, Claudia Ucros, Ede Frecska, Mihaly Péter, Brian King, Katalin E. Kiss, and Tim Jay have done much to improve earlier versions of the manuscript.

I owe a great deal to the participants, both students and guests, of my seminar "The Language of Emotion" in the Department of Psychology at the University of Massachusetts at Amherst in the fall of 1987 for their interest, insights, and criticism. More generally, this department, and especially the chair Sy Berger, provided me with an extremely pleasant atmosphere for both teaching and working on the book. I am thankful for his and the university's generosity.

The final phase of the research for this book was supported by a grant from the Fulbright Foundation, which made it possible for me to spend the fall semester of 1987 in Amherst as a visiting scholar.

I feel I should also acknowledge a great deal of intellectual debt to reviewers and critiques of my earlier related publications. Some of the comments made primarily by Anna Wierzbicka and Andrew Ortony have forced me to change my earlier views on some points. Although I am sure they still disagree with me on more points than they agree, they should know that I have a great deal of respect for their work.

Last but not least, I want to thank my wife, Judit Farkas, for her love, support, and encouragement. Without her, this book could not have become a reality and I would know less about emotion.

Zoltán Kövecses
Budapest, Hungary

Contents

1 Introduction

This chapter briefly describes the general goals of the book, introduces the most fundamental features of the methodology that is employed to achieve these goals, and gives an outline of the structure of the book. A more detailed account of the goals and methodology is presented in chapters 2 and 3, respectively.

What the Book Is About

The main objective of this study is to attempt to answer the question: How do people understand their emotions? As we shall see in the next chapter, a large number of scholars have tried to provide answers to this question. The interest in the way people understand their emotions has led scholars to the issue of the nature of emotion concepts and emotional meaning. Since the notion of understanding involves or presupposes the notions of concept and meaning, it was only natural for scholars with an interest in the way people understand their emotions to turn their attention to emotion concepts and the meaning associated with emotion terms. So the broader issue has often become more specific. For example, Davitz in his *The Language of Emotion* formulated the central question in the following way: "What does a person mean when he says someone is happy or angry or sad?" (Davitz 1969: 1).

This book is *not* about the emotions as such: It is about the nature of emotion concepts. Emotion concepts have been studied for a long time in a variety of disciplines. There is, I think, a common thread that runs through most of the research directed at emotion concepts. I believe that the common thread is that a particular conception of semantics is assumed by most of the various approaches; namely, that semantics in general is a matter of necessary and sufficient features. According to this view, to study emotion concepts is to find out what those necessary and sufficient features are for each emotion concept. Thus, in these types of approaches, emotion concepts are seen as having a simple structure (a small set of features) and minimal conceptual content (just enough content to distinguish each emotion concept from every other emotion concept).

The study of emotion concepts is, as we have just seen, couched in the traditional conception of categories in general. This has the consequence that if there is something wrong with this more general classical view (as the traditional conception of concepts has become known), then there is also something wrong with the more specific view of emotion concepts as sets of necessary and sufficient conditions. In what follows, I will try to show that emotion concepts have a more complex and elaborate structure and have a much richer conceptual content than is suggested by the classical view on which descriptions of emotion concepts are, knowingly or unknowingly, based.

In particular, six specific emotion concepts will be examined. Four of them are basic-level emotion concepts: anger, fear, pride, and respect. The fifth is the subordinate concept of romantic love and the sixth is the superordinate category of emotion.

There are two notions that are particularly relevant to the study of the structure and content of emotion concepts as visualized in the present approach: those of prototype and cognitive model (or frame). The idea that concepts are best defined in terms of best examples, or prototypes, goes against the view of concepts as minimal sets of features, and the notion of cognitive models is invoked to represent what the prototypes might look like. Thus, I take emotion concepts to be prototypical cognitive models. (This of course implies that there are also nonprototypical cognitive models associated with particular emotions. More of this in subsequent chapters.)

One very important characteristic of the cognitive models that I am interested in is that they represent our folk understandings of emotion. In this regard, they are opposed to what can be called "scientific theories," or "expert theories," of emotion. It may be objected: "What is the use of a scientific (linguistic) analysis of our folk theories of emotion?" "What is the purpose of uncovering what particular emotions are widely thought to be (the folk models), as opposed to what they really are (the expert theories)?" First of all, I would like to believe that there is a great deal of intrinsic interest in this kind of endeavor. In any case, it seems to me that there is certainly not less interest in it than in the study of emotion concepts along the classical lines. Second, I will try to show that, at least in the domain of emotion, folk and expert theories are interrelated in interesting and important ways. It seems that folk conceptualizations of emotions can affect or at least motivate scientific thinking. In order to begin to understand these relationships, it is absolutely necessary to get clear about our folk theories of emotion as well. (More discussion of this issue can be found in the last two chapters.)

Methodology

At the heart of the methodology with which I propose to study emotion concepts is language. The basic idea here is that the conventionalized language we use to talk about the emotions can be an important tool in discovering the structure and contents of our emotion concepts and that, furthermore, the emotion concepts we have can reveal a great deal about our experiences of emotion. Thus, in its global outline, though not in some of the details, our program and methodology are very much in line with the program and methodology recently proposed by philosopher Rom Harré. He says in this connection

> that two social matters impinge heavily on the personal experience of emotion. These are the local language and the local moral order. The philosophical analysis of the emotion concepts carried by local vocabularies is supposed to reveal the deep grammatical rules by which we can express the conventions for their use. (Harré 1986: 9–10)

In our case, the local vocabulary of emotion is that of English, and it is through this vocabulary that we try to probe into the nature of emotion concepts in the community of English speakers.

There is a recent upsurge of interest among psychologists in language as a possibly useful source of information concerning emotion concepts (see, for example, Scherer et al. 1986, Shaver et al. 1987, Duck and Pond 1988). A large body of their research is conducted by making use of a questionnaire method. The emotion prototypes are elicited by a series of questionnaire prompts. However, I believe that the use of conventionalized language (i.e., that of the local vocabulary, in Harré's terminology) in uncovering emotion prototypes helps us eliminate two possible weaknesses associated with the questionnaire method. The first weakness of the questionnaire method is that the subjects who answer the prompts may employ various psychological mechanisms (especially ego-defense) with the result of distorting their responses (Scherer et al. 1986). Since the collection and study of emotion vocabulary can essentially be done independently from the participation of subjects in experimental situations, the proposed methodology can eliminate the subjective factors that characterize the questionnaire method. Second, the kinds of prompts that are asked will also bias the answers that are given (Shaver et al. 1987). That is, the biases of the researcher are projected into the subjects. If, however, we rely only on the use of conventionalized language with both the researchers (and their biases) and the subjects removed, we seem to have a better chance of reconstructing our culturally defined emotion concepts.

A major part of the methodology I am suggesting is its reliance on such figures of speech as metaphor and metonymy. In this respect, too, there has been an increasing amount of awareness on the part of researchers investigating a variety of psychological phenomena. For example, Roedigger (1980) investigated metaphors for memory, Gentner and Grudin (1985) studied psychologists' metaphors of the nature and functioning of the mind in the past 90 years, and Reddy (1979) explored what he called the "conduit" metaphor for communication.

Metaphors also play a significant role in the way we conceive of the emotions. Still, only a few scholars have paid close attention to them and have studied them systematically. A major exception and a pioneer in taking metaphors seriously in the study of emotion is Jim Averill. Averill (1974) showed that psychophysiological symbolism has had a major influence on past and present thinking concerning emotion and bodily change. In a more recent study, he examined six groups of emotion metaphors on which six dominant theories of emotion can be assumed to be based (Averill, in press). Chapter 11, coauthored with Jim Averill, is a more systematic linguistic analysis and a reworking of that paper. In yet another paper (Averill, Catlin, and Chon, in press) performed an exhaustive analysis of metaphors for hope that are found in various clichés, sayings, and proverbs in English. Thus, Averill is perhaps the first to recognize and appreciate the full significance of metaphor in both our everyday and scientific understandings of emotion.

The present study also regards metaphors as playing an important role in our folk and scientific conceptualization of emotion, but also goes beyond it in several ways. First, not only metaphors but also metonymies are seen as contributing to our conceptions of emotion. Second, it will be claimed that at least some emotion concepts incorporate some other emotion concepts, that is, some emotion concepts can be inherent in other emotion concepts (see especially the chapter on romantic love in this connection). Third, it will be proposed that emotion concepts mainly emerge from the three sources we have mentioned so far: metaphors, metonymies, and inherent concepts.

What I mean by saying that emotion concepts mainly emerge from these three sources is that it is the conceptual content of the metaphors, metonymies, and inherent concepts that converge on and hence produce certain prototypical cognitive models associated with particular emotions and with the abstract category of emotion. It is these prototypical cognitive models that can be said to represent, or embody, emotion concepts. The first study along these lines was Lakoff and Kövecses (1983), which, in a slightly revised form, is reproduced here as chapter 4. A paper by Barcelona Sanchez (1985) on sadness and King (1989) on emotion metaphors in Chinese is in the same spirit. A major attraction of this way of thinking about the structure and contents of emotion concepts is that it enables us to have a more comprehensive view of emotion than we are used to. The cognitive models produced by the metaphors, metonymies, and inherent concepts suggest a broad, rich, and detailed view of emotion in which the antecedents, cognitions, subjective feelings, physiological and behavioral responses, control mechanisms, and so forth associated with emotion all find their natural place within the same model. These comprehensive (cognitive) models can thus point up the often one-sided attempts in our theorizing about emotion.

Structure of the Book

The chapters of the book can be logically divided into four parts.

The first part includes the first three chapters and is intended to provide a general introduction to the study of emotion concepts. The present chapter gives the reader an idea of the issues and goals and the methodology with which these goals can be accomplished in a sketchy and informal way. The second chapter is a survey of the most important and representative works in the study of emotion concepts in psychology, linguistics, philosophy, anthropology, and psychiatry, and it attempts a general criticism of previous approaches. The third chapter provides a detailed account of the methodology and discusses the works that approach emotion concepts in a way similar to the present one.

The second group of chapters begins with chapter 4, the study of anger, and ends with chapter 8, which concentrates on a single aspect of romantic love. This group comprises studies of specific emotion concepts; namely, anger, fear, pride, respect, and romantic love. The general purpose here is to show how particular emotion concepts differ from and are similar to each other in terms of conceptual content and to discuss some select aspects of emotion concepts in detail.

The third group of chapters is concerned with the abstract category of emotion with the main aim of showing two things: (a) what the prototype of the superordinate category of emotion is (chapter 11) and (b) that there is a close relationship between the metaphors of emotion found in ordinary language and expert theories of emotion (chapters 9 and 10). Chapter 9 is a detailed study of perhaps the most pervasive metaphor for emotion: the CONTAINER metaphor. Chapter 10 is a systematic survey of other emotion metaphors and that of some corresponding expert theories of emotion. In chapter 11, I describe the prototype of emotion as it emerges from the linguistic materials discussed in chapters 9 and 10.

The concluding chapter (chapter 12), in addition to being a summary, provides a discussion of the most important issues raised in the introductory chapters and attempts to draw out some of the implications of the new view of emotion concepts for further research.

2
The Language of Emotion: A Critical Overview

What I would like to do in this chapter is to provide a critical assessment of the main body of research in the "language of emotion" tradition as it relates to the question of how we understand the emotions. The rest, and, as we will see, for our purposes the more significant part, of the research will be discussed in the next chapter. In particular, I will here first present the relevant work in a number of disciplines, and then point out some of the advantages and the major weaknesses, drawbacks, and disadvantages of the approaches under consideration. Proceeding in this fashion, by the end of the chapter we shall be in a position to see the breadth and depth of what is involved in the attempt to answer our question in a serious way.

In section 1 and section 2, I will describe in some detail some of the psychological, anthropological, linguistic, and philosophical works in the "language of emotion" tradition. I will present my general conclusions and offer a critique of these works in section 3. In essence, the critique will be based on the idea that, in one way or another, each of the studies surveyed in these two sections employs componential analysis and that componential analysis is not an adequate way of analyzing the meaning of emotion terms. The detail in which the following works are presented is necessary in order for us to see exactly what kind of componential analysis is employed. In the remaining sections, I will describe some other approaches to emotional meaning in anthropology, philosophy, and psychiatry. Only the most representative examples of the research on emotion concepts and emotional meaning will be discussed in these sections.

Emotion Concepts in Psychology and Anthropology

Let us begin our survey with Davitz's (1969) analysis of the meaning of 50 emotion terms. From the linguistic material of written reports and interviews in which subjects described their emotional experiences, Davitz isolated 556 statements that occurred most often. The statements described various aspects of such emotional states as anger, fear, love, pride, and so forth. This check list of descriptive statements contained such items as there is a heavy feeling in my stomach, *"I sweat," "My heart pounds," "I'm in tune with the world," "There is a sense of accomplishment,"* and *"It's a state of release."* Davitz then asked the subjects to check each statement that described the emotional experience in question. This procedure yielded a definition in terms of descriptive statements for each of the 50 emotion terms. The definitions thus obtained represent the first level of Davitz's analysis of the meaning of the 50 emotion terms.

Davitz observed that the statements did not form isolated units in the definitions, but tended to cluster together. That is, if a given item occurred in the definitions of certain terms, then there were other items that also occurred in most of the same definitions. This observation led Davitz to perform a cluster analysis of items. For example, he found that the item *"There is a lump in my throat"* was present in the definition of four emotions and the item *"I feel choked up"* was present in that of seven terms, including all four definitions in which the former item appeared. The cluster analysis of the statements in the definitions produced twelve clusters. These were labeled activation (e.g., *"There is an extra spurt of energy," "There is a sense of vitality"*), hypoactivation (e.g., *"I feel heavy," "I feel empty"*), hyperactivation (e.g., *"My blood pressure goes up," "There is an excitement"*), moving toward (e.g., *"There is a unity with another person," "I want to help another person"*), moving away (e.g., *"I want to be alone," "There is a sense of unrelatedness to others"*), moving against (e.g., *"There is an impulse to strike out," "I want to say something nasty"*), comfort (e.g., *"There's a mellow comfort," "I'm in tune with the world"*), discomfort (e.g., *"There's a clutching feeling in my chest," "There's an inner ache"*), tension (e.g., *"My whole body is tense," "I'm wound up inside"*), enhancement (e.g., *"I feel bigger," "There is a feeling that I can do anything"*), incompetence: dissatisfaction (e.g., *"Seems that nothing I do is right," "There is a desire for change"*), and inadequacy (e.g., *"There is a sense of being unable to cope with the situation," "A sense of not knowing what to do"*). The labels for the clusters as given are claimed to reflect the central meaning of the items (i.e., descriptive statements) that were found to co-occur.

The clusters and the supposed concepts that correspond to them (for example, moving against, enhancement) represent another level in the analysis of the meaning of the emotion terms under consideration. It will be instructive if we look at some of the meaning definitions that Davitz arrived at by performing the cluster analysis of descriptive statements. Since in this study I am going to examine the meaning of such emotion terms as *anger, pride, love,* and *fear,* it is reasonable to take these emotions as examples. Thus, the cluster analysis of these four terms yielded the following results: The meaning of anger was defined as hyperactivation, moving against, tension and inadequacy; that of fear as hyperactivation, moving away, tension, incompetence: dissatisfaction, and inadequacy;

that of love as activation, hyperactivation, moving toward, comfort, enhancement, and inadequacy; and that of pride as activation, hyperactivation, comfort, and enhancement. I will assess these definitions as representations of the meaning of anger, fear, love, and pride later in the chapter.

As a third step in the analysis, Davitz noticed that not only did the specific items tend to co-occur, but also the clusters appeared to be related to each other. As regards their content, the clusters can be viewed as constituting four dimensions of emotional meaning: activation (which includes activation, hypoactivation, and hyperactivation), relatedness (which includes moving toward, moving away, and moving against), hedonic tone (which includes comfort, discomfort, and tension), and competence (which includes enhancement, incompetence: dissatisfaction, and inadequacy). Thus, the dimensions are abstractions derived from the clusters, in the same way as the clusters are abstractions derived from the descriptive statements. Given these dimensions, an emotion like anger can be characterized by placing it at hyperactivation on the activation scale, at moving against on the relatedness scale, at tension on the hedonic tone scale, and at inadequacy on the competence scale. In other words, we get the same results that were obtained by the cluster analysis.

De Rivera's (1977, de Rivera and Grinkis 1986) structural theory of emotion focuses on a different set of dimensions. Specifically, the theory is based on the following six dimensions of emotional meaning: The first dimension enables us to distinguish those emotions in which the person is the subject of the emotion's movement (these are called "it" emotions) from those in which the person (the person's self) is the object of the movement (these are called "me" emotions). In anger the person who is angry is the subject of the movement toward another (who is the object), while in depression the movement is self-directed, with the depressed person as the object. The second dimension specifies whether the movement is toward or away from the person or the other. Loving someone involves moving toward him or her and being afraid of something involves moving away from it. The third dimension concerns whether the self moves toward or away from the other or another is moved towards or away from the self (whose position remains unchanged). For example, in the case of desire it is the object of desire that is moved toward the self (by the self) and in fear it is the person that moves. The fourth dimension has to do with three major types of human (psychological) relations, namely, belonging, recognition, and being. Each emotion can be said to govern a particular relation. Thus, for example, love, desire, anger, and fear govern belonging: In, say, anger the self doesn't want the other to belong to him (wants to remove him). Recognition is governed by emotions like esteem, admiration, contempt, and horror. While, for example, in fear the person does not want to belong to the other (so fear is a belonging emotion), in horror "we pull back from another whom we cannot recognize, another who is so distorted that we can no longer indentify him as a member of our group'' (de Rivera, 1977: 55). Similarly, we feel pride when an ''implicit other'' admires (recognizes) us. The third relation, being, is governed by such emotions as wonder, joy, and sorrow. De Rivera suggests that for something to *be* for us, it must both exist and have some meaning for us. If follows that, according to the theory, wonder is an emotion in which we cannot fully understand something (i.e., we cannot grasp its full meaning) and joy occurs when another person or object becomes present for us, that is filled with meaning. The fifth dimension is intended to capture the degree of our involvement in the emotion. For example, the use of the word angry indicates more emotional involvement than that of the word exasperated. So here the choices are involved, or deep, on the one hand and not-so-involved, or surface on the other. The sixth dimension is concerned with whether the movement characteristic of the emotion can or cannot be easily performed. This provides us with an express-inhibit, or fluid-fixed choice. Let us take anger and hate as examples. In anger, de Rivera suggests, we are able to push the object of anger away (so anger is regarded as a fluid emotion), whereas in hate we are unable to do anything about it (which makes it a fixed emotion). The same seems to apply to fear and terror, respectively.

Thus, on this analysis, we have six choices (five of them binary and one trinary) in terms of which each particular emotion can be characterized. For example, the characterization of anger in terms of the six dimensions would look as follows: It is an ''it'' emotion, its movement is directed away from the self, it is the other's position that is altered, it governs a belonging relation, it is involved, and it is fluid. Pride, on the other hand, can be seen as an emotion with the following features: It is a ''me'' emotion, its movement is extension (toward), the position of the object is altered, it governs a recognition relation, it implies deep involvement, and it is fluid.

A more recent study of emotion with a cognitivist orientation and along dimensional lines is Smith and Ellsworth (1985). They claim that the emotional experiences associated with the 15 emotions they investigated can be and are differentiated in terms of the following cognitive appraisal dimensions: pleasantness, anticipated effort, certainty, attentional activity, self-other responsibility/control, and situational control. In other words, they suggest that the experience of emotion is, in part, a result of the appraisal of one's circumstances along these dimensions. The proposed dimensions were taken over from previous researchers, and the method of investigation was to have subjects recall past experiences of emotion and to have them rate the experiences along the dimensions. The main finding was that the dimensions were systematically used to characterize similarities and differences among the 15 emotions.

Fillenbaum and Rapoport (1970) had subjects rate 15 emotion names in terms of their similarity. Four different techniques of data collection and analysis were used. Roughly the same mean results (for the 15 subjects) were obtained by using the four methods. It was found that people judged fear and worry, joy and love, anger and envy, contempt and disgust, sadness and grief to be most similar to each other and that, consequently, these pairs form the bases of any larger clusters. Two superclusters emerged, one corresponding to what we usually think of as pleasant emotions (including love, joy, etc.), and one corresponding to what we usually think of as unpleasant emotions (including anger, fear, etc.). Thus, the only dimension that arose from the use of this maximally reliable methodology was that of pleasantness. These are, as the authors readily admit, rather meager results as far as substantive issues are concerned. However, the main burden of the paper was methodological; more specifically, to show how certain methods of data collection and analysis used by previous researchers had led to (unjustifiable) claims about the existence of a number of dimensions, which were not borne out by the data and the method of analysis.

Storm and Storm (1987) and anthropologists Wallace and Carson (1973) employ a very similar approach to study emotion concepts. Since Storm and Storm's primary goal was to arrive at a hierarchical model (a taxonomy) of *groups* of emotion terms with similar meanings and not so much to discriminate semantically among *particular* emotion terms, I will only be concerned with the study by Wallace and Carson. Wallace and Carson investigated three issues: the size of emotion vocabularies in a sample of English speakers, the meaning of the terms to these speakers, and the semantic differences between psychiatrists and psychologists in the use of emotion words. Of particular interest for the present study is the second issue, which concerns the question of meaning. To begin, Wallace and Carson make a distinction between a "core vocabulary" and a "marginal vocabulary" in people. The core vocabulary consists of items that a subject uses regularly and readily, while the marginal vocabulary is made up of items that he or she would use only occasionally and for specialized purposes. Considering the large size of the marginal vocabulary in English speakers (ranging from about 2^7 to about 2^9), only the core vocabulary (ranging from about 2^6 to 2^7) was taken into account in the job of trying to determine what the terms meant to the subjects. A sorting task was performed. With each term of the core vocabularies printed on cards, the subjects were asked to "arrange the cards in any way that makes logical sense to you" (p. 13). Questions were asked about the principles of sorting. The principles can be regarded as (mostly binary) conceptual features in terms of which the meanings of the terms can be discriminated. Despite the "substantial individual differences in the principles used in differentiating the terms" (p. 15), most subjects carried out the sorting task in four similar steps, employing the general dimensions of quality and intensity. The first step involved distinguishing "positive" from "negative'' emotions. At the second step, more specific qualitative distinctions were used that helped the subject to distinguish both the positive and the negative terms. These distinctions included such choices as whether the emotion in question is directed toward the self or toward another person or object, whether another person is present or absent, or whether the situation that gives rise to the emotion is past, present, or future in relation to the emotional state. The third step involved further qualitative distinctions. The major qualitative distinctions employed in the second step were subdivided by more refined qualitative criteria. The fourth and final step usually involved an arrangement of the terms according to intensity; that is, the terms in the qualitatively distinguished groups were placed along an intensity scale relative to each group.

These were some of the psychological and anthropological works that addressed themselves in an explicit way to the issue of emotional meaning. Since all of these works show a great deal of similarity in their approach to emotional meaning in that they use componential analysis and since they also have much in common with some linguistic and philosophical approaches, I will assess all four of them together after a brief look at the relevant linguistic and philosophical research.

Emotion Concepts in Linguistics and Philosophy

Most of the linguistic work relating to the study of emotional language focuses on the way the various emotions are expressed in and through language. The kind of meaning that is expressed through the use of diverse linguistic devices is called ''affective'' or ''emotive meaning.'' For example, Ogden and Richards (1923) draw a distinction between the referential and the emotive meanings of words and expressions. Thus two words may have the same reference, but differ in their emotive meaning (e.g., *horse* and steed).

However, there are at least some notable exceptions to the above generalization about the language of emotion as studied by linguists and students of the philosophy of language. In one of the most original works on the meaning of emotion terms, Wierzbicka (1972) begins her inquiry with the following question:

> What is the meaning of such words as *joy, sorrow, regret, fear, irritation, admiration, jealousy, pity, gratitude, worry?* Is it possible to define these words, i.e., to explain their meaning by means of semantically simpler ones and to make manifest the structural relations which obtain between the names of various emotions? (p. 57)

Wierzbicka's answer is that emotion names are best conceived of as "shorthand abbreviations for complex expressions, i.e., descriptions of some kind" (p. 59). That is, the words for various emotions *describe* emotions. But what are these "complex expressions" like? They are, she suggests, descriptions of characteristic or standard situations in which particular emotions may emerge. Thus the definition of, for example, anger is given as follows: "X feels angry = X feels as one does when one thinks that someone has done something bad and when one wants to cause this person to do something he doesn't want to do" (p. 62). The definitions of this kind proposed by Wierzbicka have some interesting characteristics. First, the definition of an emotion name is identified with the description of a standard situation that characteristically gives rise to the emotion in question. In the case of anger, this situation can be glossed, according to Wierzbicka, as "when one thinks that someone has done something bad" (p. 62) or in the case of fear as "when one thinks that something bad can happen to one which one cannot cause not to happen and which one diswants to happen" (p. 63). Second, the definition is based on a comparison as captured by the expression "X feels as one does when. . . ." In other words, we are encouraged to imagine what we would feel in the situation that is specified by the description. This property of the definitions follows from the author's assumption (which ultimately goes back to Wittgenstein) that "thoughts have a structure which can be rendered in words, but feelings, like sensations, do not. All we can do, therefore, is to describe in words the external situations." (p. 59). Third, the definitions are made up of what are called "semantic primitives" (in fact, Wierzbicka's book bears the title *Semantic Primitives*), that is, components of meaning that are supposedly simpler and more basic than the words they define. The concepts of think, desire, want (and diswant), bad, and good are among the most important components (or semantic primitives) in Wierzbicka's system.

The semantic primitives think, want, and desire also show up in Searle's (1983) analysis of emotional (or in Searle's terminology "intentional") states. Think seems to correspond to "belief," and want and desire to "desire" in Searle's system. His hypothesis is that all intentional states contain a belief or a desire component or both. The analysis of fear and pride, for example, are given as follows (Bel stand for belief, Des for Desire, $\Diamond$ for possibility, and p is propositional content):

Fear (p) $\rightarrow$ Bel ($\Diamond$p) & Des (˜p)
Pride (p) $\rightarrow$ Bel (p) & Des (p) & Bel (p is connected to me) & Des (others know that p)

That is, if I fear something (p) I must believe that it is possible that p and must want it to be the case that not p. And if I am proud of p I must believe that it is the case that p and must want p to be the case and must believe that p is connected to me and must want others to know that p is the case.

One major advantage of these ways of defining emotional meanings is that they allow us to capture the (structural) relations between the meanings of emotion words with particular clarity. Let us take the terms *dissatisfaction* and *disappointment* as analyzed by Wierzbicka. Dissatisfaction is defined as "X feels as one does when one thinks that what has happened is worse than one has wanted" and disappointment as "X feels as one does when one thinks that what one has desired to happen and thought would happen has not happened" (p. 62). These definitions provide us with a very clear statement of the way the two emotions are related: In disappointment [*what I have desired to happen has not happened,*] while in dissatisfaction [*what has happened is worse than I have wanted.*] That is, we have a contrast between desire (in disappointment) and want (in dissatisfaction) on the one hand and a desired event which has not happened (in disappointment) and a wanted event which is worse than expected (in dissatisfaction) on the other.

The Componential Analysis of Emotional Meaning

So far we have surveyed some of the psychological, anthropological, linguistic, and philosophical research that deals directly with the meaning of emotion terms. It is now time to stop and make an assessment of the results as presented. No matter how diverse the ways of defining the meaning of emotion terms appear to be in the various approaches we have reviewed, they seem to have a number of things in common. Thus, although Davitz talks about "clusters" like activation, moving against, and enhancement, de Rivera about "choices" like self moves: other moves, Wallace and Carson about "qualitative distinctions" like presence or absence of another person, it can be claimed that these authors have the same *kind* of conceptual entities in mind that the more linguistically oriented Wierzbicka calls "semantic primitives" (other terms that are commonly used synonymously are "semantic components," "semantic features," etc.). It is important to note that in the dimensional approach it is not the *dimensions* themselves that I take to correspond to components, or features: Rather, what I take to be the corresponding entities are the (binary or trinary) *choices* that are provided by the particular dimensions. For example, one of Davitz's dimensions is "relatedness." This consists of moving away, moving toward, and moving against. As we have seen above, it is these that occur in the definitions of emotional meaning, that constitute binary or other contrasts with each other, and that the application of which results in minimal definitions. The aims of both the dimensional and featural analyses are also the same. As Smith and Medin put it: "Regardless of whether dimensions or features are used to describe concepts, the goal is the same: to make apparent the relations between concepts" (Smith and Medin 1981: 14)

In evaluating this line of research on the meaning of emotion words, I will not be concerned with the adequacy of the particular analyses. Instead, my aim is to enumerate and discuss the elements that are common to the various analyses and give a critique of componential analysis as such. If this more general criticism is successful, then by implication it will falsify or at least considerably weaken the particular analyses of emotional meaning as based on componential analysis.

We have to begin with a digression into semantics. It is commonly assumed in semantics that word meaning involves two parts: a *core* (often identified with sense) and a *periphery,* or connotative meaning (see, for example, Smith and Medin 1981). To the extent that the works that have been reviewed focus on establishing minimal conceptual differences between emotion terms and to the extent that they attempt to accomplish this by using a limited (or minimal) number of simple and basic concepts (or conceptual components), they are all concerned with *core meaning* and they all employ *componential analysis* as a technique. Indeed, componential analysis and the study of "meaning as sense" go hand in hand. To study core meaning is to employ componential analysis. *It is my contention that it does not suffice to limit the study of emotional meaning to core meaning and that componential analysis is unsatisfactory, or at least incomplete, as a method in the analysis of emotional meaning.*

If we look back to some of the analyses of emotional meaning, we can see that they are all attempts to define meaning in minimal terms, with the idea of distinguishing each emotion word from every other emotion word. We have seen that, for example, Davitz defines anger as hyperactivation, moving against, tension, and inadequacy; on de Rivera's analysis pride has the features me-emotion, extension, object's position altered, recognition, deep involvement, and fluid; and Searle conceives of the meaning of fear as *believe that it is possible that p, desire that not p.* Furthermore, we have seen that these short, elegant, and economical formulations of meaning allow us to capture and state the structural relations that obtain between the items. In other words, the kind of meaning that is described in these attempts seems to be core, rather than peripheral, meaning.

But what is wrong with studying core meaning alone? What is wrong with drawing a sharp line between a core and a periphery? And what can possibly have made the study of the core more important and appealing to scholars than the study of the periphery? The critique of minimal definitions of meaning that follows is in large measure based on Kövecses (1989).

To begin with, it seems that in many cases it is simply not possible to isolate the core. The notion of core meaning is based on the idea that all categories are defined by essential properties (i.e., properties that make the thing what it is). For example, the category of square can only be defined as (a) closed figure, (b) four sides, (c) sides equal, and (d) angles equal (Smith and Medin 1981). These are then the features that are individually necessary and jointly sufficient for something to be a square. But as research since Wittgenstein has revealed, the majority of our categories are not like this. The categories of game (Wittgenstein 1953), cup (Labov 1973), climb (Fillmore 1982), mother (Lakoff 1987)—to name just a few—do not seem to be definable in terms of essential properties. And if we cannot identify essential properties in many cases, the very basis for the separation of essential from nonessential properties and hence the separation of core from peripheral meaning is called into question.

A further objection to limiting the study of meaning to core meaning is that the core alone cannot capture the totality of our experiences in connection with given aspects of the world (like the emotions, for example). Of course, here I am not talking about individual experiences; these are likely to remain unique to each individual. What I have in mind are the experiences that are defined by culture and are thus shared by members of a particular culture. The core is a reflection of just a tiny part of these (culturally) structured experiences. The definition of, for example, anger in terms of five semantic components, like hyperactivation and moving against, and so forth is a gross oversimplification and a complete distortion of our experiences of this emotion. There is a lot more to our culturally defined experiences of anger than what the above five meaning components indicate: Anger typically arises as a result of a deliberate offense to the self; the offense has various degrees; the self sees himself as a victim; the intensity of the emotion also has various degrees; it is based on the idea of retributive justice where the offense, the intensity of the emotion, and the retribution correlate with each other, to mention only a few characteristics of the culturally defined typical scenario of anger, which are not and could not be captured by sense components alone. And the same applies to the analyses of the other emotions and to the study of "meaning as core meaning" in general. Let us now take a nonemotional example. Consider the word *woman*. The sense of this word is often defined as +HUMAN, +ADULT, and −MALE. This definition of the meaning of the word seems to me to be extremely impoverished because it lacks all the culturally defined conceptual richness associated with this word. Our stereotypes of women tell us that, in addition to being human, adult, and female, women are also thought of as emotional, skirt-wearing, cowardly, talkative, gregarious, and much more (cf. Leech 1972). Without these latter attributes the meaning components (like human, etc.) merely add up to a skeleton of meaning. But, it can be argued, the sense components have been designed for a special purpose: namely, to successfully discriminate words from each other. Fair enough, but then we should not claim that the components represent the meanings of words—they merely discriminate them. And that is a very different matter.

To return to the emotions, it has to be noted that, despite their commitment to a core, some authors are aware of the difficulty associated with the core as a sole representation of the meaning of emotion terms. For example, de Rivera writes

> . . . there is bound to be a tension between these two poles—the one insisting that the investigator be faithful to experience, the other requiring the sparse elegance of precise relations between a few abstract constructs. One of the best tests of structural theory is whether it can continue to parsimoniously relate the structures of particular emotions as these structures become more precisely specified (de Rivera 1977: 121).

When de Rivera writes about being faithful to experience, he is obviously concerned with what might be considered the periphery, and when he states that precise relations between a few abstract constructs are required, what in all probability he has in mind is a core and the (elegant and parsimonious) relations among core meanings (i.e., sense relations). Clearly, in this passage he expresses his dissatisfaction with a purely core-based view of meaning and emphasizes the need for supplementing this with a more connotative view (i.e., a view that lays more emphasis on the periphery), which helps us capture our experiences more faithfully. Despite this dissatisfaction, de Rivera, together with others, appears to be primarily concerned with core meaning.

However, I believe that the preference of a core to a periphery is based on an erroneous assumption. It is a commonly held belief by advocates of the componential analysis of core meaning that the adoption of a more periphery-oriented view of meaning would commit us to the "impossibly vast study of everything that is to be known about the universe in which we live" (Leech 1982: 8). The claim is that there is no natural stopping point in accumulating knowledge about the referents of linguistic expressions and hence about the peripheral attributes of referents, and so we would have to characterize peripheral meaning (or connotation) by means of infinitely long lists of referential attributes (like skirt-wearing, emotional, talkative, etc., in the case of *woman*). The same scholars maintain that, by contrast, in the componential analysis of the core we only need a minimal number of components, that is, just enough to discriminate a word from every other word. This second alternative has been especially appealing to scholars with reductionist orientation (which means most scholars). It seems to me that these two extremes, infinitely long lists of attributes on the one hand and a minimal number of components on the other, are not the only alternatives we have. There is a middle-ground between the two extremes: A level where concepts are characterized by features that are neither too numerous nor too few. I will call concepts characterized in this way "folk models." Folk models are human-sized, which means that they are specified by no more and no less features than ordinary people in everyday life use for the understanding of a given area of experience (on folk models, see Holland and Quinn 1987). The number is of course determined by particular cultures. But here again we have to allow for a great deal of individual variation. The size, as well as the content and structure of the folk models corresponding to anger, fear, love, pride, and respect, will be dealt with in detail in the following chapters.

The next reason that is often mentioned in defense of the view that the core rather than the periphery is or should be regarded as the central aspect of meaning concerns the structure of meaning. It is claimed that the core has structure while the periphery does not. The structure of core meaning is seen as arising from a variety of sources. We have already seen that only a minimal number of conceptual components are used in the characterization of meaning as the core. Since, the argument goes, we need an infinite number of features to characterize the periphery, core meaning is the only kind of meaning that can be represented in a clear, precise, and economical way. This is the first aspect of the structure of meaning as sense (or core meaning). However, as has just been pointed out, the number of features necessary for the characterization of the periphery need not be infinite and thus we can represent the periphery just as clearly and precisely as the core. The question of economy is a tricky one. The principle of parsimony (as regards the number of features) only makes sense if it does not incur significant losses in capturing the totality of meaning. But, it seems that it does. Although on the basis of a core we can discriminate words from each other (at least in some, though not all, cases), at the same time we fail to account for the connection between words and our experiences of the world. Thus, economy is not necessarily a good guiding principle in matters of meaning. Second, it is claimed that there is a system of conceptual components where each component stands in opposition to another component. The opposition is mostly binary contrast (like MALE vs. FEMALE), but other kinds of opposition are also recognized. The semantic components that are necessary for the definition of the meaning (the core) of particular items are taken from this system. We have seen that, for example, Davitz found twelve components in terms of which the 50 emotion terms could be defined. But, as will be shown in the following chapers, a lot more features than twelve are needed even for the characterization of the meaning of the six emotion words under consideration in this study. In addition, each of these emotion terms has some unique features that are not shared by any of the other terms. The third source of considering the core more structured than the periphery is that while the components of the core consist of mostly binary contrasts, most of the peripheral attributes do not stand in (any such neat) oppositions to each other. But I do not think that this makes peripheral meaning less structured. The idea of and the search for binary contrasts in meaning has grown out of the desire to be able to distinguish each item from every other item in a systematic way. However, in the analyses to follow, I will try to demonstrate that it is possible to discriminate between items without necessarily limiting our analyses of meaning to the employment of (mostly) binary contrasts. In sum, I will be proposing that peripheral meaning can be seen as just as structured as the core, though in different ways. The simplistic structure of meaning in terms of conjoined components will be replaced by cognitive models that consist of a number of entities and predicates and that are organized in complex ways. If this proposal is correct, then the "core is more structured than the periphery" argument cannot be used to justify the primacy of a core over a peripheral meaning as regards the characterization of emotional meaning.

In the same way as it is claimed by the advocates of core meaning that the core has structure whereas the periphery does not, it is also claimed that the conceptual components of the core can be arrived at in a systematic and principled way that is not available for obtaining peripheral attributes. Let me illustrate how this technique works with an example. Consider the words *man, woman, boy, girl, gander,* and *goose*. Suppose we want to find out what some of the conceptual components are that make up the sense of these items. The following procedure can be employed. We can say that man is to woman as boy is to girl and as gander is to goose. That is, certain common features can be extracted from these words. Man, boy, and gander share the conceptual component +MALE, while woman, girl, and goose have in common −MALE (or FEMALE). This is essentially the same method that de Rivera uses when he suggests that, for example, anger is to hate as disapproval is to disrespect and as approval is to respect. The conceptual components that emerge from these sets are fluid and fixed. Anger, disapproval, and approval are emotions that flow (i.e., as de Rivera puts it, their instructions are realized) and thus contain the conceptual component fluid. By contrast, hate, disrespect, and respect are emotions that are static (i.e., their instructions are blocked) and thus contain the component fixed. Thus we have a simple but principled methodology that enables us to identify core components in a systematic way. It is assumed furthermore that, by contrast, it is not possible to study the periphery in this manner. There does not exist any such simple mechanism with which we could systematically isolate peripheral attributes. I would like to suggest in the next chapter that the study of what could be viewed as peripheral meaning can be systematic as well. But, of course, since we are looking for a different kind of meaning structure in the case of cognitive models (which also include peripheral attributes) than in the case of core meaning, the systematicity of the study of cognitive models will have to be different from that of the study of the core. Thus, here again, to the extent that the so-called peripheral attributes can be studied systematically (as parts of cognitive models), the claim that we should concentrate on the core because it is only the core that can be studied in a principled way loses much of its force.

Last but not least, let me mention one more reason why I find the notion of a core problematic. It has been noted previously that core meaning is represented by a minimal number of conceptual components. Another property of core meaning is that not only is it composed of a minimal number of components but the number of components is fixed; that is, there is a set of singly necessary and jointly sufficient conditions in all cases that have to be met if the category is to be used appropriately (these are also called criterial features). A weaker version of the same view is that there is at least one component that appears in each instance when the category is used. Recently a number of linguists have shown (cf. Lakoff 1987, among others) that this is not always the case. The findings of the present study also indicate that there is no fixed set of components that characterize the meaning of emotion terms and that in the majority of cases no one component is shared by each instance of the use of the category (but, see the chapter on love). Another consequence of the view that core meaning is composed of a fixed number of components is that, if the claim is true, there can be no better or worse examples of a category. However, as recent research on cognitive prototypes indicates, people do conceive of certain instances of a category as better examples of the category than others. (More is said about this in chapter 3.) The present study will also suggest that some instances of an emotion category are more central than others. This is a view that would not be possible if we limited our anlaysis of emotional meaning to a core as defined by a fixed number of conceptual components. (A recent study by Armstrong et al. (1983) has shown that the simultaneous existences of internal structure (i.e., prototypicality) and criterial features are independent of each other, that is, they suggest we can have better or worse examples for a category even in the case of the category having a fixed set of conditions. For example, the category of even number can be defined in terms of a fixed set of conditions and yet it will show prototype effects. Even if valid, this claim does not affect our claim that emotion categories are best seen as being organized around prototypes. It merely requires us to change our argument as given above.

We should simply say that emotion categories have a prototype structure independently of whether they can be defined in terms of criterial features and argue that they, or at least most of them, do *not* in fact have criterial features. Fehr and Russell (1984) and Lakoff (1987) answer this challenge in detail.)

To conclude, in light of the foregoing discussion it seems to me that it is a mistake to limit the study of meaning to the study of a core, and consequently to base the study of emotional meaning on the *core* meaning of emotion terms. The study of the core has to be replaced, or at least supplemented, by an approach to emotional meaning that also takes into account the periphery. It is only in this way that a better fit between emotion words and our emotional experiences of the world can be guaranteed.

We can now move on to other fields and take a look at their contributions to "language of emotion" studies.

Anthropology

We continue our survey with anthropology. We have already looked at a study by Wallace and Carson. Since these authors are anthropologists by profession, we would have been justified in discussing their work in this section. As has been noted, componential analysis as a technique is just as popular in anthropology as in psychology or linguistics. (In fact, it was anthropologists who started componential analysis.) However, in this section I will be concerned with a different approach to emotional meaning as it is pursued by other anthropologists.

In a study of the emotion language used by the A'ara of the Solomon Islands, White (1979) characterized emotional meaning in terms of the social events that lead to particular emotive responses. The study deals with the meaning of three emotion words corresponding to anger, shame, and sadness in the ritualized context of "disentangling." Disentangling is a meeting "designed to allow the public expression of pent-up emotions and repair damaged social relationships" among the A'ara people (p. 8). The social events that produce the particular emotions are seen as definable in terms of the following properties: (a) moral evaluation: The action is assigned the quality or value of "rule violation"; (b) role structure: This involves the speaker, the agent, or the perpetrator of the rule violation, and the person affected by the rule violation; (c) social relations among the speaker and participants; (d) responsibility for the action; and (e) intentionality: This concerns whether the action is considered intentional. Given these properties of social events, *anger,* for example, is defined in the following way (reproduced in a somewhat simplified form):

Rule violation (perpetrator, affected)
Responsible (perpetrator, rule violation)

Intended (perpetrator, rule violation) → Anger (affected)
Not related (perpetrator, affected)
Equal status (perpetrator, affected)
Presupposition: Speaker = Affected or Related
(speaker, affected)

In contrast, shame can be characterized as differing from anger in the following ways: The perpetrator and the affected are related, they are of unequal status, and the speaker equals the perpetrator (or the speaker and the perpetrator are related).

This means that emotion concepts in A'ara are seen as representable by such sets of propositions as the above for anger and shame. Moreover, White views the propositions as instantiations of the more schematic proposition:

$$\text{Social Behavior } (SB_x) \rightarrow \text{Emotive Response } (ER_y) \rightarrow \text{Intended Reaction } (IR_z)$$

Given this schema and the specific propositions that characterize social events producing emotive responses as well as the intended reactions resulting from these responses, two sorts of inference can be and are made by the A'ara. One is "backward-looking" and the other is "forward-looking." As an example, let us take the sort of inference that looks backward at a social event. An assertion of a specific kind of emotive response (e.g., *"I am angry"*) will communicate a great deal about the way the speaker conceives of the situation that produced the emotive response in him. In the case of anger, it will indicate that the speaker has categorized an event as a rule violation, that he holds the agent of the action responsible, that he (the speaker) is not related to the perpetrator, and so forth. That is, statements about emotion may be viewed as revealing how the speaker interprets the preceding social events.

Lutz (1987) attempts to capture the meaning of Ifaluk emotion words in terms of two major theoretical constructs, "events" and "goals." She regards emotion concepts in Ifaluk society as knowledge that is structured by salient events in everyday life and by culturally defined goals associated with particular words. She represents these knowledge structures by way of cognitive schemata that vary in their degrees of generality from the very general to the very specific. Lutz distinguishes between four general schemata that are used by the Ifaluk for emotional understanding. They are:

1. If Event X, then Emotion Y.
2. If we experience Emotion X, then we may do Act Y.
3. If we experience Emotion X, then another person should or might experience Emotion Y.
4. If we experience Emotion X, then we may later experience Emotion Y.

The following specific propositions are possible corresponding instantiations of these schemata: (a) "Travel from the island" leads to *fago* (compassion/love/sadness), (b) *song* (justifiable anger) leads to "refusal to eat," (c) *song* (justifiable anger) in one person leads to *metagu* (fear/anxiety) in another, and (d) *ker* (happiness/excitement) leads to *metagu* (fear/anxiety). Of the four general schemata instantiated by these four specific propositions it is the first that is central. For the Ifaluk people the determination of which emotion concept applies appropriately to a situation is largely a matter of which social event is present in the situation (Compare this with the Wierzbicka/Wittgenstein view quoted on p. 12.) Thus, the Ifaluk tend to treat emotions as primarily social phenomena and not as internal psychophysiological feelings.

Lutz claims furthermore that emotion words used by the Ifaluk entail culturally defined goals. The goals can be of two types, "action goals" and "disclosure goals." Action goals are motives to act. For example, the action goal associated with *song* (justifiable anger) is "change the situation by altering the behavior of the offending party" and with *fago* (compassion/love/sadness) it is "change the situation by filling the need of the unfortunate party.") The disclosure goals have to do with whether or not the various emotions can be expressed verbally. The general disclosure goal in relation to the emotion domain encourages the verbal expression of emotions. This follows from the Ifaluk attitude to the emotions. In general, the Ifaluk consider the emotions as a sign of maturity and intelligence. However, certain pragmatic constraints on the verbal expression of emotions are also recognized. Thus, in a given situation the expression of a particular emotion may be discouraged.

But, Lutz also observes that, often, emotional meaning does not simply arise from the schemata associated with social events. In many cases, a particular situation can be interpreted in more than one way; that is, the same person or different individuals may imbue the same situation with different emotional meanings, or a person may question the appropriateness of the emotion felt by another. In other words, emotional meaning is often negotiated rather than mechanically computed from the schemata. Negotiation takes place simultaneously on two levels: one semantic, the other pragmatic. Negotiation on the semantic level is an attempt to decide "the extent to which an event is a prototypical or good example of a particular emotion" (Lutz, 1987: 307). Negotiation on the pragmatic level, on the other hand, is concerned with the question of whether "it is appropriate to use a particular emotion concept with particular others in particular contexts" (p. 307).

In another paper, Lutz (1980) raises the issue of which factors contribute to the content of categories in general and emotional categories in particular. Following Rosch (1977), she proposes that the content of categories is determined by correlational structures in the real world. Thus, the main elicitors of the emotion *fago* (compassion/love/sadness)—death, infancy, and famine—correlate highly in Ifaluk society. The understanding of these and other related correlations requires an understanding of a variety of things, including various sociological facts, the assumptions the Ifaluk have about the nature of the self and the other, historical factors, cultural institutions and values, and so on. For example, the high rate of sterility, which is supposedly a matter of involving both sociology and history, has created a situation in which the Ifaluk are greatly concerned with feeding and caring for children. Feeding and caring for children are major components of the meaning of *fago*. Thus, these constituents of the meaning of *fago* can be seen as arising from some of the special features of Ifaluk society.

These accounts of emotional meaning in anthropology can now be critically evaluated and compared with the account I am going to propose. We can begin with some comparisons. However, the comparisons will of necessity have to remain sketchy, and a full appreciation of the similarities and differences will have to wait until the last chapters.

The foregoing studies of emotional meaning and the account to be proposed here share a number of features. Most important, perhaps, they share an interest in uncovering the folk theories, or ethnologies of emotion, rather than in trying to construct a scientific model. However, on the whole, anthropologists are interested in describing the entire (ethno)system of emotional meaning, though less frequently they may also present detailed accounts of particular emotions (e.g., Lutz 1988). By contrast, I will mainly be concerned with particular emotion categories like anger, pride, love, and fear. As we shall see in a moment, this emphasis on particular emotions is based on more than just taste.

Further, the folk theories, both on the general level of emotion and one on that of particular emotions, are seen as being built up of similar parts in the two approaches. It is not surprising that both approaches view emotions as having a causal aspect (the "social events" in the terminology above and "causes" in the terminology I will use); as having a purposive aspect ("goals" vs. "desire," or "purposive aspect"); and as having an actional aspect ("intended reactions" vs. "behavioral reactions"). Thus, there seems to be a great deal of overlap between the contents of the folk theories as seen by the two approaches. Nevertheless, my contention will be that we need to go into much more detail than anthropologists ordinarily do in the characterization of particular emotion concepts if we wish to capture most of our emotional experiences associated with particular emotions.

The anthropological approach to emotion concepts as described above offers at least one distinct advantage over the approach I am advocating. This advantage stems from two sources, sources that have been mentioned above. The first is that aspect of meaning that places emphasis on how meaning is negotiated. The ethnotheory proposed by these anthropologists is superior to a purely cognitively based ethnotheory in that it is capable of showing how emotional meaning arises in particular contexts in the process of meaning negotiation. The second source is that anthropological ethnotheories of emotion (or at least some of them, like the work of Lutz) attempt to capture the entire system of emotional meaning, in contrast to the meaning of particular emotion words. This emphasis on the emotional domain as a whole makes it possible for anthropologists to investigate the interaction between the domain of emotion and the larger system of cultural values. As we have seen, the examination of this aspect of emotion may provide (partial) explanation for how and why particular emotion concepts have the content that they have.

What is an advantage from one point of view may turn out to be a weakness from another. In their effort to model the interaction of concepts within the domain of emotion on the one hand and the interaction of the emotion system with the larger system of cultural values on the other, these anthropologists have paid less attention than necessary to the detailed examination of the structure and content of particular emotion concepts. The detailed examination of particular concepts is necessary because this examination may always reveal fine details that link up a particular emotion concept with broader cultural values, and if we do not go into these details the connections between the two are lost. Consider, for example, the cases of love and anger. The folk models obtained from the detailed analysis of the linguistic expressions we use to describe these emotions seem to contain elements that reflect deeply embedded cultural values. One of the linguistically based conceptual metaphors of love in English is LOVE IS A VALUABLE COMMODITY (IN AN ECONOMIC EXCHANGE). As an examination of the linguistic examples of this metaphor suggests (see Kövecses 1988), it is this metaphor that gave rise to the idea that (ideal) love should be mutual. The idea of mutuality, or "balance," is an extremely general cultural value that found its way into the concept of love. And the same applies to anger, where we have the idea of retributive justice. Again, there are a number of linguistic expressions that point to the existence of this notion in our concept of anger. The notion of retributive justice also reflects general cultural values. However, these connections between the concepts of love and anger on the one hand and our larger system of cultural values on the other hand would have gone unnoticed had we not analyzed the concepts in great detail and had we begun the job with seeking these connections straight away. The point is that although anthropologists may have different goals from the ones I have, they nevertheless cannot afford to ignore the detailed analyses of *particular* emotion concepts.

There is, I think, another weakness in the anthropological works that have been surveyed. It concerns the kind of knowledge in terms of which a particular area of experience is understood. Knowledge can be conceived of as existing in at least two forms, propositional and image-schematic. The anthropological studies that have been reviewed seem to view the knowledge associated with emotions as limited to propositional knowledge (but see Lutz 1988). As we have seen, this knowledge was (re)presented in the form of either general or specific propositions. However, the studies of the various emotions such as anger, pride, and love to be presented in this work will show that there is at least one type of image-schematic knowledge that plays a very significant role in the conceptualization of emotions. This is the container image-schema. It seems that most of our emotions are conceptualized in terms of some kind of metaphorical SUBSTANCE IN A CONTAINER (which corresponds to the body). The implications of this way of viewing the emotions and ourselves will be examined in some detail in the chapters on anger, fear, and, primarily, the concept of emotion (Chapter 9).

To round up our survey of anthropological work on the language of emotion, mention must be made of another line of research. Here authors are concerned with cross-cultural differences and similarities in the use and understanding of emotion terms. We have already seen that Lutz (1987) notes that on Ifaluk, people understand their emotions with reference to the social events and situations in which these emotions are likely to occur. She also points out that in contrast to this Americans tend to define their emotions primarily in terms of internal, private psychophysiological feelings and sensations, an observation she owes to Davitz (1969). In her study of the Javenese, Geertz (1959) found that of the universally potential repertory of emotional experience the Javanese emphasize respect. Rosaldo's (1980) description of Ilongot anger suggests dramatic differences in the way the Ilongot and Americans conceptualize this emotion. While, as the study on anger in chapter 4 will indicate, Americans have an ambivalent attitude to anger, Briggs (1970) describes anger among the Utku Eskimos as an inferior way of being, characteristic only of people such as children, whites, and the mentally retarded.

The major problem with this kind of research is that the studies fail to provide a systematically arrived at and sufficiently detailed conceptual model of the emotions under study. Consequently, the comparisons across cultures are to a large extent based on subjective assessments of how a given emotion is conceptualized in the two cultures.

Philosophy

Philosophers working in the language of emotion tradition appear to be primarily concerned with (a) emotion terms and the concept of emotion itself, and (b) emotion statements. Of more relevance for our purposes is their work on emotion terms. This work is devoted in large part to making subtle conceptual distinctions between the various senses of such words as emotion and feeling, and between the meaning of various emotion terms like love, fear, anger, and pride. We have seen how Searle (1983) tries to discriminate among a variety of emotion terms by making use of such components as belief and desire. His work can then be considered as exemplifying emotion term studies of the latter kind.

Several philosophers address the issue of the meaning of the words emotion and feeling. In trying to get clear about what these words mean, they pursue the type of linguistic analysis characteristic of the Oxford school of philosophy. They search for conceptual differences on the basis of the correct use of the words in ordinary language. This "logic of language" leads to the discovery of subtle shades of meaning.

In his classic work on the subject Ryle (1949) claims that when we use the word emotion we mean by it at least three different kinds of things: "inclinations" or "motives" (like vanity, avarice), "moods" (like happy, depressed) including "agitations" (like disturbed, upset), and "feelings" (like thrills, twinges, pangs). Inclinations or motives lead us to perform more or less intelligent actions, moods and agitations merely give rise to certain aimless movements, and feelings are only signs of agitations and as such they are not typically used to explain human behavior. Furthermore, inclinations or motives and moods are propensities, while feelings are occurrences. Motive words signify long-term tendencies to act in certain ways, whereas mood terms refer to shorter conditions during which we act and feel in relation to the world in particular ways. Feelings, on the contrary, cannot be viewed as long or short tendencies or dispositions as they signify momentary episodes or occurrences in the body.

In his book on emotion Lyons (1980), following Alston (1967), makes a similar distinction between dispositions and occurrent states. However, while Ryle seems to refer moods and feelings back to inclinations or motives, Lyons considers the occurrent sense of emotion terms as being more prototypical or paradigmatic of emotion terms than the dispositional sense. But, as he also points out, this does not mean that all emotion terms with a dispositional meaning will have an occurrent sense as well. He demonstrates this with the emotion words love, rage, and anger. According to Lyons, love is only used in a dispositional sense, while rage is confined to an occurrent sense. However, the term anger seems to be applicable in both senses.

Philosophers in the linguistic analysis tradition examine the way we talk about particular domains of experience. Ryle, for example, notes that we talk about (emotional) feelings in terms of bodily sensation like twinges, throbs, pangs, glows, thrills, itches, and many others. So we can describe a person's feelings by saying that *"He felt a glow of pride."* However, this description will be very different from the description *"He is vain."* The difference lies in the use of the two expressions *a glow of pride* and *vain*. We can use the second but not the first to explain the motives of higher-level human behavior. "When a man is described as vain, considerate, avaricious, patriotic or indolent, an explanation is being given of why he conducts his actions, daydreams and thoughts in the way he does" (Ryle, 1949: 85). The use of the expression *a glow of pride* cannot serve as an explanation of behavior in the same sense. It is linguistic reasons like this that lead Ryle to his paradigm of speech about emotion, a paradigm involving inclinations, motives, moods, agitations, and feelings.

But some philosophers, such as James F. Brown (1982), among others, have recently criticized the way Ryle talks about emotion, or more simply, the Ryleian paradigm of emotion. Brown's criticism focuses on a particular part of Ryle's system: the notion of feeling. Brown gives several reasons for his dissatisfaction with Ryle's treatment of feeling. The major objection seems to be that Ryle arbitrarily confines the meaning of feeling to bodily sensation. This, Brown argues, follows from the mistaken idea that for Ryle the only grammatically correct usage of feel is when it is used with cognate objects in sentences like: *"He felt a glow of pride,"* and *"She felt a twinge of remorse."* These are the same kind of cases as *strike a blow,* where the verb and the noun express the same thing. Brown's point is that, although Ryle appears to recognize some other uses of feel as well, he reduces feelings to bodily movements on the basis of prescribing, rather than describing, ordinary language use. The apparent counterexamples that Brown cites are *feelings of joy* or *feelings of despair,* which are perfectly correct grammatically. Just as importantly, Brown notes, joy and despair cannot be reduced to mere bodily sensations. Brown points out another weakness in Ryle's paradigm. It is that Ryle seems to think of feelings as merely momentary physical episodes in the body. What is wrong with this, Brown maintains, is that feelings can last a long time as well. In his own words: "We do speak of feelings, for example, of joy and despair, lasting and enduring for long periods of time" (p. 36). It should be noted that here again the argument is based on *how we speak* about feelings. A third weakness, according to Brown, is that not only does Ryle confine feelings to bodily sensations and to isolated moments in time but he appears to want to locate them in actual places in the body, whether it be within the body (like throbs, sinkings), on the body (like itches, prickings), or throughout the body (like glows, thrills). Brown says that in many cases (like loneliness or frustration) it would be difficult or even impossible to locate the feeling in strictly physical terms.

Brown goes on to argue that the reduction of feelings to physical phenomena has some disastrous consequences. One such consequence is that feeling and cognition will be seen as two irreconcilably distinct faculties. Second, and more important for my immediate purpose, the equation of feelings with purely physical phenomena ignores a host of other experiences that, again on the basis of ordinary language use, form inalienable parts of feelings. Feelings, in addition to being of the body, are associated with a variety of intellectual, physical, and emotional experiences, in either conscious or unconscious form. Brown states this succinctly: "Feelings may be of the body, but they are also beyond it" (p. 34). However, at this point the question arises: How can we get at these nonphysical experiences? Brown's answer is that we should take a closer look at the way we talk about feelings. Here is where he proposes his new paradigm.

This alternate paradigm of speech about feelings consists of four types. The types refer to the ways we talk about feelings. In the first type, Brown takes note of the fact that in ordinary language use we often describe feeling as *changing, lasting,* or *enduring* through time. This is in sharp contrast with Ryle's idea that feelings are merely sudden, momentary bodily movements. Consider, for example, the use of the verb feel in the sentence *I have felt depressed for the last few years* (p. 68). The sentence does not say anything about twinges or pangs (though of course on occasion they may also accompany feelings), and more to the point, what we have here is a state that lasts a long time, rather than a momentary episode. Cases like this could not be easily accommodated in the Ryleian paradigm of feeling since Ryle appears to think of feelings in terms of short-lived physical episodes within the body.

Type two arises from the recognition that we also speak of feelings as being *confused, unclear, mixed up, muddled,* or, conversely, *clear*. Examples for this type can be found in sentences like *"I am not really clear about my feelings."* Brown suggests that type two typically occurs when we rush into some new situation and are not able to quickly assess our own affective reaction to it (p. 76). In this respect, feelings come close to what we call "first impressions" and that can also be clear or unclear. But this way of talking about feelings has another important property. It is that, since here feelings are reactions to certain situations, feelings are directed at something in the world. Again, this is an aspect of feelings that the view of feelings as bodily sensations could not account for. While type two emphasizes the ambiguous nature of feelings in relation to a new situation in the world, type three highlights their complexity. When I say *"I have very mixed feelings about my country"* (p. 76), the sentence typically indicates all the complexities that go into the creation of my feelings, among them history, education, positive and negative experiences, and my judgment of the political and economic affiliations of the country. My feelings can also be mixed at this level, but the confusion or unclear nature of the feelings does not arise from the inability to quickly assess a new situation. It stems from the difficulties in assessing matters in life that are inherently complex and complicated. At this level, emphasis is again on objects, persons, events, and so forth that affect us in particular ways. However, the complexity of feelings has an aspect closely related to this. It is that we affect the world as well. One of Brown's examples to illustrate the point is: *How I feel toward my supervisor, or how I affect her, is difficult to say* (p. 80). That is, in addition to the passive sense of feeling, which is perhaps the more popular sense, there is also an active sense that highlights how "we feel *toward* or *for* someone or something, as well as how we are made to feel *by* or *about* someone or something" (p. 81). These are aspects of meaning that Ryle's treatment does not cover at all.

Type four is a mode of speaking that indicates the close association of feeling with understanding, or insight. Consider the following examples given by Brown:

He shows a real feel for that period.
He has captured the spirit of that period. He has insight into it.
He understands that period.

To the extent that these sentences can be said to have similar meanings, it can be claimed that feeling involves some kind of knowledge, or understanding, and that real understanding is not imaginable without having a feel(ing) for whatever the object of knowledge is. It is clear that an account of feelings as based on their physical aspects is too narrow to capture these properties of the meaning of the word feeling.

This discussion of feelings is obviously broader and subtler than that offered by Ryle. The main point is that ordinary language use suggests feelings cannot be limited to bodily sensations. However, we can now ask: Is this all language tells us about feelings and emotions? And the answer is that, just as obviously as Brown's paradigm of speech about feelings uncovers more than Ryle's model, a further examination of certain aspects of ordinary language can reveal more about feelings and emotions than Brown's paradigm. Apparently, Brown does not seem to attach any significance to the existence of the hundreds of linguistic expressions that, in some way, are related to feelings and emotions. He is content with examining some of the linguistic contexts in which the word feeling occurs and with establishing a number of senses for the word on the basis of these linguistic contexts. As an unfortunate consequence, he ignores most of what constitutes the concept of feeling.

The word feeling occurs in a host of linguistic contexts other than the ones Brown examines. If the ones he examines are worthy of attention, then there seems to be no reason why these other contexts and the large number of related expressions should be disregarded. If there is a systematic relationship between a concept and the words and phrases that are related to it (as I would like to believe there is; see the next chapter in this connection), then it is essential that we should examine *all* or *most* of these expressions. It is only this way that we can get a relatively complete picture of the various aspects of a concept like feeling or emotion. If it is true that most of our nonphysical reality is structured, understood, and created by metaphors (and a large and growing body of literature seems to suggest this), then a systematic examination of metaphors relating to the concepts feeling and emotion is not just something extra that we can do but something that we *must* do. The examination of expressions like *over-*

whelmed by feelings and *struggling with feelings* may turn out to be just as informative as the examination of expressions like *unclear feelings* and *have a feel for* something. But we cannot stop with metaphors. There are also metonymies, idioms of various kinds, and many other types of linguistic expressions. They all seem to contribute something to our understanding of whatever concept we are studying. The studies below will be devoted to just this task.

Psychiatry

In psychiatry, the language of emotion is studied from at least two perspectives. In one, scholars address the issue of how we talk about the emotions both in everyday life and on the level of metapsychology, and they also try to determine the adequacy of these languages. The second line of research is concerned with the way we express our emotions in a psychiatric (therapeutic) context, and with the use that can be made of the various expressive devices for the purpose of curing patients. It is clearly the first issue that is of more relevance for our purposes. So, let us briefly look at the general nature of the work done in this area and provide some examples. We have seen that philosophers are interested in the various paradigms of speech about emotions and feelings. The speech models that reflect our conceptualizations are based on the examination of ordinary language. Schafer (1976) also examines the language we use to talk about the emotions and concludes that this language reflects some very strange ways of conceptualizing our emotions. For example, the use of expressions like *"Love glows," "Love grows,"* and *"Love withers"* suggests that it is not *us* who love, who love more, and who love less. The use of the noun *anger* suggests that anger is an entity that exists independently of us. And the use of expressions like *"Fear grips us"* suggests that we endow fear with the property of agency. Schafer offers both a criticism of and an alternate paradigm to these ways of talking about and conceptualizing the emotions. A major portion of the work to be presented in this book will be devoted to such and similar analyses of ordinary language expressions.

In the view of the scholars who work on the issue of how we express our emotions, the therapeutic interview can be considered as language material elicited on the part of the therapist for the purpose of discovering the variety of emotions that underlie human relationships. Understandably, this material has received a great deal of attention by analysts, psychiatrists, and, to some extent, linguists as well. Extensive studies have been done on the signals, or reflection, of the psychological states of the patient in verbal behavior. As an example, we mention Labov and Fanshell's (1977) work, which investigates both the lexical content and the several nonlexical aspects of the interview. From the present point of view, the problem with these studies seem to be that they do not provide any clear answer to the question of how we conceptualize our emotions. The meaning of emotion terms is simply taken for granted. The reason why these studies do not shed any light on conceptualization is that at the present time we know very little about the relationship between (emotional) expression (in the sense of signals) and (emotional) conceptualization (if there is anything to know at all). As has been indicated, it can be assumed that there is some positive relationship between description and conceptualization—in the sense that description reveals conceptualization. But it is not clear how expression and conceptualization are related. A further issue is how expression and description are related: How does one influence the other? Until we have a satisfactory account of these issues it seems more important to study the descriptions of the emotions than the signals we use in speech to express them if our goal is to gain a better understanding of how the emotions are conceptualized. (Some of the complexities involved in determining the nature of the relationship between expression and description are dealt with by Alston (1985).

Summary and Conclusions

Let me now try to summarize what has been done so far. Given that we are interested in the way people understand their emotions and emotional experiences and that the notion of meaning plays a crucial part in this, the following objections have been made to studies of emotional meaning in the various disciplines (the disciplines with respect to which the objections were made are given in brackets):

- The study of emotional meaning cannot be limited to the study of the core meaning of emotion words. (psychology, linguistics)
- The peripheral, or connotative aspects of emotional meaning do not commit us to characterizing meaning in terms of infinitely long lists of features. (psychology, linguistics)
- Not only the core but also the connotative meaning of emotion words has structure, though a different kind. (psychology, linguistics)
- Not only core components but also peripheral attributes of emotions can be studied and arrived at in a systematic way (this will be justified in the next chapter). (psychology, linguistics)
- Prototype effects in emotion concepts cannot be accounted for on the basis of meaning as a minimal number of conceptual components. (psychology, linguistics)
- We cannot discover the full range of cultural values built into our emotion concepts unless we perform detailed analyses of particular emotion concepts. (anthropology)
- The study of emotional meaning cannot be confined to the study of propositional knowledge. (anthropology)

- In uncovering emotion concepts it does not do to base the analyses on the linguistic behavior of a single emotion word and/or a small number of arbitrarily selected linguistic expressions related to the concept in question. (philosophy)
- The signals reflecting emotional states do not seem to provide us with any (or enough) insight into how the emotions are conceptualized. (psychiatry)

If these objections are valid (as I have tried to argue that they are), then the opposites and complementaries of the objections yield a fairly detailed positive program for studying emotional meaning. In particular:

- The study of emotional meaning must be based on *both the core and peripheral aspects* of meaning. It is only this broadening of focus that can ensure a better fit between emotional meaning and emotional experience.
- The characterization of emotion concepts should involve uncovering cognitive models (or scenarios) associated with emotion terms *that are human-sized and are used for the purposes of everyday life.*
- We should attempt to discover the structure of both the core and the periphery of meaning associated with emotion terms. *This structure is likely to be more complex than the structure associated with the core* as construed by most scholars, but it is likely to reflect our emotional experiences more faithfully than the core (sense) alone.
- We should find ways of studying what in the classical view would be considered connotation, or peripheral meaning associated with emotion terms *in a systematic way,* just as there are systematic ways of studying the core.
- It seems that our emotion concepts, similarly to other concepts, are organized around prototypes. Consequently, it should be our goal to identify and describe the *paradigmatic, or prototypical cases of emotion concepts,* together with the set of deviations from these prototypes.
- If we wish to account for the interaction between the emotion domain and the system of cultural values, then we should study *particular emotion concepts in great detail.*
- The study of emotional meaning must be based on more than propositional knowledge, including *image-schematic knowledge* of various kinds.
- In order for us to come to know an emotion concept in its detailed entirety, we have to examine, in addition to the various uses of a single emotion word, *the entire range of words and expressions related to the concept in question,* including metaphors, metonymies, idioms, and many more.
- The goal of understanding emotional experience requires us to investigate the (linguistic) *descriptions of the emotions,* rather than the signals used to express them.

3 The Theoretical and Methodological Background

In the previous chapter we saw some of the weaknesses (and also some of the advantages) of the most prevalent approaches to the study of emotional meaning in a variety of disciplines. To the extent that the objections raised are valid, the criticism gives us a detailed positive program on the basis of which the investigation of the structure and contents of emotion concepts can be placed in a new light. The items that make up this new program were listed at the end of chapter 2. The list consists of items that have to do with both theoretical and methodological issues. The present chapter takes up each of these issues in more detail, and thus attempts to provide most of the theoretical and methodological background to the particular analyses that follow. In the course of presenting this background, we will have occasion to mention the work of those scholars whose ideas have had the most influence on the present approach. (Some of this has already been mentioned. See primarily Lutz 1988.)

Prototypes

One view concerning lexical meaning that I will rely on heavily throughout this study is that the members of a category are organized around one (or in some cases more than one) central member (the prototype). The prototype view of categorization has a long history (for a survey, see Lakoff 1987). In recent years a number of linguists, anthropologists, and psychologists have argued that the prototype view has several distinct advantages over traditional componential analysis (e.g., Berlin and Kay 1969; Rosch 1973, 1975, 1977; Rosch and Mervis 1975; Fillmore 1975; Lakoff 1972, 1987; Lakoff and Johnson 1980). This view goes against the idea that the meaning of a lexical item can be represented in terms of a fixed set of necessary and sufficient conditions.

Prototype theory has also found its way into emotion research, as exemplified by the work of scholars like Ekman, Alston, and J.A. Russell. Interestingly enough, however, there are considerable differences in their purposes and in the way these researchers make use of prototype theory. The main focus of Ekman's research was to find out which emotions have consistent correlates in facial expressions across cultures (Ekman 1971; Ekman, Wallace, and Ellsworth 1972). He concluded that of all the subtle emotions that we have, and have words for, only happiness, sadness, anger, fear, surprise, and interest correlate universally with facial gestures. What renders this research "prototype-oriented" is that these basic emotions appear to function as the central examples of an entire category of concepts. In the next chapter, we will see that, for example, wrath, cold anger, and rage can all be seen as shades or variations of basic anger.

Alston (1967) focuses attention on the concept of emotion itself and arrives at a "prototype" definition. He claims that the concept of emotion can be characterized by the following six factors: (a) a cognition of something as in some way desirable or undesirable; (b) feelings of certain kinds; (c) marked bodily sensations of certain kinds; (d) involuntary bodily processes and overt expressions of certain kinds; (e) tendencies to act in certain ways; and (f) an upset or disturbed condition of mind or body. It is this list of typical features that brings out what sort of thing an emotion is. Some of these (but different ones) are present in all cases, there is no one feature that is present in all cases, and only the central members of the category (the paradigm cases) exhibit all the features. What is clear from this way of defining emotion is that there is no fixed set of necessary and sufficient conditions that characterizes each and every situation that we would consider a case of emotion. I will return to this and related issues in chapter 11, where the concept of emotion itself will be discussed.

All the latest accomplishments of prototype theory have been utilized by James Russell and his associates in a series of linguistic tasks (Fehr and Russell 1984; Fehr, Russell, and Ward 1982). The main burden of their experiments was to determine whether the concept of emotion has any internal structure (i.e., whether membership in the category is a matter of degree or all-or-none) and whether there is or is not a sharp boundary that separates members from nonmembers. It was shown that the category has a great deal of internal structure and lacks sharp boundaries. The studies indicate that emotions like anger, fear, love, happiness, and sadness are viewed as better examples of emotion than awe, respect, calmness, and boredom.

Now we are in a position to see how these "prototype-based" approaches differ from each other. Ekman and his associates tried to find the prototypical emotions on the basis of facial expressions. Russell and his associates tried to do the same but by using a variety of linguistic tasks. Alston proposed six typical features in order to define the paradigm case of emotion.

The reason why I have emphasized these differences is that they provide a good background to the understanding of what I will try to do in this book. Part of my purpose is to take some carefully selected emotion concepts (anger, fear, pride, respect, and love) and discover what their respective prototypes are on the basis of the language that we use to talk about them. Thus, although I follow the prototype approach in emotion research in general, the specifics differ from the endeavors of other researchers: namely, in my concentration on finding out what the central cases of *particular* emotion concepts are and in the *methodology* that I use to achieve this goal. A variety of particular emotion concepts will be discussed in subsequent chapters and the methodology will be dealt with in the final sections of this chapter.

Cognitive Models

In addition to trying to show that the emotion concepts under investigation are organized around central members, I also will try to show that these central members are best conceived as elaborate cognitive models. In other words, the claim is that emotion concepts are not mere *collections* of features and that they are not *minimal* sets of features. In fact, in most cases the material that makes up cognitive models does not even seem to consist of *features* as these are traditionally thought of. Instead, cognitive models are taken to be propositional and image-schematic knowledge that is neither infinitely large nor minimally small, and that is composed of certain entities and certain predicates, the combinations of which may be organized in some (here, usually temporal) order. This means then that I view concepts as prototypically organized cognitive models. This view obviously owes a great deal to some recent work in the cognitive semantics tradition (see especially Lakoff 1987; Johnson 1987).

Here again, one can find some clear antecedents in emotion research. I believe that de Sousa (1980) has the same idea in mind when he talks about "paradigmatic scenarios" in connection with particular emotions. In this expression "scenario" is a commonly used alternative, together with "frame," "model," "script," and "schema," to the notion of cognitive model. More important, as is clear from the term paradigmatic scenario, de Sousa also sees the need to link the notion of prototype with that of models (scenarios) in order to gain more insight into what an emotion concept is and how it is structured. Fehr and Russell (1984) also mention the possibility that emotion concepts have a "script-like" structure. However, in their studies they do not attempt to specify the structure and contents of these concepts. Following their lead, Shaver et al. (1987) try to do exactly this. Shaver and his associates used questionnaires to elicit accounts of actual and typical episodes of six cognitively basic-level emotions, and the representations of the internal structure and contents of the emotion concepts under investigation were based on these accounts. As regards the goal of trying to specify the exact internal organization and the precise contents of emotion categories, it is the study done by Shaver and his associates (1987) that comes closest to the present endeavour.

In order to see what it means for a concept to contain neither too much nor too little information, to be composed of entities and predicates, and to have a temporal order, let us consider the following prototypical love scenario, taken from Kövecses (1988):

1. True love comes along.
   The other attracts me irresistibly.
   The attraction reaches the limit point on the intensity scale at once.
2. The intensity of the attraction goes beyond the limit point.
3. I am in a state of lack of control.
   Love's intensity is maximal.
   I feel that my love gives me extra energy.
   I view myself and the other as forming a unity.
   I experience the relationship as a state of perfect harmony.
   I see love as something that guarantees the stability of the relationship.
   I believe that love is a need.
   that this love is my true love.
   that the object of love is irreplaceable.
   that love lasts forever.
   Love is mutual.
   I experience certain physiological effects: Increase in body heat, increase in heart rate, blushing, and interference with accurate perception.
   I exhibit certain behavioral reactions: Physical closeness, intimate sexual behavior, sex, and loving visual behavior.
   I experience love as something pleasant.
   I define my attitude to the object of love through a number of emotions and emotional attitudes: Liking, sexual desire, respect, devotion, self-sacrifice, enthusiasm, admiration, kindness, affection, care, attachment, intimacy, pride, longing, friendship, and interest.
   I am happy.

The entities that are used to represent the concept of love are, for instance, the self (I), the object of love (the other), and, at least metaphorically, love itself. The predicates are of two kinds: relations and properties. The relations characterize various relationships between the entities (like "love gives me extra energy," "the other attracts me"), and the properties describe particular entities (like "the object of love is beautiful," "love lasts forever"). What I am suggesting then is that a cognitive model, like that of love, is composed primarily of knowledge that consists of combinations of entities and predicates (i.e., propositions). This view of the makeup of concepts goes against the view that concepts are made out of conceptual "building-blocks" or conceptual "primitives." It also goes against some versions of prototype-theory, versions that define the prototype of all categories in terms of mere clusters, or collections of features.

As we saw in chapter 2, for most purposes of componential, or feature, analysis the order of elements that are assumed to constitute a concept does not play a part. There may be more or less "logical" or economical ways of presenting components, or features, but this is usually not a crucial issue (and for the purposes of componential analysis it need not be one). In contrast, in the present view cognitive models are seen as having a great deal of organization and order. This is not because order is considered superior to lack of order per se, but because it is thought that it is in the nature of concepts to code information in an organized and orderly fashion. This order need not of course correspond to the way things "really" are, but reflect "only" a projected reality. In fact, one could perhaps even say that concepts *are* this projected reality. Most of the time love may not occur according to the three temporally arranged stages as given in the (prototypic) model, yet perhaps most of us think of love that way.

Perhaps the most conspicuous difference between a componential and cognitive model approach lies in the amount of encoded information. For example, for Davitz (1969), love is composed of the components activation, hyperactivation, moving toward, comfort, enhancement, and inadequacy. This is what I have called a minimal definition. It is designed to distinguish love from every other emotion in the most minimal terms possible. However, if we insist on a view of meaning that can capture common, culturally given experiences and not just minimal distinctions between concepts, then the componential view of meaning becomes unconvincing. It captures only a fraction of our culturally determined experiences of, say, love. It is for this reason that I see the need for a more periphery-oriented view of emotional meaning, a view that emphasizes the relationship between words and our experiences in the world. Cognitive models (which include both core and peripheral features—and more) are taken to be a reflection, and to some degree also a determinant, of experience.

As was noted in chapter 2, a common objection in linguistics to taking the study of peripheral meaning seriously is that there are infinitely many attributes the referents of words have; that is, our (potential) knowledge of referents (i.e., of the world) is infinite. While strictly speaking this might be true, it does not seem to be true of the world as it exists for us in our ordinary conceptual system. By virtue of this conceptual system we assume a simplified or idealized world. We do so as long as we do not perceive a conflict between this world and the "real" world. When we do, we get nonprototypical cases. The cognitive model presented above represents a piece of the simplified or idealized world, a piece that we call love. This cognitive model does not consist of an infinitely large number of features; rather it is composed of as many propositions as seem to be justified on the basis of the examination of ordinary linguistic usage about love. The study of ordinary talk about love gives rise to a fairly complex cognitive model that contains more than a minimal and less than an infinite number of features (or rather, propositions). Models like this contain a more or less complete repertory of culturally defined love experiences.

Despite the many similarities and overlapping features between this model and the definitions offered by the authors discussed in chapter 2, it should be clear that the cognitive model of love as conceived here represents and allows for a significantly larger number of love experiences than the definitions based on minimal sets of features. That there is a true love; that true love comes along; that love should be mutual, or reciprocal; that there is liking, respect, friendship, and sexual desire between the lovers are all aspects of love that minimal definitions of love do not contain. Nevertheless, these are aspects that form a large part of our conception of love. It is in this sense that we can claim that prototypical cognitive models of the emotions are, in general, more information-rich than are the corresponding minimal definitions.

Interestingly enough, however, there is a clear tendency even among those who analyze emotional meaning in terms of minimal-sense components to try to make their componential definitions "more faithful" to emotional experience. We saw an example of this in chapter 2, when de Rivera (1977) expressed the need for a closer fit between sense components and (emotional) experience. In his scheme, he used six choices, or dimensions, to account for emotional meaning. Solomon (1976) increased the number of dimensions to thirteen in his attempt to capture more of emotional experience. Frijda's (1986) scheme provides even more dimensions, with the clear intention of narrowing the gap between emotional meaning and emotional experience. Although all of these attempts represent major steps toward capturing emotional meaning and emotional experience, they cannot be successful because they assume, explicitly or implicitly, the basic principles of componential analysis; namely, the ideas that the study of meaning can and should be limited to core meaning, that the core can be described in terms of a small number of conceptual components that *minimally* distinguish every word from every other word, and that the components come from a finite system of components. In chapter 2 we saw that these assumptions can be criticized on several grounds. But, the point here is that even those who work within the componential analysis tradition find it important to try to capture emotional experience in its entirety, but that they are prevented from achieving this goal by the very method that they employ.

In this section various features of cognitive models have been discussed. It has been noted, for example, that cognitive models consist of entities and predicates, they are neither minimal or infinitely large, and a great deal of experience is packed into them. It is a further feature of cognitive models that they represent not an "objective," "scientific" conception of a domain but a folk understanding of it. Understandings of this kind have come to be known as "folk," or "cultural models" (on these, see Holland and Quinn 1987). I have emphasized throughout that the experiences that prototypical cognitive models incorporate and embody are culturally defined. What this is intended to mean is that prototypical cognitive models are defined in large part by conventionalized language use. In a similar vein, De Sousa (1980) sees what he calls "paradigm scenarios" as emerging in three stages: first, from our daily and everyday interactions with adults as small children; second, from the stories and fairy tales we are exposed to; and third, through literature and art. Needless to say, a major part of our interactions with and exposure to adults, stories, and literature is based on language. Thus, through language we build up a conceptual universe, which represents "reality" in a simplified and/or idealized form. The product is a cultural one (in the sense of folk, or everyday) and not something that we acquire as a result of formal education and/or scientific procedures.

At this point it might be asked: Does the language we use to talk about the emotions accurately reflect current beliefs about the emotions? This is a question that we will be in a better position to answer in a later section in this chapter (see the section on the lexical approach to emotion concepts below).

The Structure of Emotional Concepts

The discussion of emotional meaning so far must lead one to the conclusion that emotion concepts are fairly complex constructs with a sophisticated structure. It has been mentioned, for example, that they are constituted by a variety of entities and predicates, that the combinations of entities and predicates (i.e., propositions) follow some order, that they embody a great deal of experience, and that they arise in large part from metaphor. This view of emotional meaning is sharply opposed to a very influential theory of emotion. Schachter and Singer (1962) claimed that the kind of emotion we are about to experience is determined by two factors: physiological arousal and our appraisal of the situation in which we are aroused. Depending on our evaluation of certain situational cues we choose the appropriate label and attach it to the situation. On this account of emotion, emotion words do not have any cognitive content—they are mere labels that lack all the characteristics of emotion concepts that have been found important so far in this chapter. The studies of particular emotions in subsequent chapters will also indicate that the Schachter–Singer position is not acceptable in its present form. To conceive of emotion names as mere labels is to ignore a large body of evidence that points to a contrary conclusion.

So far I have claimed that emotions have a great deal of conceptual content with a great deal of structure. We have seen the prototypical cognitive model of love as an example. But at this point we have to go even further. I would like to suggest that a large number of emotion concepts have an even more complex structure with at least the following parts (Kövecses, 1986):

1. a system of conceptual metonymies associated with the emotion concept in question;
2. a system of conceptual metaphors associated with the emotion concept in question;
3. a set of concepts linked to the emotion concept in question; and
4. a category of cognitive models, one or some of which are prototypical.

So far in the chapter we have seen only an example for a part of 4. The cognitive model of love described in the previous section is just one member of the category of cognitive models we have for love. It represents a prototypical model that is an ideal. There is also another prototype for love and that prototype is a typical model (see Kövecses 1988). In addition to these prototypes that are at the center of the concept of love, there exist a number of nonprototypical models for this concept that also belong to the category of cognitive models associated with love. (A detailed description can be found in Kövecses 1988.)

Perhaps it is reasonable to suggest that of the four parts that seem to make up emotion concepts it is the prototypical cognitive models that represent the concept as we commonly think of it. Thus, the other parts, listed in 1., 2., and 3., can be seen as providing a certain "depth" to this "front" or "surface"; that is to say, we can view these other parts of the structure of emotion concepts as somehow being "behind" what actually appears "on the surface" of thought. This view immediately raises two issues: (a) What is the connection between the category of cognitive models on the one hand and the conceptual metonymies, conceptual metaphors, and related concepts on the other? (b) In what ways are the metonymies, metaphors, and related concepts related to each other? These issues will be taken up in the next two sections.

Now, it might be useful to see some examples for each of these parts. By conceptual metonymies are meant behavioral and physiological reactions that in our folk models are assumed to accompany an emotion; thus, the corresponding linguistic expressions can stand for the emotion (concept). For example, expressions like "Don't be *upset*" can metonymically stand for anger because physical agitation is a part of our folk theory of anger (which does not, of course, mean that a person needs to be angry in order to be considered upset). Conceptual metaphors will be discussed in detail below. Here, suffice it to mention only some examples: love as insanity (e.g., "I am *crazy* about you"), love as war (e.g., "He *conquered* her"), anger as fire (e.g., "That comment just *added fuel to the fire*"), fear as an opponent (e.g., "I was *struggling* with my fear"), and many more. Finally, related concepts are ones that form a part of the network of concepts associated with the concept in question. Romantic love, for example, seems to have a very large and elaborate network of concepts, including friendship, respect, intimacy, affection, sexual desire, enthusiasm, and others. The chapter on love will mainly focus on this aspect of emotion concepts.

The idea that the structure of most emotion concepts consists of the four parts as given in 1., 2., 3., and 4., gives us a picture of the nature and structure of emotional concepts that is very different from the one we saw in chapter 2. Indeed it is so different that it requires a great deal of justification. Most of this book will be devoted to just this task. For the time being, however, we must turn our attention to some methodological issues.

A Lexical Approach to the Structure of Concepts

It is a basic assumption of this work that a large part of our conceptual system can be uncovered through a detailed study of most of the lexical expressions that are related to particular concepts. The principle that underlies this assumption is that language, particularly its lexicon, is a reflection of our conceptual system. An approach to concepts that is based on the study of lexical expressions can be called a "lexical approach" (cf. Verschueren 1985), and the models of concepts that we arrive at in this manner can be termed "language-based" (folk) models.

This approach to the conceptual system can be regarded as a continuation of some respectable traditions in the study of cognitive systems. One tradition I have in mind is what is called "linguistic analysis" as represented in the works of Wittgenstein (1953), Austin (1961), Ryle (1949), and others. These philosophers use ordinary language for discovering subtle conceptual distinctions among such philosophically interesting categories as "action," "meaning," "mind," "emotion," and so forth. We saw examples of this kind of analysis in the previous chapter. The other tradition comes from ethnography and anthropology. Ethnographers and anthropologists who are interested in the cognitive systems of various peoples look at language as an important tool in the job of learning about these cognitive systems. Researchers in this area owe a great deal to the pioneering work of Sapir (1949) and Whorf (1956). One of the most influential recent advocates of this methodology, Charles Frake, sees the role of language in this connection in the following way:

The analysis of a culture's terminological systems will not, or course, exhaustively reveal the cognitive world of its members, but it will certainly tap a central portion of it. Culturally significant cognitive features must be communicable between persons in one of the standard symbolic systems of the culture. A major share of these features will undoubtedly be codable in a society's most flexible and productive communicative device, its language. (in Dil, ed., 1980: 3)

Similarly, my assumption in this study will be that it is possible to uncover a portion of our conceptual system by studying the way we talk about various aspects of the world. However, there are also some major differences between these traditions and the methodology that I am proposing.

One point of divergence concerns the goals that the methods are aimed at. In the philosophical and anthropological approaches mentioned above the goal of researchers is to discover the most important conceptual distinctions that are coded into the language (especially into its vocabulary). That is, these researchers are searching for the main dimensions along which concepts can be shown to be related to and especially to differ from each other. By contrast, my main emphasis will be on how a single concept like "anger," "fear," "pride," "respect," or "love" is structured internally. In short, while the main aim of the former approaches is to point out conceptual differences between items, my focus of interest is on the conceptual organization of a single item. (This does not mean, however, that the lexical approach I am working with cannot lead to some interesting "inter-item" issues.) It seems to me that it is this difference in emphasis that is mainly responsible for the impoverished view of meaning as predominantly core meaning. Concentrating on differences between items results in a skeleton of meaning for an item. On the other hand, I would like to believe that if we focus on the detailed internal structure of an item the conceptual features responsible for the differences will fall out as well and will do so in a natural way. The emphasis on internal structure also opposes the lexical approach to those anthropological works that try to capture the interaction between the domain of emotion *as a whole* and the system of cultural values in a society. It was pointed out in the previous chapter that we cannot expect to find the connections between these two domains without going into great detail in the analysis of *particular* concepts.

Another difference between the two approaches is closely related to the first. In accordance with their goals as given above, the philosophers and anthropologists in question try to find those conceptual dimensions that provide systematic (preferably binary) *contrasts* that apply to a large portion of the lexicon. The lexical approach as conceived of in the present study does not seek such systematic contrasts. When it is proposed, for example, that the proposition "I view myself as forming a unity with the other," which characterizes love, is a part of the conceptual model of love, it is not expected that this feature has a (binary or any other kind of) counterpart and that it will show up in other items in the lexicon. The idea of contrast is simply irrelevant here. Nevertheless, as we shall see, these nonsystematic features play just as important a role as systematic core components in defining what we mean by emotion words.

Finally, the philosophical and anthropological approaches are deficient in an important respect. This is the fact that they do not seem to recognize the special relevance of metonomy, metaphor, and what was termed "related concepts" to the makeup of some concepts. I do not wish to claim that these are all relevant to each concept or that they are relevant to the same degree, but I certainly wish to claim that the analysis of a large number of concepts would be deficient without taking at least some of them into account.

Since one reflection of our conceptual system is language, the examination of the linguistic expressions that have to do with anger, fear, pride, respect, and love should prove to be a fruitful approach to the study of the conceptual models of these emotions. Since I am primarily concerned with the everyday conception of anger, fear, pride, respect, and love—as opposed to scientific and artistic conceptions—I focus attention on what might be viewed as everyday linguistic expressions associated with these emotions. The material on which this study is based is composed of those linguistic expressions that are commonly used by and are familiar to most, if not all, native speakers of English, that is, those expressions that do not belong to the sphere of either scientific or artistic discourse. As a result, the expressions we will be looking at often will be well-worn, clichéd or even hackneyed. However, this need not cause the least concern, since the goal is to make explicit our most everyday conception of anger, fear, respect, pride, and love. I will be referring to expressions of this kind as "conventionalized" (or "standardized," as Frake puts it (Dil, ed., 1980: 4) linguistic expressions. Thus, a twofold distinction is intended. First, I would like to draw a distinction between conventionalized language and conventional language. In a sense, most expressions of a language can be regarded as conventional (except, maybe, sound-imitating words). However, not all conventional expressions are also conventionalized, that is, worn-out or clichèd, for instance. This distinction will become clearer as we go along. The second distinction is intended to capture the difference between conventionalized expressions on the one hand and creative, novel, unconventional, or nonstandardized expressions on the other. In the case of love, for example, such expressions could be used by a good poet when he or she writes about love.

The conventionalized expressions of a language consist of a wide variety of expression types. These include metaphors, metonymies, idioms, clichés, sayings, proverbs, collocations (typical co-occurences of words), and more. Let us take love as an example. The number of conventionalized expressions about love in many languages is considerable. In English it is roughly 300. Here are some examples from Kövecses (1988):

Love is blind.
She carries a torch for him.
We are one.
It was a torrid love story.
He caressed her gently.
I am crazy about you.
She gave him her heart.
He worships the ground she walks on.
The magic is gone.
Love lasts forever.
She pursued him relentlessly.
He was given new strength by love.
I am so happy with you.

My claim is that inherent in these and similar expressions is a conceptual model of love, which we can make explicit if we examine the way in which the expressions are related to each other and which aspects of love they capture. A further contention is that, contrary to the practice of some philosophers and anthropologists, each and every expression related to a concept has to be examined if we wish to uncover the minute details of the concept.

The expressions above and other similar ones are not isolated. It is a methodologically important property of lexical items associated with emotion concepts that they come in systems. We can distinguish two major kinds of system: a metaphorical and a metonymical one. The metaphorical system is constituted by a variety of conceptual metaphors (like "Love is war") and the metonymical system by a variety of conceptual metonymies (like "Physical agitation stands for anger"). Since the various idioms, clichés, sayings, proverbs, and collocations are often metaphorical or metonymical in nature, they also often fall into these two major systems. For example, the expression "He worships the ground she walks on" is an idiom, but it is an idiom that is also a metaphor. In this case the conceptual metaphor is THE OBJECT OF LOVE IS A DEITY.

It would seem then that the task is to group all the lexical expressions associated with a given emotional concept into conceptual metaphors and metonymies. This results in a system of conceptual metaphors and metonymies, which represents two of the parts that were given in the previous section as constituting the structure of most emotion concepts. For example, in some situations the sentence "He caressed her gently" might be used to indicate, or suggest, love. Lexical expressions like *caress gently* and other similar items make up the INTIMATE SEXUAL BEHAVIOR STANDS FOR LOVE conceptual metonymy. The expression *torrid love* story is a part of another conceptual metonymy: BODY HEAT STANDS FOR LOVE. We often conceptualize love as insanity. The expression *I am crazy about you* is an example of the LOVE IS INSANITY conceptual metaphor. The third part of the structure of emotion concepts was given as "related concepts." The expression "I am so happy with you" can, in certain situations, be taken to indicate love. This is possible because love and happiness are related concepts. If I am in love and my love is returned, I am also happy. In general, in most cases related concepts are like conceptual metonymies; expressions referring to them (e.g., "I am so *happy* with you") can be used to mean the concept to which they are related (e.g., love).

Thus, we seem to have a large number and wide variety of conventionalized expressions that can be grouped into various conceptual metaphors and metonymies. The conceptual metaphors and the conceptual metonymies including related concepts form two large systems. This is one aspect of the systematic nature of the methodology. The other aspect involves the question of how these two systems (comprising the *three* parts—1., 2., and 3.—of the structure of emotion concepts), on the one hand and the category of cognitive models, on the other, are related. At this point, we can simply say that the two systems converge on the category of cognitive models and especially on the prototypical cognitive models. The amount of conceptual content that prototypical models incorporate is often a function of how richly a given concept is conceptualized in metaphorical and metonymical terms. We have seen that, for example, INTIMATE SEXUAL BEHAVIOR is a conceptual metonymy of (romantic) love and thus also appears as a part of the prototypical cognitive model. Happiness, a related concept of love, is another part of that model. The convergence of conceptual metonymies and related concepts onto cognitive models is fairly obvious in most cases. The same process is less obvious in the case of conceptual metaphors. This issue will be dealt with in the next section.

It is appropriate to close this section with a tentative answer to a question raised at the end of a previous section. The question was whether the conventionalized language we use to talk about the emotions accurately reflects current beliefs about the emotions. (This issue was raised by Ortony 1988.) It can be argued that, for example, from the use of conventionalized language like "The sun came up" and "The sun went down" it does not follow that we believe today that the earth is stationary and the sun moves up and down with respect to it. This example would seem to suggest that our folk models based on language do not reveal current beliefs and so our claim that we can uncover valid folk models of emotion from language is not justified. However, I do not think that our conceptions of the earth/sun and of emotion are comparable. The major difference, from our point of view, is that, as a result of certain scientific discoveries, our educational system has spent several centuries on changing our geocentric view of the relationship between the earth and the sun. The consequence is that, despite our language use, anyone with at least some elementary education would refuse the geocentric view as his or her folk model of the earth/sun relationship. Nothing like this has been the case with the emotions. No such large-scale attempts have been made to change our thinking about them (though there have been *some* attempts like the human potential movement). As a result, we pretty much believe what we say about them. We have some experimental evidence that suggests that, for example, in the case of romantic love the language-based folk model is very close to what a large number of people actually believe about love (Averill and Boothroyd 1977). It seems then that, as far as the emotions go, we still live by and think in terms of a geocentric emotional universe.

Metaphor

Metaphors play an important role in the study of emotional meaning and experience for a variety of reasons. First, they are pervasive in the language we use to describe the emotions. Second, and this is closely related to the first, a large part of our emotional understanding seems to be based on metaphor. Third, it is often hardly noticeable that we understand aspects of emotions in metaphorical terms. Fourth, in many cases the metaphors that we use for emotional understanding have subtle consequences that can affect thought and behavior in subtle ways.

The first point is the easiest to demonstrate. We can continue to use love as an example. Among the expressions that are related to love we can find a large number of metaphorical expressions. Even the small sample of conventionalized language about love in the previous section contains several metaphors: "We are one," "I am crazy about you," "She gave him her heart," "The magic is gone," "She pursued him relentlessly," "He was given new strength by love," "She carries a torch for him," and so on.

To see how metaphors are utilized in the understanding of a variety of emotional experiences, we can take the last example. The expression *carry a torch for someone* is not the only one that has to do with fire. There are several other conventionalized expressions that indicate that we often conceptualize the concept of love as fire. Let us see some more examples for the LOVE IS FIRE conceptual metaphor:

LOVE IS FIRE.
My heart's *on fire*.
He was *burning* with love.
The old-time *fire* is gone.
She *set* my heart *on fire*.
There were *sparks*.
She is his latest *flame*.
The *fire* slowly *went out*.
That *kindled* love in his heart.
I don't want to get *burned* again.

He was *consumed* by love.
I just *melted* when she looked at me.
She carries a *torch* for him.

When expressions from one domain (in this case, fire) are used to capture aspects of another domain (in this case, love), we have conceptual metaphors (Lakoff and Johnson 1980). Conceptual metaphors involve two concepts, one of which is typically abstract and the other typically concrete. The more difficult (i.e., the more abstract) concept is called the "target domain," and the concept in terms of which we try to understand this concept is the "source domain." Not only the target domain but also the source domain can be characterized by several (prototypical and nonprototypical) cognitive models, or schemas. Typically, it is the prototypical schema (i.e., the most familiar conceptual content) of the source domain that is utilized in the process of mapping this content onto the target domain. One (prototypical) schema associated with fire could be given as follows:

Event A causes a thing B to burn.
Thing B is burning. (Fire exists)
The fire is burning with intensity.
The thing burning (B) is unable to function normally.
The fire can cause physical pain in person C.
The fire may go out (of existence).

The concept of love, as structured by various (prototypical and nonprototypical) schemas, may, among other things, contain the following parts:

Person A causes person B to love A.
Person B loves person A. (Love exists)
The love is intense.
The person in love (B) is unable to function normally.
Love can cause emotional pain in a person in love (C).
Love can go out of existence.

Since the concept of love may contain all these parts, the LOVE IS FIRE conceptual metaphor can map all the parts of the fire domain onto the corresponding parts of the love domain. This is what is meant by saying that a concept is understood in terms of another concept that is in some way more simple or easier to understand. This formulation of the process of mapping assumes that the parts of the target domain must exist independently of the conceptual metaphor. But this may not always be the case. It is perhaps also possible that mappings from one domain onto another can also take place when the target domain does not have previously existing corresponding parts. In fact, it is questionable whether "The person in love (B) is unable to function normally" or the "Love can cause emotional pain in a person in love (C)" parts of the concept of love exist independently of the fire metaphor. I will return to this issue in a moment.

Thus the following mappings, or correspondences between the fire and love domains, can be specified.

1. The cause of the fire is the cause (source) of love.
2. The existence of the fire is the existence of love.
3. The intensity of the fire is the intensity of love.
4. The inability of the thing burning to function normally is the inability of the person in love to function normally.
5. The physical pain caused by the fire is the emotional pain caused by love.
6. The going out (of existence) of the fire is the going out of existence of love.

It is these correspondences on the basis of which we can make sense of the expressions from the domain of fire when they are used to talk about love:

Correspondence	Expressions made sense of
1.	*set one's heart on fire; kindle love*
2.	*one's heart is on fire; burn with love*
3.	*sparks; flame; carry a torch*
4.	*consumed by love; melt*
5.	*get burned*
6.	*fire goes out; fire is gone*

The correspondences also show which aspects of love are addressed by the LOVE IS FIRE conceptual metaphor. They include the beginning of love, the existence of love, the intensity of love, and so forth. The special significance of examining most of the linguistic examples of a given conceptual metaphor is that they can direct our attention to aspects of a concept in an explicit way.

Let us now return to the important theoretical question of whether the parts of the concept of love exist independently of the fire metaphor or it is the fire metaphor that *creates* these aspects. This is a very difficult question, which touches upon the third reason why metaphors must be taken very seriously in the study of emotions; namely, that emotional meaning and experience are often metaphorical in imperceptible ways. In general, my suggestion will be that conceptual metaphors, like LOVE IS FIRE, actually *create* several aspects of emotional concepts like love. However, since this is one of the major claims that I would like to make in this book and it is one that requires ample documentation, at this point it would be premature to discuss the issue any further. And since the fourth reason for the serious study of metaphor in emotion is dependent on the acceptance of the third, we should also delay the explicit discussion of how metaphorical understandings of emotions can affect thought and behavior until the last chapter.

It was mentioned in the previous section that the conceptual material of the metonymic and metaphoric systems converges on one or more prototypical cognitive models. We have seen some metonymic examples for this process. Now we can also see how the process of convergence applies to the materials that are produced by the conceptual metaphors. It has been shown that one of the things that the LOVE IS FIRE metaphor maps onto the concept of love is that love is a very intense experience (cf. words like *flame* and *sparks*). The same aspect of love can be found in the prototypical model. Similarly, the inability of a person in love to function normally (cf. words like *consume* and *melt*) shows up in the proposition "I am in a state of lack of control." In other words, some of the propositions that get mapped from the concept of fire onto the concept of love via the LOVE IS FIRE metaphor end up in the prototypical cognitive model. This is what I mean when I say that the conceptual material of the metaphoric system (and also that of the metonymic system) converges on the (prototypical) cognitive models. But, of course, not all of this material ends up in the prototypes. The conceptual metaphors may contain correspondences between the source and target domains that contradict our prototypes. Since, for example, our ideal version of romantic love maintains that (romantic) love lasts forever, the partial contribution of the fire metaphor that love goes out of existence simply won't find its way into the ideal model. When this happens, the metaphor can be regarded as producing nonprototypical cases. We return to the discussion of this issue in the last chapter.

Conclusions

An attempt has been made to show that emotion concepts have a much more complex structure than has been previously suggested. This structure consists of conceptual metonymies, conceptual metaphors, related concepts, and a category of cognitive models with one or more prototypical models in the center. The key notions relevant to this view have been introduced; namely, those of prototype, cognitive models, and conceptual metaphors. It has been suggested that what has been called a "lexical approach" can be a useful method in the systematic study of emotional meaning and experience. The next chapter—the examination of the concept of anger—is a detailed demonstration of this approach.

4
Anger

Emotions are often considered to be feelings alone, and as such they are viewed as being devoid of conceptual content. As a result, the study of emotions is usually not taken seriously by students of semantics and conceptual structure. A topic such as The Logic of Emotion would seem on this view to be a contradiction in terms, since emotions, being devoid of conceptual content, would give rise to no inferences at all, or at least none of any interest. We would like to argue that the opposite is true, that emotions have an extremely complex conceptual structure, which gives rise to a wide variety of nontrivial inferences.

The Conceptualization of Anger

At first glance, the conventionalized expressions used to talk about anger seem so diverse that finding any coherent system would seem impossible. For example, if we look up anger in, say, *Roget's University Thesaurus,* we find about three hundred entries, most of which have something or other to do with anger, but the thesaurus does not tell us exactly what. Many of these are idioms, and they too seem too diverse to reflect any coherent cognitive model. Here are some example sentences using such idioms:

He *lost his cool.*
She was *looking daggers at* me.
I almost *burst a blood vessel.*
He was *foaming at the mouth.*
You're beginning to *get to* me.
You make by *blood boil.*
He's *wrestling with* his anger.
Watch out! He's *on a short fuse.*
He's just *letting off steam.*

Try to *keep a grip on* yourself.
Don't *fly off the handle.*
When I told him, he *blew up.*
He *channeled* his anger into something constructive.
He was *red* with anger.
He was *blue in the face.*
He *appeased* his anger.
He was *doing a slow burn.*
He *suppressed* his anger.
She kept *bugging* me.
When I told my mother, she *had a cow.*

What do these expressions have to do with anger, and what do they have to do with each other? We will be arguing that they are not random. When we look at inferences among these expressions, it becomes clear that there must be a systematic structure of some kind. We know, for example, that someone who is foaming at the mouth has lost his cool. We know that someone who is looking daggers at you is likely to be doing a slow burn or be on a short fuse. We know that someone who has channeled his anger into something constructive has not had a cow. How do we know these things? Is it just that each idiom has a literal meaning and the inferences are based on the literal meanings? Or is there something more going on? What we will try to show is that there is a coherent conceptual organization underlying all these expressions, and that much of it is metaphorical and metonymical in nature.

Metaphor and Metonymy

The analysis we are proposing begins with the common cultural model of the physiological effects of anger:

The physiological effects of anger are increased body heat, increased internal pressure (blood pressure, muscular pressure), agitation, and interference with accurate perception.

As anger increases, its physiological effects increase.

There is a limit beyond which the physiological effects of anger impair normal functioning.

We use this cultural model in large measure to tell when someone is angry on the basis of their appearance—as well as to signal anger or hide it. In doing this, we make use of a general metonymic principle:

The physiological effects of an emotion stand for the emotion.

Given this principle, the cultural model given above yields a system of metonymies for anger:

BODY HEAT
Don't get *hot under the collar.*
Billy's a *hothead.*
They were having a *heated* argument.
When the cop gave her a ticket, she got all *hot and bothered.*

INTERNAL PRESSURE
Don't get a *hernia!*
When I found out, I almost *burst a blood vessel.*
He almost had a *hemorrhage.*

Increased body heat and/or blood pressure is assumed to cause redness in the face and neck area, and such redness can also metonymically indicate anger.

REDNESS IN FACE AND NECK AREA
She was *scarlet* with rage.
He got *red* with anger.
He was *flushed* with anger.

AGITATION
She was *shaking* with anger.
I was *hopping* mad.
He was *quivering* with rage.
He's all *worked up.*
She's all *wrought up.*

INTERFERENCE WITH ACCURATE PERCEPTION
She was *blind* with rage.
I was beginning to *see red.*
I was so mad I *couldn't see straight.*

Each of these expressions indicates the presence of anger via its supposed physiological effects.

The cultural model of physiological effects, especially the part that emphasizes heat, forms the basis of the most general metaphor for anger: ANGER IS HEAT. There are two versions of this metaphor, one where the heat applies to fluids, the other where it is applied to solids. When it is applied to fluids, we get: ANGER IS THE HEAT OF A FLUID IN A CONTAINER. The specific motivation for this consists of the HEAT,

INTERNAL PRESSURE and AGITATION parts of the cultural model. When ANGER IS HEAT is applied to solids, we get the version ANGER IS FIRE, which is motivated by the heat and redness aspects of the cultural theory of physiological effects.

As we shall see shortly, the fluid version is much more highly elaborated. The reason for this, we surmise, is that in our overall conceptual system we have the general metaphor:

THE BODY IS A CONTAINER FOR THE EMOTIONS
He was *filled with* anger.
She couldn't *contain* her joy.
She was *brimming with* rage.
Try to get your anger *out of your system.*

The ANGER IS HEAT metaphor, when applied to fluids, combines with the metaphor THE BODY IS A CONTAINER FOR THE EMOTIONS to yield the central metaphor of the system:

ANGER IS THE HEAT OF A FLUID IN A CONTAINER
You make my *blood boil.*
Simmer down!
I had reached the *boiling point.*
Let him *stew.*

A historically derived instance of this metaphor is:

She was *seething with* rage.

Although most speakers do not now use *seethe* to indicate physical boiling, the boiling image is still there when *seethe* is used to indicate anger. Similarly, *pissed off* is used only to refer to anger, not to the hot liquid under pressure in the bladder. Still, the effectiveness of the expression seems to depend on such an image.

When there is no heat the liquid is cool and calm. In the central metaphor, cool and calmness corresponds to lack of anger:

Keep *cool.*
Keep *calm.*

As we will see shortly, the central metaphor is an extremely productive one. There are two ways in which a conceptual metaphor can be productive. The first is lexical. The words and fixed expressions of a language can *code,* that is, be used to express aspects of, a given conceptual metaphor to a greater or lesser extent. The number of conventionalized linguistic expressions that code a given conceptual metaphor is one measure of the productivity of the metaphor. In addition, the words and fixed expressions of a language can *elaborate* the conceptual metaphor. For example, stew is a special case in which there is a hot fluid in a container. It is something that continues at a given level of heat for a long time. This special case can be used to elaborate the central metaphor. "Stewing" indicates the continuance of anger over a long period. Another special case is "simmer," which indicates a low boil. This can be used to indicate a lowering of the intensity of anger. Although both of these are cooking terms, cooking plays no metaphorical role in these cases. It just happens to be a case where there is a hot fluid in a container. This is typical of lexical elaborations.

Let us refer to the HEAT OF FLUID IN A CONTAINER as the source domain of the central metaphor, to anger as the target domain. We usually have extensive knowledge about source domains. A second way in which a conceptual metaphor can be productive is that it can carry over details of that knowledge from the source domain to the target domain. We will refer to such carryovers as metaphorical entailments. Such entailments are part of our conceptual system. They constitute elaborations of conceptual metaphors. The central metaphor has a rich system of metaphorical entailments. For example, one thing we know about hot fluids is that when they start to boil, the fluid goes upward. This gives rise to the entailment:

WHEN THE INTENSITY OF ANGER INCREASES, THE FLUID RISES
His pent-up anger *welled up* inside him.
She could feel her *gorge rising*.
We got a *rise* out of him.
My anger kept *building up* inside me.
Pretty soon I was in a *towering* rage.

We also know that intense heat produces steam and creates pressure on the container. This yields the metaphorical entailments:

INTENSE ANGER PRODUCES STEAM
She got all *steamed up*.
Billy's just *blowing off steam*.
I was *fuming*.

INTENSE ANGER PRODUCES PRESSURE ON THE CONTAINER
He was *bursting with* anger.
I could barely *contain* my rage.
I could barely *keep it in* anymore.

A variant of this involves keeping the pressure back:

I *suppressed* my anger.
He *turned* his anger *inward*.
He managed to keep his anger *bottled up* inside him.
He was *blue in the face*.

When the pressure on the container becomes too high, the container explodes. This yields the entailment:

WHEN ANGER BECOMES TOO INTENSE, THE PERSON EXPLODES
When I told him, he just *exploded*.
She *blew up* at me.
We won't tolerate any more of your *outbursts*.

This can be elaborated, using special cases:

Pistons: He *blew a gasket*.
Volcanos: She *erupted*.
Electricity: I *blew a fuse*.
Explosives: She's *on a short fuse*.
Bombs: That really *set* me *off*.

In an explosion, parts of the container go up in the air.

WHEN A PERSON EXPLODES, PARTS OF HIM GO UP IN THE AIR
I *blew my stack*.
I *blew my top*.
She *flipped her lid*.
He *hit the ceiling*.
I *went through the roof*.

When something explodes, what was inside it comes out.

WHEN A PERSON EXPLODES, WHAT WAS INSIDE HIM COMES OUT
His anger finally *came out*.
Smoke was *pouring out of his ears*.

This can be elaborated in terms of animals giving birth, where something that was inside causing pressure bursts out:

WHEN A PERSON EXPLODES, WHAT WAS INSIDE HIM COMES OUT

She was *having kittens*.
My mother will *have a cow* when I tell her.

Let us now turn to the question of what issues the central metaphor addresses and what kind of ontology of anger it reveals. The central metaphor focuses on the fact that anger can be intense, that it can lead to a loss of control, and that a loss of control can be dangerous. Let us begin with intensity. Anger is conceptualized as a mass, and takes the grammar of mass nouns, as opposed to count nouns. Thus, you can say:

How much anger has he got in him?

but not

*How many angers does he have in him?

Anger thus has the ontology of a mass entity, that is, it has a scale indicating its amount, it exists when the amount is greater than zero, and it goes out of existence when the amount falls to zero. In the central metaphor, the scale indicating the amount of anger is the heat-scale. But, as the central metaphor indicates, the anger scale is not open-ended; it has a limit. Just as a hot fluid in a closed container can only take so much heat before it explodes, so we conceptualize the anger scale as having a limit point. We can only bear so much anger, before we explode, that is, lose control. This has its correlates in our cultural theory of physiological effects. As anger gets more intense the physiological effects increase and those increases interfere with our normal functioning. Body heat, blood pressure, agitation, and interference with perception cannot increase without limit before our ability to function normally becomes seriously impaired and we lose control over our functioning. In the cultural model of anger, loss of control is dangerous, both to the angry person and to those around him. In the central metaphor, the danger of loss of control is understood as the danger of explosion.

The structural aspect of a conceptual metaphor consists of a set of correspondences between a source domain and a target domain. These correspondences can be factored into two types: ontological and epistemic. Ontological correspondences are correspondences between the entities in the source domain and the corresponding entities in the target domain. For example, the container in the source domain corresponds to the body in the target domain. Epistemic correspondences are correspondences between knowledge about the source domain and corresponding knowledge about the target domain. We can schematize these correspondences between the fluid domain and the anger domain as follows:

Source: HEAT OF FLUID IN CONTAINER
Target: ANGER

Ontological Correspondences:

- the container is the body
- the heat of fluid is the anger
- the heat scale is the anger scale, with end points zero and limit
- container heat is body heat
- pressure in container is internal pressure in the body
- agitation of fluid and container is physical agitation
- the limit of the container's capacity to withstand pressure caused by heat is the limit on the anger scale
- explosion is loss of control
- danger of explosion is danger of loss of control
- coolness in the fluid is lack of anger
- calmness of the fluid is lack of agitation

Epistemic correspondences:

Source: The effect of intense fluid heat is container heat, internal pressure, and agitation.
Target: The effect of intense anger is body heat, internal pressure, and agitation.

Source: When the fluid is heated past a certain limit, pressure increases to the point at which the container explodes.
Target: When anger increases past a certain limit, pressure increases to the point at which the person loses control.

Source: An explosion is damaging to the container and dangerous to bystanders.
Target: A loss of control is damaging to an angry person and dangerous to other people.

Source: An explosion may be prevented by the application of sufficient force and energy to keep the fluid in.
Target: A loss of control may be prevented by the application of sufficient force and energy to keep the anger in.

Source: It is sometimes possible to control the release of heated fluid for either destructive or constructive purposes; this has the effect of lowering the level of heat and pressure.
Target: It is sometimes possible to control the release of anger for either destructive or constructive purposes; this has the effect of lowering the level of anger and internal pressure.

The latter case defines an elaboration of the entailment WHEN A PERSON EXPLODES, WHAT WAS INSIDE HIM COMES OUT:

ANGER CAN BE LET OUT UNDER CONTROL
He *let out* his anger.

I *gave vent* to my anger.
Channel your anger into something constructive.
He *took out* his anger on me.

So far, we have seen that the cultural theory of physiological reactions provides the basis for the central metaphor, and that the central metaphor characterizes detailed correspondences between the source domain and the target domain—correspondences concerning both ontology and knowledge.

At this point, our analysis enables us to see why various relationships among idioms hold. We can see why someone who is in a towering rage has not kept his cool, why someone who is stewing may have contained his anger but has not gotten it out of his system, why someone who has suppressed his anger has not yet erupted, and why someone who has channeled his anger into something constructive has not had a cow.

Let us now turn to the case where the general ANGER IS HEAT metaphor is applied to solids:

ANGER IS FIRE
Those are *inflammatory* remarks.
She was *doing a slow burn.*
He was *breathing fire.*
Your insincere apology just *added fuel to the fire.*
After the argument, Dave was *smoldering* for days.
That *kindled* my ire.
Boy, am I *burned up!*
He was *consumed* by his anger.

This metaphor highlights the cause of anger (*kindle, inflame*), the intensity and duration (*smoldering, slow burn, burned up*), the danger to others (*breathing fire*), and the damage to the angry person (*consumed*). The correspondences in ontology are as follows:

Source: FIRE
Target: ANGER

- the fire is anger
- the thing burning is the angry person
- the cause of the fire is the cause of the anger
- the intensity of the fire is the intensity of anger
- the physical damage to the thing burning is mental damage to the angry person
- the capacity of the thing burning to serve its normal function is the capacity of the angry person to function normally
- an object at the point of being consumed by fire corresponds to a person to a person whose anger is at the limit

• the danger of the fire to things nearby is danger of the anger to other people

The correspondences in knowledge are:

Source: Things can burn at low intensity for a long time and then burst into flame.
Target: People can be angry at a low intensity for a long time and then suddenly become extremely angry.

Source: Fires are dangerous to things nearby.
Target: Angry people are dangerous to other people.

Source: Things consumed by fire cannot serve their normal function.
Target: At the limit of the anger scale, people cannot function normally.

Putting together what we have done so far, we can see why someone who is doing a slow burn has not hit the ceiling yet, why someone whose anger is bottled up is not breathing fire, why someone who is consumed by anger probably cannot see straight, and why adding fuel to the fire might just cause the person you are talking to to have kittens.

The Other Principal Metaphors

As we have seen, the ANGER IS HEAT metaphor is based on the cultural model of the physiological effects of anger, according to which increased body heat is a major effect of anger. That cultural model also maintains that agitation is an important effect. Agitation is also an important part of our cultural theory of insanity. According to this view, people who are insane are unduly agitated—they go wild, start raving, flail their arms, foam at the mouth, and so on. Correspondingly, these physiological effects can stand, metonymically, for insanity. One can indicate that someone is insane by describing him as foaming at the mouth, raving, going wild, for example.

The overlap between the cultural models of the effects of anger and the effects of insanity provides a basis for the metaphor:

ANGER IS INSANITY
I just touched him, and he *went crazy.*
You're *driving me nuts!*
When the umpire called him out on strikes, he *went bananas.*
One more complaint and I'll *go berserk.*
He got so angry, he *went out of his mind.*

When he gets angry, he *goes bonkers.*
She went into an *insane rage.*
If anything else goes wrong, I'll *get hysterical.*

Perhaps the most common conventional expression for anger came into English historically as a result of this metaphor:

I'm *mad!*

Because of this metaphorical link between insanity and anger, expressions that indicate insane behavior can also indicate angry behavior. Given the metonymy INSANE BEHAVIOR STANDS FOR INSANITY and the metonymy ANGER IS INSANITY, we get the metaphorical metonymy:

INSANE BEHAVIOR STANDS FOR ANGER
When my mother finds out, she'll *have a fit.*
When the ump threw him out of the game, Billy started *foaming at the mouth.*
He's *fit to be tied.*
He is about to *throw a tantrum.*

Violent behavior indicative of frustration is viewed as a form of insane behavior. According to our cultural model of anger, people who can neither control nor relieve the pressure of anger engage in violent frustrated behavior. This cultural model is the basis for the metonymy:

VIOLENT FRUSTRATED BEHAVIOR STANDS FOR ANGER
He's *tearing his hair out!*
If one more thing goes wrong, I'll start *banging my head against the wall.*
The loud music next door has got him *climbing the walls!*
She's been *slamming doors all morning.*

The ANGER IS INSANITY metaphor has the following correspondences:

Source: INSANITY
Target: ANGER

- the cause of insanity is the cause of anger
- becoming insane is passing the limit point on the anger scale
- insane behavior is angry behavior

Source: An insane person cannot function normally.
Target: A person who is angry beyond the limit point cannot function normally.

Source: An insane person is dangerous to others.
Target: A person who is angry beyond the limit point is dangerous to others.

At this point we can see a generalization. Emotional effects are understood as physical effects. Anger is understood as a form of energy. According to our cultural understanding of physics, when enough input energy is applied to a body, the body begins to produce output energy. Thus, the cause of anger is viewed as input energy that produces internal heat (output energy). Moreover, the internal heat can function as input energy, producing various forms of output energy: steam, pressure, externally radiating heat, and agitation. Such output energy (the angry behavior) is viewed as dangerous to others. In the insanity metaphor, insanity is understood as a highly energized state, with insane behavior as a form of energy output.

All in all, anger is understood in our cultural model as a negative emotion. It produces undesirable physiological reactions, leads to an inability to function normally, and is dangerous to others. The angry person, recognizing this danger, views his anger as an opponent.

ANGER IS AN OPPONENT (IN A STRUGGLE)
I'm *struggling* with my anger.
He was *battling* his anger.
She *fought back* her anger.
I've been *wrestling* with my anger all day.
I was *seized* by anger.
I'm finally *coming to grips with* my anger.
He *lost control over* his anger.
Anger *took control* of him.
He *surrendered* to his anger.
He *yielded* to his anger.
I was *overcome* by anger.
Her anger has been *appeased*.

The ANGER IS OPPONENT metaphor is constituted by the following correspondences:

Source: STRUGGLE
Target: ANGER

- the opponent is anger
- winning is controlling anger
- losing is having anger control you
- surrender is allowing anger to take control of you
- the pool of resources needed for winning is the energy needed to control anger

One thing that is left out of this account so far is what constitutes "appeasement." To appease an opponent is to give in to his demands. This suggests that anger has demands. We will address the question of what these demands are below.

The OPPONENT metaphor focuses on the issue of control and the danger of loss of control to the angry person himself. There is another metaphor that focuses on the issue of control, but whose main focus is the danger to others. It is a very widespread metaphor in Western culture, namely, PASSIONS ARE BEASTS INSIDE A PERSON. According to this metaphor, there is a part of each person that is a wild animal. Civilized people are supposed to keep that part of them private, that is, they are supposed to keep the animal inside them. In the metaphor, loss of control is equivalent to the animal's getting loose. And the behavior of a person who has lost control is the behavior of a wild animal. There are versions of this metaphor for various passions—desire, anger, and so forth. In the case of anger, the beast presents a danger to other people.

ANGER IS A DANGEROUS ANIMAL
He has a *ferocious* temper.
He has a *fierce* temper.
It's dangerous to *arouse* his anger.
That *awakened* my ire.
His anger *grew*.
He has a *monstrous* temper.
He *unleashed* his anger.
Don't let your anger *get out of hand*.
He *lost his grip* on his anger.
His anger is *insatiable*.

An example that draws on both the FIRE and DANGEROUS ANIMAL metaphors is:

He was *breathing fire*.

The image here is of a dragon, a dangerous animal that can devour you with fire.

The DANGEROUS ANIMAL metaphor portrays anger as a sleeping animal that is dangerous to awaken; as something that can grow and thereby become dangerous; as something that has to be held back; and as something with a dangerous appetite. Here are the correspondences that constitute the metaphor.

Source: DANGEROUS ANIMAL
Target: ANGER

- the dangerous animal is the anger
- the animal's getting loose is lose of control of anger
- the owner of the dangerous animal is the angry person
- sleeping for the animal is anger near the limit

Source: It is dangerous for a dangerous animal to be loose.
Target: It is dangerous for a person's anger to be out of control.

Source: A dangerous animal is safe when it is sleeping and dangerous when it is awake.
Target: Anger is safe near the zero level and dangerous near the limit.

Source: A dangerous animal is safe when it is very small and dangerous when it is grown.
Target: Anger is safe near the zero level and dangerous near the limit.

Source: It is the responsibility of a dangerous animal's owner to keep it under control.
Target: It is the responsibility of an angry person to keep his anger under control.

Source: It requires a lot of energy to control a dangerous animal.
Target: It requires a lot of energy to control one's anger.

There is another class of expressions that, as far as we can tell, are instances of the same metaphor. These are cases in which angry behavior is described in terms of aggressive animal behavior.

ANGRY BEHAVIOR IS AGGRESSIVE ANIMAL BEHAVIOR
He was *bristling* with anger.
That *got my hackles up*.
He began to *bare his teeth*.
That *ruffled her feathers*.
She was *bridling with anger*.
Don't *snap* at me!
He started *snarling*.
Don't *bite my head off!*
Why did you *jump down my throat?*

Perhaps the best way to account for these cases would be to extend the ontological correspondences of the ANGER IS A DANGEROUS ANIMAL metaphor to include:

The aggressive behavior of the dangerous animal is angry behavior.

If we do this, we can account naturally for the fact that these expressions indicate anger. They would do so via a combination of metaphor and metonymy, in which the aggressive behavior metaphorically corresponds to angry behavior, which in turn metonymically stands for anger. For example, the snarling of the animal corresponds to the angry verbal behavior of the person, which in turn indicates the presence of anger.

Aggressive verbal behavior is a common form of angry behavior, as *snap, growl, snarl,* and so forth indicate. We can see this in a number of cases outside of the animal domain:

AGGRESSIVE VERBAL BEHAVIOR STANDS FOR ANGER
She gave him a *tongue-lashing*.
I really *chewed* him *out* good!

Other forms of aggressive behavior can also stand metonynically for anger, especially aggressive visual behavior:

AGGRESSIVE VISUAL BEHAVIOR STANDS FOR ANGER
She was *looking daggers* at me.
He *gave me a dirty look.*
If *looks could kill,* . . .
He was *glowering* at me.

All these metonymic expressions can be used to indicate anger.

As in the case of the OPPONENT metaphor, our analysis of the DANGEROUS ANIMAL metaphor leaves an expression unaccounted for—"insatiable." This expression indicates that the animal has an appetite. This "appetite" seems to correspond to the "demands" in the OPPONENT metaphor, as can be seen from the fact that the following sentences entail each other:

Harry's anger is *insatiable*.
Harry's anger cannot be *appeased*.

To see what it is that anger demands and has an appetite for, let us turn to expressions that indicate causes of anger. Perhaps the most common group of expressions that indicate anger consists of conventionalized forms of annoyance: minor pains, burdens placed on domestic animals, etc. Thus we have the metaphor:

THE CAUSE OF ANGER IS A PHYSICAL ANNOYANCE
Don't be a *pain in the ass*.
Get *off my back!*
You don't have to *ride me so hard*.
You're *getting under my skin*.
He's a *pain in the neck*.
Don't be a *pest!*

These forms of annoyance involve an offender and a victim. The offender is at fault. The victim, who is innocent, is the one who gets angry.

There is another set of conventionalized expressions used to speak of, or to, people who are in the process of making someone angry. These are expressions of territoriality, in which the cause of anger is viewed as trespasser.

CAUSING ANGER IS TRESPASSING
You're beginning to *get to* me.
This is where I *draw the line!*
Don't *step on my toes!*

Again, there is an offender (the cause of anger) and a victim (the person who is getting angry). In general, the cause of anger seems to be an offense, in which there is an offender who is at fault and an innocent victim who is the person who gets angry. The offense seems to constitute some sort of injustice. This is reflected in the conventional wisdom:

Don't get *mad,* get *even!*

In order for this saying to make sense, there has to be some connection between anger and retribution. Getting even is equivalent to balancing the scales of justice. The saying assumes a model in which injustice leads to anger and retribution can alleviate or prevent anger. In short, what anger "demands" and has an "appetite" for is revenge. This is why warnings and threats can count as angry behavior:

If I get mad, watch out!
Don't get me angry, or you'll be sorry.

The angry behavior is, in itself, viewed as a form of retribution.

We are now in a position to make sense of another metaphor for anger:

ANGER IS A BURDEN
Unburdening himself of his anger gave him a sense of *relief.*
After I lost my temper, I felt *lighter.*
He *carries* his anger around with him.
He *has a chip on his shoulder.*
You'll feel better if you *get it off your chest.*

In English, it is common for responsibilities to be metaphorized as burdens. There are two kinds of responsibilities involved in the cultural model of anger that has emerged so far. The first is a responsibility to control one's anger. In cases of extreme anger, this may place a considerable burden on one's "inner resources." The second comes from the model of retributive justice that is built into our concept of anger; it is the responsibility to seek vengeance. What is particularly interesting is that these two responsibilities are in conflict in the case of angry retribution: If you take out your anger on someone, you are not meeting your responsibility to control your anger, and if you do not take out your anger on someone, you are not meeting your responsibility to provide retribution. The slogan "Don't get mad, get even!" offers one way out: retribution without anger. The human potential movement provides another way out by suggesting that letting your anger out is okay. But the fact is that neither of these solutions is the cultural norm. It should also be mentioned in passing that the human potential movement's way of dealing with anger by sanctioning its release is not all that revolutionary. It assumes almost all of our standard cultural model and metaphorical understanding, and makes one change: sanctioning the "release."

Some Minor Metaphors

There are a few very general metaphors that apply to anger as well as to many other things and are commonly used in comprehending and speaking about anger. The first we will discuss has to do with existence. Existence is commonly understood in terms of physical presence. You are typically aware of something's presence if it is nearby and you can see it. This is the basis for the metaphor:

EXISTENCE IS PRESENCE
His anger *went away*.
His anger eventually *came back*.
My anger *lingered on* for days.
She couldn't *get rid of* her anger.
After a while, her anger just *vanished*.
My anger slowly began to *dissipate*.
When he saw her smile, his anger *disappeared*.

In the case of emotions, existence is often conceived of as location in a bounded space. Here the emotion is the bounded space and it exists when the person is in that space:

EMOTIONS ARE BOUNDED SPACES
She flew *into* a rage.
She was *in* an angry mood.
He was *in* a state of anger.
I am not easily roused *to* anger.

These cases are relatively independent of the rest of the anger system, and are included here more for completeness than for profundity.

The Prototype Scenario

The metaphors and metonymies that we have investigated so far converge on a certain prototypical cognitive model of anger. It is not the only model of anger we have; in fact, there are quite a few. But as we shall see, all of the others can be characterized as minimal variants of the model that the metaphors and metonymies converge on. The model has a temporal dimension, and can be conceived of as a scenario with a number of stages. We will call this the "prototype scenario": it is similar to what de Sousa (1980) calls the "paradigm scenario." We will be referring to the person who gets angry as S, short for the Self.

Stage 1: Offending event

There is an offending event that displeases S. There is a wrongdoer who intentionally does something directly to S. The wrongdoer is at fault and S is innocent. The offending event constitutes an injustice and produces anger in S. The scales of justice can only be balanced by some act of retribution. That is, the intensity of retribution must be roughly equal to the intensity of offense. S has the responsibility to perform such an act of retribution.

Stage 2: Anger

Associated with the entity anger is a scale that measures its intensity. As the intensity of anger increases, S experiences physiological effects; increase in body heat, internal pressure, and physical agitation. As the anger gets very intense, it exerts force upon S to perform an act of retribution. Because acts of retribution are dangerous and/or socially unacceptable, S has the responsibility to control his anger. Moreover, loss of control is damaging to S's own well-being, which is another motivation for controlling anger.

Stage 3: Attempt at control

S attempts to control his anger.

Stage 4: Loss of control

Each person has a certain tolerance for controlling anger. That tolerance can be viewed as the limit point on the anger scale. When the intensity of anger goes beyond that limit, S can no longer control his anger. S exhibits angry behavior and his anger forces him to attempt an act of retribution. Since S is out of control and acting under coercion, he is not responsible for his actions.

Stage 5: Act of retribution

S performs the act of retribution. The wrongdoer is the target of the act. The intensity of retribution roughly equals the intensity of the offense and the scales are balanced again. The intensity of anger drops to zero.

At this point, we can see how the various conceptual metaphors and metonymies we have discussed all map onto a part of the prototypical scenario, and how they jointly converge on that scenario. This enables us to show exactly how the various metaphors are related to one another, and how they function together to help characterize a single concept. This is something that Lakoff and Johnson (1980) were unable to do.

The course of anger depicted in the prototype scenario is by no means the only course anger can take. In claiming that the scenario is prototypical we are claiming that according to our cultural theory of anger, this is a normal course for anger to take. Deviations of many kinds are both recognized as existing and recognized as being noteworthy and not the norm. Let us take some examples:

- Someone who "turns the other cheek," that is, who does not get angry or seek retribution. In this culture, such a person is considered virtually saintly.
- Someone who has no difficulty controlling his anger is especially praiseworthy.
- A "hothead" is someone who considers more events offensive than most people, who has a lower threshold for anger than the norm, who cannot control his anger, and whose acts of retribution are considered out of proportion to the offense. Someone who is extremely hotheaded is considered emotionally "unbalanced."

On the other hand, someone who acts in the manner described in the prototypical scenario would not be considered abnormal at all.

Conclusion

We have shown that the expressions that indicate anger in American English are not a random collection, but rather are structured in terms of an elaborate cognitive model that is implicit in the semantics of the language. This indicates that anger is not just an amorphous feeling devoid of any conceptual content, but rather that it has an elaborate cognitive structure.

5 Fear

In the previous chapter we saw how the two systems of metonymies and metaphors jointly produce the prototypical cognitive model of anger. In this chapter I would like to show what it would mean if only one of these systems were taken into account in our effort to reconstruct the prototypical model of fear; in particular, what it would mean to base the reconstruction on the *metonymic* system of fear alone. I will try to demonstrate that the result would be a drastic loss of conceptual content. The reason why I have chosen to show the poverty of the metonymic—as opposed to the metaphoric—system in the production of prototypical cognitive models is not completely arbitrary, especially not in the case of fear. Fear is often defined as a dangerous situation accompanied by a set of physiological and behavioral reactions that typically ends in flight. While this (in our terms) metonymy-based definition of the folk understanding of fear is correct so far as it goes, it does not tell us the whole story of fear. That is mostly provided by the metaphors. The poverty of an exclusively metonymy-based model will be evident by the end of the chapter.

Another issue that the present chapter is concerned with is that there are emotions that can be represented by more than one prototypical cognitive model. Anger was shown to have only one prototype, but it might be the case that it has more than one. In fact, it was suggested that the "don't-get-mad-get-even" case is regarded by some people as an alternative to the prototype. The possibility that there may exist at least two prototypical models of fear will be raised and the two models will be discussed in some detail.

Finally, a comparison between anger and fear will be offered. The study of the way the two emotions are conceptualized will enable us to see some of the differences between anger and fear. It will be shown that metaphorical understandings of these emotion concepts account for some of the major differences.

Metonymies of Fear

Fear is an emotion that appears to be characterizable for the most part by a rich system of its physiological effects and behavioral reactions. These include the following:

PHYSICAL AGITATION
He was *shaking* with fear.
She was *trembling like a leaf.*
Tom had the *jitters* when he had to go outside alone.
The arrival of the railroad caused much *fear and trembling* among the Indians.
That gave him the *shakes.*
Snakes give me the *shivers.*
Our enemies must be *trembling in their shoes.*
She *quaked* at the thought of leaving the house at night.
Dick *quivered* like a rabbit.

INCREASE IN HEART RATE
His heart *pounded* with fear.
My heart began to *race* when I saw the animal.
The student got up to make his first speech *with his heart in his mouth.*
My *heart leapt into my throat.*
I had *my heart in my mouth* when I went to the bank to ask for more money.

LAPSES IN HEARTBEAT
His *heart stopped* when the animal jumped in front of him.
You made *my heart miss a beat* when you said you had left the money at home.

BLOOD LEAVES FACE
She turned *pale.*
You are *white* as a sheet.
His face *blanched* with fear at the bad news.
He was *grey* with fear.

SKIN SHRINKS
That man gives me the *creeps.*
A shriek from the dark gave me *goosebumps.*
The sound of someone coming towards the door made *my flesh creep.*
His skin was *prickling* with fear.
I felt *my flesh crawl* as he described the murder.
This is a *creepy* old house, let's get out of here.

As a result of this physiological effect, one has the subjective impression that one's hair straightens out:

HAIR STRAIGHTENS OUT
The story of the murder *made my hair stand on end.*
That was a *hair-raising* experience.
It was *hairy* driving down that narrow road in the darkness.

INABILITY TO MOVE
I was *rooted to the spot.*
He was so terrified he *couldn't move.*
She was scared *stiff.*
He was *paralyzed* with fear.
My *legs turned to rubber.*
He *has rubber legs.*
I was *petrified.*
He was *numbed* by fear.

DROP IN BODY TEMPERATURE (see p. 72) and INABILITY TO MOVE jointly produce

She was *frozen in her boots.*
I was *frozen in my tracks.*

INABILITY TO BREATHE
She was *breathless* with fear.
He *gasped* with fear.

INABILITY TO SPEAK
I was *speechless* with fear.
He was *struck dumb.*

INABILITY TO THINK
My mind went blank with fear.
You scared me *out of my wits.*
She was *out of her mind* with fear.
I was frightened *out of my senses.*

(INVOLUNTARY) RELEASE OF BOWELS or BLADDER
I was *scared shitless* when I saw the man with the knife coming towards me.
You scared *the shit out of* me.
Don't be a chicken *shit.*
My mother *was shitting bricks* waiting for me to come home.
She *has the squitters* every time a dog barks at her.

I was almost *wetting myself* with fear.
Don't *pee in your pants* just because you see a snake.

SWEATING
The cold *sweat* of fear broke out.
There were *sweat beads* on his forehead as the animal approached.
Her palms were *damp* as she entered the boss's office.

NERVOUSNESS IN THE STOMACH
He got *butterflies in the stomach.*
A cold fear *gripped him in the stomach.*

DRYNESS IN THE MOUTH
My *mouth was dry* when it was my turn.
He was scared *spitless.*

SCREAMING
She was *screaming* with fear.

WAYS OF LOOKING
There was *fear in her eyes.*

DROP IN BODY TEMPERATURE
Just the face of the monster was enough *to make my blood run cold.*
I heard a *blood-curdling* scream.
It *chilled my blood* to hear a man I thought had been dead for years.
The blood turned to ice in his veins.
I *was chilled to the bone.*
He wanted to dance with her but *got cold feet* and he didn't.
Her blood froze when she had to walk through the cemetery at night.
He *froze* with fear.
I felt *icy* fingers going up my spine.
It was *spine-chilling* to learn that there was a murderer in our neighborhood.
That movie was a real *chiller.*
The man broke out in *cold sweat* as a gun was put to his head.
I was going to apply for that job but I got *cold feet.*

STARTLE
That noise nearly made me *jump out of my skin!*
The touch on his shoulder *made him start.*
You gave me quite a *turn* when you shouted out like that.
You made me *jump.*

FLIGHT
When he heard the police coming, the thief *took to his heels*.
The mouse *scurried into its hole* when the cat appeared.
The army sent the enemy *scuttling*.
He *fled* from persecution.

Since these expressions indicate fear (without directly referring to it), we get the metonymic principles:

The physiological effects of fear stand for fear
The behavioral reactions of fear stand for fear

These principles are special cases of the general metonymic principles:

The physiological effects of an emotion stand for the emotion
The behavioral reactions of an emotion stand for the emotion

The various kinds of physiological effects and behavioral reactions do not indicate the same level of intensity. For example, PHYSICAL AGITATION indicates the presence of more fear than INCREASE IN HEART RATE and A DROP IN BODY TEMPERATURE more than PHYSICAL AGITATION. Or, INABILITY TO MOVE suggests a more intense form of fear than STARTLE. These and similar observations give us the following principle in our folk model of fear:

As fear increases, its physiological effects
and behavioral reactions increase

Thus, terror is characterized by, for example, INABILITY TO MOVE and RELEASE OF BOWELS but less so, for example, by INCREASE IN HEART RATE. On the other hand, INCREASE IN HEART RATE seems to pair off with a common but less intense form of fear.

The intensity of fear has another closely related aspect. The examples given can show more or less fear even *within the same kind* of effect or reaction. Thus, for example, the expression *get cold feet* in the physiological effect of DROP IN BODY TEMPERATURE indicates less fear than, say, the expression *make one's blood run cold* or *blood-curdling*. This means that the *same kind* of effect or reaction can characterize *different forms* of fear, depending on what level of intensity is indicated. In other words, the reaction DROP IN BODY TEMPERATURE can be viewed as characterizing both terror and a less intense form of fear.

As we shall see later, the concept of fear is likely to have more than one prototype, or central case. One of these central members seems to be associated with less intense physiological and behavioral reactions. This is a type of fear which seems to be characterized in the main by PHYSICAL

AGITATION, INCREASE IN HEART RATE, DRYNESS IN THE MOUTH, ABSENCE OF BLOOD IN THE FACE, NERVOUSNESS IN THE STOMACH, SWEATING, and to some extent also by DROP IN BODY TEMPERATURE, SKIN SHRINKS, and (INVOLUNTARY) RELEASE OF BOWELS or BLADDER. There is, of course, also FLIGHT and WAYS OF LOOKING. However, a more precise reconstruction of even a metonymy-based prototype of the concept of FEAR requires us to take into account more than just the most common physiological effects and behavioral reactions.

We have seen in some of the examples given under these effects and reactions that fear is generally thought of as arising from some kind of danger. Danger is considered as the primary cause of fear. It can be described as a situation that presents some threat to the self—be it physical, psychological, social, or whatever.

The observations we have made so far about the metonymies and the causes of fear allow us to propose a cognitive model of fear:

1. Danger

   There is some danger.

2. Fear exists

   S experiences certain physiological effects: physical agitation, increase in heart rate, blood leaves face, nervousness in the stomach, dryness in the mouth, sweating, (to a smaller degree; drop in body temperature, skin shrinks, involuntary release of bowels or bladder).

   S exhibits certain behavioral reactions: ways of looking, (inability to breathe, inability to speak)

3. Flight

   S flees from the danger

This is a metonymy-based model of fear. But the question arises: Is this all language tells us about fear? If we look at the metaphors, the answer must be an obvious no.

Metaphors of Fear

There are a large number of metaphorical expressions that we use to talk about fear. Let us now look at these in some detail. We can begin with the metaphor FEAR IS A FLUID IN A CONTAINER, which is a special case of the very general metaphor THE EMOTIONS ARE FLUIDS IN A CONTAINER. A version that applies to fear seems to be much less interesting than the one that applies to anger. Consider the following examples:

FEAR IS A FLUID IN A CONTAINER
Fear was *rising in* him.
The sight *filled* her with fear.
She could not *contain* her fear.
He was *full of* fear.

Just like the case of anger, the fluid corresponds to the emotion (in this case fear) and the container to the body of the person who is in the emotional state (here, fear). But unlike in anger, in this metaphor there is no indication that the fluid is hot. As we shall see in the last section of this chapter, this fact leads to some interesting consequences. The main focus of this metaphor, as typical of the CONTAINER metaphor in general, is the existence of the emotion. In addition, the CONTAINER metaphor suggests that fear exists as an independent mass entity inside the self.

So far we have only said that the typical cause of fear is danger. We can learn more about some of the details of this danger if we study further the metaphorical expressions we use to talk about fear. This can give us a more precise idea of the typical causes of fear. Let us take the VICIOUS ENEMY metaphor first:

FEAR IS A VICIOUS ENEMY (HUMAN or ANIMAL)
There was a fear *lurking* in her heart that she wouldn't succeed.
Fear slowly *crept up on* him.
He was *choked by* fear.
He was *hounded by* the fear that the business would fail.
The fear that things wouldn't work out continued *to prey on* her mind.
She managed to *harness* her fear.

This metaphor portrays fear as an enemy/opponent that, for instance, lurks around, preys on, creeps up on, or hounds the self. An enemy/opponent of this kind presents a threat to the self's survival.

FEAR IS A TORMENTOR
They were *tortured by* the fear of what was going to happen to their son.
Her parents were *tormented by* the fear that she might drown.

According to this metaphor, fear is a person who can afflict the self with great pain.

FEAR IS AN ILLNESS
She was *sick with* fright.
I have *recovered from* the shock slowly.
He couldn't *get over* his fear.
The town was *plagued by* fear.

The implication of the ILLNESS metaphor seems to be that either fear is an illness or it can cause illness in the self.

FEAR IS A SUPERNATURAL BEING (GHOST, etc.)
She was *haunted by* the fear of death.
Let's get out of here, this is a *spooky* place!
His *dark* fears lingered on.
It was a *ghastly* scene.

The metaphor depicts fear as a supernatural entity that can cause a great deal of mental anguish to the self.

In general, these metaphors make us view fear as an entity that can cause either death or much physical or mental suffering. But, this is not the single most important feature of these metaphors. Equally important is the fact that the metaphors highlight certain of the large number of possible causes of fear: namely, death and physical or mental pain. Thus, there seems to be an interesting relationship between the cause of fear and the way fear itself is conceptualized. Some of the causes of fear—a vicious enemy, a tormentor, illness, and a supernatural being—also serve the purpose of understanding what fear itself is. In the process of this way of conceptualizing fear, fear is also created: It becomes an entity with a number of properties that all define a negative relationship between the emotion and the self—threatening his life, causing pain, and so forth. In other words, our notion of what produces fear becomes a part of our conception of fear. Furthermore, because of this relationship, the metaphors enable us to see what the most characteristic causes of fear are thought to be. This is possible because it can be assumed that the metaphors are not based on rare and random causes of fear. If this conclusion is correct, then we have a purely linguistic way of finding out what the *typical* causes of an emotion are: they are those causes that appear in the metaphorical conceptualization of the emotion itself.

We have just seen how some of the metaphors we use in the conceptualization of fear can be viewed as providing us with the most typical causes of fear. As a result, instead of the general category of "danger" we can now describe the causes of fear in a more detailed way. But this is just one example of how the metaphors can contribute to our understanding of a concept. Let us review further the other principal metaphors of fear.

Given that fear is conceptualized as an entity that can threaten our lives and cause great physical or mental suffering, it is only natural that it is also viewed as an OPPONENT that we have to defeat. Another reason why we think of fear in terms of an OPPONENT may be the social expectation that people (especially men) should not display fear or should not be afraid at all. The OPPONENT metaphor is a very productive one in the case of fear:

FEAR IS AN OPPONENT
He was *wrestling with* his fear.
Her fear *overcame* her.
Fear *took hold of* him.
I was *gripped by* fear.
He could not *control* his fear any longer.
She was *besieged by* fear.
They were *seized by* fear.
She eventually *suppressed* her fear.
I was *struggling with* fear.
He was *fighting* his fear but fear *won out*.
She was *attacked by* fear.
He was *in the clutch of* fear.
I was *incapacitated by* fear.
Fear *gripped* the village.
Panic *overtook* them.

The ontological correspondences of the metaphor are obvious. The opponent is fear. The physical struggle between the self and the opponent corresponds to the psychological struggle for emotional control. Defeating the opponent is understood as controlling fear and losing to the opponent as fear controlling the self. As can be seen, most of the examples have to do with loss of control over fear. To the extent that these examples sound natural and thus reflect psychological reality, this can only mean that in our folk model of fear the natural course for fear to take implies our losing control over it. That is, in the same way as in the case of anger, the prototypical example of fear is one in which, despite the self's efforts, fear gains control over the self.

Let us now briefly look at some additional metaphors which, like the CONTAINER metaphor, are fairly general for the various emotions. We can begin with the BURDEN metaphor, which we have already seen in the chapter on anger. The version that applies to fear can be illustrated by examples like the following:

FEAR (DANGER) IS A BURDEN
He was greatly *relieved* when the danger was over.
Fear *weighed heavily on* them as they heard the bombers overhead.
She looked around and gave a *sigh of relief*.
Her fears were *alleviated* when the neighbors came home.
He was *burdened* by the possibility of not seeing his friend anymore.

When the BURDEN metaphor is used in connection with a target domain, it indicates that the domain in question is considered unpleasant, or bad. Thus, fear and the metonymically related concept of danger are portrayed by the metaphor as unpleasant. On the other hand, it also follows that the cessation of fear (danger) is pleasant, that is, it provides a relief.

Another metaphor commonly employed in the conceptualization of emotions is the NATURAL FORCE metaphor:

FEAR IS A NATURAL FORCE (WIND, STORM, FLOOD, etc.)
Fear *swept over* him.
She was *engulfed* by panic.
There was a *surge* of fear.
He was *flooded* with fear.
I was *overwhelmed* by fear.
Fear *came over* him.
She was *carried away* by fear.

The main focus of the NATURAL FORCE metaphor seems to be that the self is passive in relation to the emotion, that the emotion affects us while we passively undergo its effects.

According to our metaphorical conceptualization of the emotions, not only do we passively undergo the effects of various natural forces (e.g., the emotions) but our emotions also force us to perform certain actions. This way of understanding the emotions emerges from the SUPERIOR metaphor. This metaphor suggests that the self is an inferior who obeys the commands of the superior. The particular version for fear can be exemplified as follows:

FEAR IS A SUPERIOR
Her fear *prevented* her *from* going into the house.
Fear *drove* him to do something he wouldn't have done normally.
His actions were *dictated by* fear.
She was *ruled by* the fear that something was going to happen.
Fear *dominated* his actions.
Fear *reigned* in their hearts.

As can be seen, what the metaphor adds to our idea of fear is that fear is something that can prevent us from doing certain things, that can cause us to perform certain actions, and that in general it is something that can dominate our behavior.

Putting all of this together, we can now see how and what the metaphors contribute to the concept of fear. The contribution is significant because it enriches our idea of fear with features and dimensions that are entirely missing from a model based solely on the most common metonymies of fear. This new and more complete model can be given as follows:

1. Danger

   There is a dangerous situation.
   It involves death, physical or mental pain.
   S is aware of the danger.
   The danger produces fear in S.

2. Fear exists

   S is passive in relation to the experience of fear.
   Fear exists as a mass entity inside S.
   S experiences certain physiological effects: increase in heart rate, physical agitation, dryness in the mouth, sweating, nervousness in the stomach, blood leaves face, (and to a smaller degree: skin shrinks, drop in body temperature, [involuntary] release of bowels or bladder).
   S exhibits certain behavioral reactions: ways of looking, (inability to breathe, inability to speak).
   The feeling is unpleasant.
   The feeling dominates S's behavior.

3. Attempt at control

   S attempts to control his fear: S makes an effort not to display fear and/or not to flee.

4. Loss of control

   S loses control over fear.

5. Flight

   S flees from the danger.
   S is safe and feels relieved.
   Fear ceases to exist.

Thus, what the metaphors contribute to the concept of fear is the following: a more precise formulation of the properties of danger in some prototypical cases, a clearer understanding of the nature (ontology) of fear, the highlighting of some additional characteristics of fear like our passive relation to it, the introduction into the model of the aspect of control, and a specification of what it involves that the danger is over. Without these, our idea of fear would not be complete.

Terror

It could be argued, however, that the model presented above is not the only prototype for fear. This, in a sense, is true. Perhaps for many people terror is just as good of an example of fear as the fear we saw in the previous section. Lakoff (1987) observes that prototypicality may arise from a variety of sources: from the fact that a member of a category is common, that it is salient, or that it is ideal, or that it is stereotypical, and so on. Perhaps the model outlined in the previous section can be viewed as our stereotype of fear. Another prototypical form of fear may be the one that is very common. This is what is called dispositional fear (as exemplified by sentences like *He is afraid that it may rain tomorrow*). A third prototype is what we call *terror*. Some people may conceive of terror as the prototype of fear due to its salience. On the whole, terror, as we commonly think of it, seems to be characterized by more intense physiological and behavioral reactions than our stereotype of fear. As we have seen, these more intense reactions include HAIR STRAIGHTENS OUT, SCREAMING, DROP IN BODY TEMPERATURE, INABILITY TO MOVE, INABILITY TO BREATHE, INABILITY TO SPEAK, and INABILITY TO THINK. These features render terror more conspicuous than the stereotype, which is accompanied by "only" such reactions as INCREASE IN HEART RATE, PHYSICAL AGITATION, and SWEATING. This would then enable us to view terror as *the* prototype of fear, or, alternatively, to have two or even three prototypes simultaneously: a stereotypical model, a typical model (which is perhaps the commonest), and a salient one.

But intensity is not the only aspect in which terror and stereotypical fear differ. In addition to the more intense manifestations of terror, the two also differ in the aspect of control. More specifically, in terror the dangerous situation seems to lead immediately to a lack of control, which is a state characterized by an inability to move, inability to think, and so forth. Again, this is suggested by our use of language. Consider the following sentences:

He was struggling with his fear.
?He was struggling with his terror.

He managed to control his fear.
?He managed to control his terror.

The sentences with the word terror somehow sound less natural than the sentences with fear. This would seem to indicate that we do not think of terror as something that we try to control. Instead, we seem to think of it as a state of complete lack of control, this state being constituted by the most salient manifestations mentioned above. The direct change from a state of calm to a lack of control in all probability contributes to our impression that terror appears to be more conspicuous than the case of fear given in the stereotypical model.

There is yet another way in which they are different. This has to do with the causes of fear. Of the causes we have seen are associated with fear, the one that is perhaps most closely associated with terror is a situation in which the self's life is in immediate danger. We are more likely to be terrified when a fierce tiger jumps in front of us than when we are having a tooth pulled. And this has to do with salience as well. The former is a more conspicuous form of danger than is the latter.

Closely related to the salience of the causes of terror is another issue. It was noted in the previous section that fear exists as an entity inside a container that corresponds to the self. It is interesting to speculate about how it gets there. To find out, let us look at language again. It is sometimes claimed that fear is an emotion that goes into a person from outside of him. This may be based on linguistic expressions (and the corresponding conceptual metaphor) like the following:

FEAR GOES INTO A PERSON FROM OUTSIDE
He *put* the fear of God *into* her.
What they heard *cast* fear *into* their hearts.
The sight *struck* terror *into* their hearts.
That *threw* a scare *into* him.

We have seen in the chapter on anger that the cause of anger is conceived of an input energy that produces internal heat. This internal heat corresponds to anger. That is to say, although the input energy necessary for bringing about anger comes from outside, the anger itself comes into being only inside the container. In the case of fear, however, the emotion seems to exist outside already and then it goes inside as a result of some force (cf. put, cast, strike, throw). That fear already exists outside the self suggests that there is a close conceptual association between the cause of fear (danger) and fear itself. Perhaps this is why we can use the word fear to describe both the emotion itself and the cause of it (cf. *my fear is that . . .*). The same cannot be done in the case of anger. We do not seem to be able to say that *my anger is that. . . .* Thus the emotion of anger appears to be kept more clearly distinct from its cause.

The expressions (*put/cast/strike/throw fear into some*) underscore another interesting property of more salient causes of fear. This has to do with the kinds of situations that typically produce intense fear. Putting, casting, striking and throwing are all momentary actions. The implication seems to be then that we view the cause of intense fear (like terror) as danger that emerges suddenly and that produces fear instantly. There are some more examples to indicate this:

He was *struck* dumb.
She was panic-*stricken*.
I was *struck* with fear that he might drown.
Her face was horror-*stricken* at the thought.

These expressions are also examples of the general metaphor EMOTIONAL EFFECT IS PHYSICAL CONTACT (Lakoff and Johnson, 1980). When this general metaphor applies to fear, it indicates that the cause of fear arises suddenly and that the danger is imminent. This accords with our intuitions concerning the paradigmatic causes of terror.

Comparison of the Language of Anger and Fear

If we examine the language we use to describe anger and the language we use to describe fear, we find that there is a considerable overlap but that there are also important differences. My major goal in this section is to investigate some of the sources for these differences and to follow up the implications of the analyses for some issues in the study of emotions. As was seen, the expressions we use to talk about anger can be conveniently grouped into two classes: metonymic and metaphorical expressions. The metonymies correspond to physiological and behavioral reactions as we think of these in our language-based folk theories of anger. The language-based folk theory of these reactions includes the following in the case of anger: INCREASE IN BODY HEAT, INTERNAL PRESSURE, REDNESS IN FACE AND NECK AREA, AGITATION and INTERFERENCE WITH ACCURATE PERCEPTION. The metaphors correspond to various other aspects of our experiences of anger. Anger seems to be characterized by the following major conceptual metaphors: ANGER IS THE HEAT OF A FLUID IN A CONTAINER, ANGER IS FIRE, ANGER IS A DANGEROUS ANIMAL, ANGER IS A BURDEN, ANGER IS INSANITY, and ANGER IS AN OPPONENT. Our everyday expressions describing fear can also be factored into metonymies and metaphors. The examination of the metonymies suggests that, for everyday purposes, fear is assumed to be accompanied by such physiological effects as INCREASE IN HEART RATE, BLOOD LEAVES FACE, SKIN SHRINKS, HAIR STRAIGHTENS OUT, SWEATING, and DROP IN BODY TEMPERATURE. The metaphors for fear also include FEAR IS A BURDEN, FEAR IS AN OPPONENT, and FEAR IS A FLUID IN A CONTAINER.

These linguistic details represent some raw facts about anger and fear and the question one might legitimately ask is this: Can we learn anything important about anger and fear, and the emotions in general, if we study the language we use to talk about them? There are, I think, three issues which can be profitably studied or better understood if we adopt the lexical approach in the analysis of anger and fear. The three issues have to do with (a) the physiology of the emotions, (b) our conceptualization of anger and fear, and (c) our attitude to these emotions as regards the aspect of control. Furthermore, I would like to claim that these three issues are not isolated but dependent on each other. We can only understand how the control aspect of anger and fear works if we get clear about how these two particular emotions are conceptualized, and an understanding of conceptualization requires us to see what our folk theory of physiological effects is.

The three issues will be dealt with in connection with three major areas of differences in the language of anger and fear. The issue of physiology will be discussed in connection with the analysis of the various metonymical expressions we use to describe the physiological effects of anger and fear. Conceptualization will be taken up when some of the differences between anger and fear metaphors are pointed out. Finally, the issue of control will be raised when some metaphorical expressions that denote various ways of controlling anger and fear are compared.

The examination of the metonymical expressions that describe the assumed physiological changes in anger and fear reveals that anger and fear share only one physiological effect: PHYSICAL AGITATION. The other parts of the folk theory of physiological effects do not seem to be interchangeable. It would be odd to describe a person's fear with the sentence *"He almost had a hemorrhage,"* the reason in all probability being that INTERNAL PRESSURE (either muscular or blood pressure) is not understood to be a part of our folk theory of fear. Likewise, it would be strange to describe a person's anger with the sentence *"His heart pounded with anger"* because it appears that INCREASE IN HEART RATE is not considered to be a part of our folk understanding of anger. Some of the other differences are even more conspicuous. In anger the face typically reddens while in fear blood leaves the face; while anger is seen as producing an increase in body temperature, fear is supposed to lead to a drop in body temperature.

We are now in a position to raise the first issue. This can be put in the following question: Are the emotions characterized by a general state of arousal or by specific bodily response patterns? The answer seems to depend on what we mean by bodily responses. If we allow the term to cover not only the traditional autonomic responses but also various neurochemical and central nervous system activities that take place during emotional states, then the answer given by recent researchers is that each emotional state like anger and fear is characterized by specific sets of these biochemical and CNS processes (cf. Frijda 1986). However, if we limit ourselves to such traditional autonomic responses as blood pressure, heart rate, respiration, and body temperature, then we can find two conflicting views in psychology. The well known experiments by Schachter and Singer (1962) in the early 1960s were taken to indicate that there is no physiological response patterning in emotion. This is still a widely held view today. And it is also popular science. For example, in a recent psychological textbook we can read the following about anger and fear: "Fear and rage are physiologically equivalent. The marked internal changes that occur in a person who has been frightened are indistinguishable from those that occur in a person who has been angered." (Sperling 1984: 157). As we have seen, this idea contrasts very markedly with language-based folk theories associated with the physiology of anger and fear. These folk theories would seem to support the rival view of physiological changes according to which emotions are characterized by specific response patterns (see, for example, Wolf and Wolff, 1947; Ax, 1953; Lacey, 1967). It thus seems that in many (though not in all) cases language can be used to support or diffract from a given idea concerning the physiological responses associated with an emotion. Another role for language can be that it can point to certain physiological changes in the body and so direct our attention to phenomena that are worth investigating by physiologists. This may sound naive but it is not completely so. In their study of six emotions (anger, fear, sadness, happiness, surprise, and disgust), Ekman and his associates (1983) found that while anger shows an increase in skin temperature, there is a decrease in the case of fear. It is thus not an accident that speakers of English (and presumably other languages as well) describe their experiences of anger and fear the way they do.

However, no simple correlation between language and physiology can be expected. In the same study, the researchers found that heart rate increases considerably both in anger and fear. This makes it a mystery why language users have not encoded this very salient physiological experience into their description of anger and, conversely, why they have encoded it in the case of fear. As we have seen, there are a number of conventionalized expressions that denote an increase in heart rate in fear, but no such expressions come easily to mind in the case of anger. We do not at present have an answer to this dilemma.

Let me now turn to another area where the language of anger differs from the language of fear in an interesting way. If we look at the metaphorical expressions that describe anger and fear, we find that many of them belong to, or express, the same conceptual metaphors. BURDEN, OPPONENT, and CONTAINER are conceptual metaphors that are common to both anger and fear. There seems to be one notable metaphor for anger that is missing from the system of metaphors characterizing fear. The conceptual metaphor is: ANGER IS HEAT. The HEAT metaphor for anger has two versions: ANGER IS THE HEAT OF A FLUID IN A CONTAINER and ANGER IS FIRE. It is the former that is of special relevance here. The ANGER IS THE HEAT OF A FLUID IN A CONTAINER metaphor is a special case of the general metaphor THE BODY IS A CONTAINER FOR THE EMOTIONS. In the case of fear, this applies as FEAR IS A FLUID IN A CONTAINER. The examples of this metaphor suggest that fear is conceptualized as a fluid or fluid-like substance that is in a container (corresponding to the body), but there is no indication whatsoever that this fluid is hot. Indeed, sentences like *"He was boiling with fear"* or *"She was seething with fear"* are completely unlikely. Why is this so? Is there a systematic explanation?

This question leads us naturally to the second issue I wish to raise. Do we conceptualize our emotions in terms of arbitrarily chosen metaphors or are the metaphors based on fact? That is, is it the case that anger just *happens* to be conceptualized in terms of a HOT FLUID IN A CONTAINER and fear merely in terms of a FLUID IN A CONTAINER? I think the no to this question can be expected from what has been said about the physiological correlates of anger and fear. Anger is experienced as hot and indeed it seems to go together with an increase in skin temperature, while fear is experienced as cold and it actually correlates with low skin temperature. The point is that in several cases the physiological correlates of the emotions (as described by the metonymies) seem to form the basis of, or motivate (in the terminology of cognitive semantics) the kinds of metaphorical conceptualizations (as described by the metaphors) that we have of the emotions. However, motivation is not to be confused with complete predictability. The increase in body temperature associated with anger motivates the HOT FLUID metaphor but does not predict it. Similarly, in the case of fear, the drop in body temperature does not automatically result in a COLD FLUID metaphor; we do not appear to have a COLD FLUID metaphor for fear. But if we had one, it would be motivated by the DROP IN BODY TEMPERATURE physiological response.

Finally, a third area of divergence between the language of anger and fear involves expressions that have to do with the control aspect of these emotions. There is a small but interesting set of expressions describing anger which do not seem to have their counterparts in fear. Consider the following metaphorical expressions for anger:

He *vented* his anger *on* his wife.
I *gave vent to* my anger.
He *let out* his anger.
She *took out* her anger on me.
He's just *letting off steam*.
Try to *channel* your anger into something constructive.
He managed to *keep* his anger *bottled up inside* him.
I could barely *keep it in* anymore.
He was *blue* in the face.
He *turned* his anger *inward*.

When I say that these expressions do not have counterparts in fear, I do not of course mean that fear does not have a control aspect. Fear can *overcome* us (to use an instance of the OPPONENT metaphor) and we can overcome fear; that is, we can both lose and gain control over fear, just as we can lose and gain control over anger. The expressions above all have to do with the aspect of control, as opposed to a loss of control. However, they elaborate the notion of control in anger in ways that are not conceptually available for fear. The controlled response suggested by *venting*, *giving vent to,* and *letting out* anger does not seem to be available for fear; nor does the conscious displacement suggested by *taking it out on* someone; nor does the controlled reduction suggested by *letting off steam;* nor does the utilization for another purpose suggested by *channeling* anger into something else; nor does the conscious containment suggested by *keeping it bottled up, keeping it in,* and *being blue in the face;* nor does the reversal of the flow of the emotion suggested by *turning* anger *inward.* These observations involve us in the third issue.

The issue is why it is that we have only a limited number of options in the conceptualization of the control aspect of fear (the *available* options for fear have not been mentioned here). The answer that I would like to propose is that this is because the two emotions are conceptualized differently: anger as the HEAT OF A FLUID IN A CONTAINER, while fear simply as a FLUID IN A CONTAINER. The conceptualization of anger gives rise to a number of metaphorical consequences that cannot arise in the case of fear. Since anger is viewed as the heat of a fluid in a container, it can metaphorically follow that intense anger produces steam, that intense anger produces pressure on the container, that, as a result, the container (i.e., the angry person) can blow up, and what was inside comes out. Consequently, we can think of anger as something that can be controlled by metaphorically letting it out under control; by metaphorically redirecting its outflow; by metaphorically reducing the pressure inside in a controlled way; by metaphorically channelling it into an activity other than angry behavior; by metaphorically preventing its outflow; or by metaphorically reversing the direction of the outflow. Since the conceptualization of fear does not have a heat component, the fluid in the container does not produce steam and pressure, there is no explosion, and nothing comes out whose outflow could be held back or reversed. Thus, the above ways of controlling anger are not available for controlling fear. The conclusion is that the conceptualization of the control aspect of an emotion may depend on the way the emotion itself is conceptualized.

Perhaps what was said at the beginning of the section makes more sense now. The physiological correlates of an emotion seem to determine (in the sense of "motivate") how the emotion itself is conceptualized, which in turn may determine the conceptualization of the various aspects of the emotion, like that of control.

Conclusions

In this chapter we have seen that metonymies play a very important role in the constitution of the concept of fear. However, perhaps the main finding was that without the rich conceptual contribution of metaphors for fear the concept would be impoverished. Furthermore, it was pointed out that we may have more than one prototype associated with fear. The prototypical cases that have been identified were: a stereotypic, a typical, and a salient model. Finally, it was shown that close comparative analyses of the conventionalized language we use to describe particular emotions can enhance our understanding of the conceptualizations of these emotions.

6
Pride

One theme that I will be concerned with in this chapter is what it means for experience to be metaphorical and to be metaphorically real. This is an important issue for my purposes because one of the claims that I make in this book is that emotional experience is to a large extent metaphorical and metaphorically real. I will try to demonstrate what this means by using the notion of enhancement, which forms an integral part of our notion of pride.

Another issue that will be addressed pertains to the causal aspect of pride. In the discussion of fear, it was noted that certain kinds or types of causes typically go with different kinds of fear. The same issue will be pursued here. In addition, an attempt will be made to show that the notion of prototype can be put to good use in understanding some of the complexities in the causal structure of pride. In particular, the notion will prove useful if we try to clarify the nature of the relationship between the self and the state of affairs that has given rise to pride. It is usually claimed that the two must be connected in some way. It will be shown that we can understand more about this connection if we approach the causes that give rise to pride from a prototype perspective.

Finally, I will examine the various conceptual metaphors that apply to pride. In doing this, special emphasis will be placed on the question of what kind of pride is characterized by which metaphors. The category of pride is a broad one. It subsumes such varied concepts as self-esteem, conceit, and vanity. My suggestion will be that each of these members of the pride category differ from the prototype of pride, differ from each other, and do so primarily in terms of the principal metaphors and metonymies that characterize them. Furthermore, the various concepts will be presented in the form of prototypical models. This form of presentation makes easily accessible the differences that emerge from the metaphors and metonymies. My contention will be that the prototype of the general category of pride is what can be termed as ''balanced'' pride as an immediate response and that the various other forms of pride can be systematically defined in relation to this.

Physiological and Behavioral Responses

Let us begin with the folk model of the physiological effects of pride. This part of the folk model maintains that the physiological effects of pride are REDNESS IN THE FACE, INCREASED HEART RATE, INTERFERENCE WITH ACCURATE PERCEPTION, AND INTERFERENCE WITH NORMAL MENTAL FUNCTIONING. Given the general metonymic principle,

The physiological effects of an emotion stand for the emotion

we get the following system of metonymies for pride:

REDNESS IN THE FACE
He *flushed with* pride.

INCREASED HEART RATE
His heart *was throbbing with* pride.
Her heart *fluttered with* pride.

INTERFERENCE WITH ACCURATE PERCEPTION
He *was blinded* by conceit.
His conceit *prevented him from seeing clearly.*
She *was blinded* by her own glory.
Winning the class election *turned his head.*

INTERFERENCE WITH NORMAL MENTAL FUNCTIONING
Success *went to his head.*

It is important to see that REDNESS IN THE FACE and INCREASED HEART RATE apply to what is called justified or proper pride, whereas INTERFERENCE WITH ACCURATE PERCEPTION and INTERFERENCE WITH NORMAL MENTAL FUNCTIONING apply to conceit, and that the latter two are more intense physiological effects than the former ones. Furthermore, INTERFERENCE WITH ACCURATE PERCEPTION and INTERFERENCE WITH NORMAL MENTAL FUNCTIONING are physiological effects that impair one's normal functioning. These observations lead to further principles in the folk model of the physiological effects of pride:

As pride increases, its physiological effects increase.
There is a limit beyond which the physiological effects of pride impair normal functioning.

The linguistically based folk model of the behavioral reactions of pride maintains:

The behavioral reactions of pride include erect posture, chest out, brightness of the eyes, smiling, telling people about one's achievements, head held unnaturally high, chest unnaturally thrust out, forms of walking, ostentatious behavior, thinking one is unique, and boasting.

Given the general principle

The behavioral reactions of an emotion stand for the emotion,

we get the following system of metonymies for pride:

ERECT POSTURE
After winning the race, he walked to the rostrum *with his head held high.*
He *stood tall* as he received the prize.

CHEST OUT
After winning the race, he *swelled* with pride.

BRIGHTNESS OF THE EYES
She *was beaming* with pride.
He *was glowing* with pride.
There was pride *in his eyes as he looked* at his son.

SMILING
He *was smiling* proudly after winning the race.

TELLING PEOPLE ABOUT ONE'S ACHIEVEMENTS
He ran home *to tell his mother about* his success.

HEAD HELD UNNATURALLY HIGH
She's going around *with her nose in the air.*
Don't *high-hat* me again!
She's *looking down her nose at* everyone.
She said, "No!", *bridling up.*

CHEST UNNATURALLY THRUST OUT
He *was bloated* with pride.
He was going around *with his chest out.*
Why is he so *puffed up?*
John's so *swelled up* with pride that I think *he'll burst*
He's *inflated* with pride.
You shouldn't be so *chesty.*

FORMS OF WALKING
The manager *strutted* along the hall.
He *swaggered* down the street after winning the fight.
She's *going around like a peacock.*
He's *walking around as if he owned the place.*

OSTENTATIOUS/THEATRICAL BEHAVIOR
She's *giving herself airs.*
The child *was putting on airs.*
You don't need *to put on the dog.*
He's just a *show-off.*
She's *flaunting* her new fur coat.

THINKING ONE IS UNIQUE
He *thinks he is it.*
You needn't *think your shit doesn't stink.*
She *thinks the sun shines out of her asshole.*

BOASTING
He's always *singing his own praises.*
Stop *bragging.*
Here he is *blowing his own horn* again.
He's always *broadcasting his own achievements.*
You like *talking big,* don't you?

Here, again, we should notice that ERECT POSTURE, CHEST OUT, BRIGHTNESS OF THE EYES, SMILING, and TELLING PEOPLE ABOUT ONE'S ACHIEVEMENTS are behavioral reactions that characterize justified pride, and that the rest of the reactions are typical of conceit. Also, the reactions that characterize justified pride are less intense and less salient reactions than the ones that typically go together with conceit. This is particularly obvious in such comparable pairs as ERECT POSTURE vs. HEAD HELD UNNATURALLY HIGH, CHEST OUT vs. CHEST UNNATURALLY THRUST OUT, and TELLING PEOPLE vs. BOASTING. This gives us another principle in the folk model of the behavioral reactions of pride:

As pride increases, its behavioral reactions increase.

A major theme of these behavioral reactions has to do with an increase in the size of the body. The increase in the intensity of pride is seen as being accompanied by an increase in the physical proportions of the body. As we shall see in the next section, this correlation has an important consequence for the way we conceptualize and also experience pride.

The Container Metaphor

After the metonymies let us now turn to some of the metaphors for pride. The discussion of the metaphors will enable us to see the different kinds of pride, the aspects of pride that they address, and the overall cognitive organization of the different kinds of pride.

Pride also has its version of THE EMOTIONS ARE FLUIDS IN A CONTAINER metaphor. The PRIDE IS A FLUID IN A CONTAINER metaphor is partially motivated by the THE BODY IS A CONTAINER FOR THE EMOTIONS metaphor. The experiential basis for the metaphor PRIDE IS A FLUID IN A CONTAINER seems to be provided by the physiological effects INCREASED HEART RATE (involving the heart as a container with blood in it) and the behavioral reaction CHEST OUT (involving the chest as a container).

PRIDE IS A FLUID IN A CONTAINER
His good performance *filled him with* pride.
Pride *welled up inside him* at the sight of his garden.
He was *full of* pride after beating the former champion.
Her pride *rose* as she watched her children perform.

In this metaphor the container is the body. There is another metaphor, where the container is the heart:

PRIDE IS (A FLUID) IN THE HEART
Her *heart swelled* with pride.
The news *filled her heart with* pride.
Pride *swelled* his heart.

These metaphors address a variety of issues concerning PRIDE. In particular, they highlight the aspect of intensity (*full of, swell with*), the change in its intensity (*rise*), that it has a cause (good performance, sight of one's garden, beating the champion, etc.), and that it has a beginning (*well up, fill*).

The FLUID IN A CONTAINER and HEART metaphors are constituted by the following ontological correspondences:

- the container is the body
- the fluid in the container is pride
- for the container to be full of fluid is for pride to be intense (cf. MORE IS UP)
- for the fluid to appear is for pride to begin to exist

An important epistemic correspondence of the CONTAINER metaphor for pride is the following. We know that when a container is filled up with a fluid, the container may swell. Indeed, the word *swell* indicates just this aspect of pride. The swelling of the container has been mentioned in connection with the HEART metaphor and also in connection with the metonymies CHEST OUT and CHEST UNNATURALLY THRUST OUT. The reason for this is that the expression *swell with pride* is both a metonymy (as a result of those behavioral reactions) and a metaphor (as a result of the above epistemic correspondence). In the chapter on anger, cases like this were called metaphorical metonymies.

What is particularly interesting about this partly metonymy, partly metaphor-based notion of "increase in physical size" is that it seems to form the basis for the notion of "enhancement" that is often given as a part of the definition of pride (e.g., Davitz 1969). It is also considered a major part of pride. In Davitz's study enhancement was the component (or cluster) in pride that received the most emphasis as measured by the number of descriptive statements in the cluster and the number of subjects who checked each of these statements.

The notion of enhancement is also very vague. It seems to cover a variety of experiences, including strength, power, and confidence. Among the statements people checked in connection with pride in the Davitz study are "I feel taller, stronger, bigger, strong inside"; "I have a sense of sureness, a sense of being important and worthwhile"; and "I have a sense of being superior, a sense of power". The concepts of strength, power, and confidence are all related to the bigness of the container in the container metaphor. Strength is something that we associate with large size; hence the metaphor STRONG IS BIG. The notion of power is conceptualized in terms of the concept PHYSICAL STRENGTH, via the STRONG IS BIG metaphor. And confidence is often viewed as a heavy object (e.g., "His confidence was shaken"), where heaviness is a part of the belief HEAVY IS BIG. The point of all this is to show that the diverse and diffuse concept of enhancement has a clear experiential grounding in the CONTAINER metaphor and that the frequently reported experience of enhancement in pride is, to a large degree, jointly produced by the metonymies and metaphors of pride.

Causes of Pride

Now let us make a brief inventory of the causes that make people proud. I will ignore many details and deal with the issues only in the depth that is necessary for my purposes in this study. If we look at the kinds of things that people typically mention as the causes for their pride, we get the following groups:

Achievements	winning the race, getting a good grade in a difficult exam, writing

	a good book, solving a problem, etc.
Possessions	owning a Mercedes, having a lot of money, having a diamond necklace, etc.
Belonging to a group	the team you play for, the university where you study, your hometown, your nation, etc.
Appearances	good looks, having a pretty face, having a shapely body, long dark hair, green eyes, etc.
Physical/mental capabilities/ skills/properties	how high you can jump, how strong you are, how fast you can read, how many things you remember, your health, etc.
Moral qualities	your honesty, that you cannot be bribed, that you have never lied in your life, etc.
Social position/status/class	you are the manager, you are a well known singer, you are an aristocrat, etc.

And the list could no doubt be continued. But this much will do. What makes the list relevant to our purposes is that the various kinds of pride seem to go together with particular causes. For example, JUSTIFIED PRIDE seems to go together typically with ACHIEVEMENTS, VANITY with APPEARANCES, and HAUGHTINESS with SOCIAL STATUS/ CLASS. Of course, this does not mean that the various kinds of pride are restricted to one particular cause. The claim is that a given form of pride favors a particular kind of cause, but less typically can also take others.

In order for a person S (short for the Self) to be appropriately proud, S must be involved in some way in one of the states of affairs given in the above taxonomy. That is, S must be the "agent" in ACHIEVEMENTS, the "owner" in the case of POSSESSIONS, or a "member" of the GROUP in order to be able to be proud of an ACHIEVEMENT, POSSESSION and GROUP, respectively. In other words, I cannot be proud of a valuable book *as such*. I can only be proud of it if I am the owner of the book. However, as we will see below, this condition can be weakened in less prototypical cases of pride.

This is, however, not sufficient for S to be proud. For S to be appropriately proud of X (=something), X must have some value. The things that can be the causes of pride either have built-in social values or the proud person assigns individual values to them. Thus, we have a scale of social values and a scale of individual values. Things with built-in social values are, for example, achievements, expensive goods, things considered beautiful in a culture, honesty, and being the manager of a company. (Many of these things are oriented UP: VIRTUE, SOCIAL STATUS, etc.) The individual rates things highly on the scale of individual values if in a given context it is difficult for him to achieve X (something). In this case, he can be justifiably proud of X. Thus, one can only be proud of X if X has a built-in social value or X can be assigned a value by the individual (=S).

The difference between built-in social values and assigned individual values can be illustrated by a simple example. Under normal circumstances, it is not an achievement to lift (in the sense of "raise") an ordinary pen. That is, lifting a pen does not have a built-in social value. If, however, S is a paralytic and after a long period of exercising he is eventually able to lift a pen, he can be justifiably proud of lifting the pen. For S, lifting the pen can be assigned a value on the scale of individual values, and thus S will consider lifting the pen as an achievement that forms a proper basis for his pride. In general, it can be maintained that individual value scales are accepted to base one's pride on when there are socially accepted extenuating circumstances for ignoring social value scales. One such extenuating circumstance that is socially accepted is one's illness.

We said that S can be proud of X if he has some direct role ("agent," "owner," "member," etc.) in one of the possible causes for pride in the above taxonomy. However, in less typical cases of pride, this is not always the case. We often hear people proudly say things like:

My son's got straight A's in school.
I know a man who can eat fifty eggs in one sitting.
Someone has an '89 Mercedes on our street.

In reporting these utterances, we could say:

He's proud of his son.
He's proud of someone he knows.
He's proud of someone living on his street.

What this suggests is that S (=he, in the examples) can be proud of X not only if he (S) has some direct role in the cause, but also if S is a relative of someone (*my son*) who plays a direct role ("agent") in the cause; or if S lives in the vicinity of someone (*someone on our street*) who has a direct role ("owner") in the cause of pride. Thus it seems that, less typically though, S can also be proud of X if S "is a relative of" P ("someone other than S"), "knows" P and "lives nearby" P, provided P plays a direct role ("agent," "owner," etc) in X. Of course, we sense a lessening in the degree of acceptability as a cause for pride between:

S "plays a direct role" ("agent," "owner," "member," etc.) in X.
S "is a relative of" P who plays a direct role in X.
S "knows" P who has a direct role in X.
S "lives nearby" P who has a direct role in X.

It is very likely that S's playing a direct role in X produces a much better example of pride than S's living nearby P who has a direct role in X. The formulations above are perhaps nothing else but more specific explications of the notion of "extended self." However, as can be seen, the notion of prototype can give a new dimension to discussions of possible causes associated with pride.

The Prototype of Pride

So far I have talked about only one scale: a value scale for actions, possessions, appearances, social positions, and so forth. This scale can be imagined as a scale that is oriented UPWARDS, and that has a threshold associated with it. The actions, possessions, appearances, social positions, and so on that are above the threshold have (social or individual) value and therefore are proper causes for pride, given that the other conditions are also met. The idea of this scale gives us an explanation for the expression *justified pride*. One's pride is justified if the cause of one's pride is above the threshold on the value scale. And we have to allow for the possibility that opinions in judging what's above and below the threshold may differ.

Now consider a sentence like:

He's more proud of it than he should be.

This sentence implies not just one, but two scales. The two scales are a value scale and a pride scale. In effect, what the speaker says is that S has more pride than is justified by X (the cause of his pride); that is, X occupies a certain position above the threshold on the value scale and S's pride is at a point on the pride scale that is higher than the point that corresponds to the point on the value scale. Notice that this is not the same case as justified pride. In justified pride, the issue is whether the cause of pride is above or below the threshold on the value scale. If it is above, the pride is justified. In the case under discussion, the issue is the *measure* of pride; that is, whether S has or does not have the amount of pride that he is entitled to, given the amount of value on the value scale. In other words, whether the pride as such is justified or not is not called into question; what is suggested is that the pride is excessive relative to its cause.

It is important to realize that the entire discussion of value in relation to actions, states, and properties is couched in metaphor. States of affairs (actions, states, and properties) are not commodities, they don't have values literally. Thus, our thinking about states of affairs seems to be metaphorical to a large extent, as the following metaphor indicates:

STATES OF AFFAIRS ARE COMMODITIES
That was a *valuable* victory.
He had *to pay a high price for* his dishonesty.
Give her some roses *in return for* her kindness.

His paper *isn't worth* looking at.
Did your plan *pay off?*
The *value* of his work is tremendous.
Just watch out! I'll *pay you back* for this.

The analysis of the kind of pride under consideration ("pride as immediate response") has to be augmented by what can be called "related concepts" (for a detailed explanation of this notion, see the chapter on love). It can be argued that pride as characterized so far has JOY as an inherent concept. This would seem to follow from at least the following linguistic evidence: First, there are certain behavioral reactions (correspondingly, certain metonymies) that are shared by both PRIDE and JOY. These include BRIGHTNESS OF THE EYES and SMILING. Second, linguistic usage seems to indicate that, on a conceptual level and at least in the kind of pride under discussion, one cannot be proud of something and not feel joy:

?He was proud of winning the race, but he was not happy.
*He was proud of winning the race, but he was happy.

It has to be noticed that the cases where PRIDE entails JOY in the most clear way are those where pride arises from achievements, rather than the other causes. The reason perhaps is that, unlike achievements, social status, appearance, possession, and so forth are permanent states or properties, which do not give rise to such immediate events as joy. It is partly this immediacy which makes "pride resulting from an achievement" a more prototypical form of pride than the forms of pride that result from other causes. (Some other reasons are discussed at the end of the chapter). And, third, pride and joy seem to appear together in such conventionalized expressions as one's *pride and joy,* which can be taken as an indication that the two concepts are closely related.

One can only feel joy if one is satisfied with what one has done, and an achievement also presupposes that one is satisfied with what one has done. Thus satisfaction is another concept inherent in pride (of the kind under investigation). Linguistically, in addition to the *but-test* (discussed in more detail in the chapter on love), this is shown by the fact that the following two sentences entail each other:

He looked at his son with pride.
He looked at this son with satisfaction.

In the light of what has been done so far, we can see the following prototypical model of pride emerge:

1. S does X.
   S is directly involved in X.
   S values X on a social value scale; X's value is high.
   S perceives X as an achievement.

2. S is proud of X.
   The pride is intense (but not inappropriately so).
   The pride scale is the same height as the value scale.
   There is a sense of enhancement.
   S experiences physiological effects: Redness of the face, increased heart rate.
   S exhibits behavioral reactions: Erect posture, chest out, brightness of the eyes, smiling, telling people about the achievement.
   Inherent concepts: Joy, satisfaction.

This model reveals pride not only as "immediate response" but also as "balanced." Many of the concepts within the domain of pride can be seen as deriving from this notion of pride.

Self-Esteem

As some of the examples we have seen so far suggest, there is a form of pride that comes about as an immediate response to a state of affairs that S perceives as an achievement (cf. *"Winning the race filled him with pride"*). However, not all forms of pride are like this. Consider the following metaphor:

PRIDE IS A PERSON
His criticism *hurt* her pride.
They *humbled* his pride.
His pride *revolted against* the treatment he received.
His national pride was *roused/awakened* by the stupid comments.
Don't say anything that may *wound* his pride.
Her pride *was deeply injured.*

The pride in this metaphor is not an immediate response to a situation. Rather, it is something that S has had for some time and that, on a given occasion, *can revolt, can be hurt,* or *can awaken,* for instance. This seems to be the kind of pride that one takes in one's possessions, one's country, one's success in a field (but not in just one achievement, which is the pride as immediate response), and so on. By and large, in these cases *self-esteem* is a synonym for *pride*. Most of the examples in the PERSON metaphor could be used with the word *self-esteem* in place of *pride* (e.g., *"His self-esteem was injured"*).

The PRIDE IS A PERSON metaphor is constituted by the following ontological correspondences:

- the person is pride
- the physical harm done to the person is emotional harm to S

- physical revolt against something is S's emotional revolt
- humbling the person is reducing S's pride
- for the person to awaken is for pride to begin or continue to function

The word *self-esteem* can be used as a synonym for the word *pride* in the following metaphor as well:

PRIDE IS A SUPERIOR; THE SELF IS AN INFERIOR
His pride *prevents him from* doing anything dishonorable.
His pride *did not allow him* to accept the aid.
Pride *did not let her* do what she wanted to do the most.

The main focus of this metaphor seems to be how pride has an influence on what we should, and in particular, on what we should not do. The issue of how pride can determine our actions shows up in other metaphorical expressions as well: *swallow one's pride, pocket one's pride,* and *set one's pride aside*. These are expressions that are not instances of the PRIDE IS A SUPERIOR conceptual metaphor. Nevertheless, the diversity of these expressions indicates that this is an important aspect of pride for us.

Although in many of the examples *self-esteem* could replace *pride,* self-esteem is, on the whole, different from pride. It has to do with one's overall evaluation of oneself. Unlike the kind of pride exemplified by the CONTAINER and HEART metaphors (which have their particular causes), the kind of pride represented by the following metaphor does not have particular causes.

SELF-ESTEEM IS AN (ECONOMIC) VALUE (WHICH A PERSON ESTIMATES HIMSELF TO HAVE)
He has *low* self-esteem.
She *values* herself *highly*.
Her achievements *boosted* her self-esteem.
Don't *overestimate* yourself.
She *underestimates* herself.
Don't let him *lower* your self-esteem.

This metaphor enables us to see self-esteem as something that can be represented on a scale: It can be *low,* it can be *boosted,* it can be *high*. When self-esteem is high, the person is proud of himself. That this is so can be seen from the following two sentences that entail each other under normal circumstances:

She has high self-esteem.
She is proud of herself.

This close relationship between pride and self-esteem is likely to be the result of the way we structure ourselves and our actions, possessions, appearances, and so forth (i.e., the causes of pride) in metaphorical terms. Since we see our actions, possessions, and so on and ourselves as having VALUES, we expect people with actions, possessions, and so on that have HIGH VALUES to see *themselves* as having *high value*, that is, as having high self-esteem. Of course, implicit here is a principle we use for understanding ourselves:

A person's self-esteem is determined by his actions, possessions, and so on.

But this takes place only indirectly, through pride. The particular actions, states and properties that have HIGH VALUES result in pride, and the particular instances of pride give rise to self-esteem. Self-esteem is thus a generalized form of pride that is not directly linked to particular causes of pride: S is just proud of himself (i.e., values himself highly), and not of some particular action, state, or property involving him.

To complete the survey of this form of pride, mention must be made of another metaphor. The metaphor is PRIDE IS AN OBJECT.

PRIDE IS AN OBJECT
His self-esteem *was shattered* when he had found out the result.
He *lost* his pride and began to implore her not to leave him.
She managed to *destroy* my self-esteem.
He *tore* her pride *to shreds*.
He *kept* his pride in the face of all adversities.
It put a *dent* in his pride.

The main focus of this metaphor is the existence of pride and how pride can play a role in determining our actions. In the discussion of the PRIDE IS A SUPERIOR metaphor, I said that our pride can have an influence on what we do. Now we can see how this works. If S has his pride (i.e. has *kept* it), then it does *not allow him* to do certain things, but if he does not have it (i.e. has *lost* it), then S does certain things he would not do otherwise.

The ontological correspondences are:

- the object is pride
- the dented object corresponds to less pride
- the destroyed object is pride out of existence
- having the object is having pride

Two epistemic correspondences deserve particular attention in this metaphor. The first gives us an idea of how the dent in one's pride can correspond to less pride. A dent evokes the image of a hollow object with rigid walls (like a car). Thus, the process of understanding the meaning of this expression involves the mapping of the more specific container image onto the concept of object. The dent in the wall of the container reduces the capacity of the container; that is, the container can hold less substance. Corresponding to this is the idea that there is less pride in the container.

But our intuitions tell us that the expression *dent in one's pride* means more than just a "lessening of one's pride." The expression also connotes that the amount of pride we lost is not recoverable, that the dent causes permanent damage to a person's self-esteem. How does this part of the meaning arise? For an answer, we have to go outside the conceptual domain of emotion. The metaphor that is relevant to a fuller understanding of the expression is PERFECT IS REGULAR; that is, we seem to comprehend the notion of perfection in terms of regularity. A perfect object is a regular object. A regular object is one without stains, spots, scars, scratches, and, of course, dents. And once there is a dent in the object, it is not a perfect object anymore. This would then seem to provide the explanation for why, in addition to a decrease in pride, we sense the meaning component "permanent damage to one's self-esteem" in the expression *dent in one's pride*.

The epistemic correspondence that accounts for *keeping* and *losing one's pride* is:

Source: An object can only work for S if S has the object.
Target: Pride can only determine S's actions if S has the pride.

The word *dignity* could be a natural replacement for *pride* in the expressions *keeping pride* and *losing pride*. This would seem to suggest that dignity is that aspect of pride (or self-esteem) that plays a role in determining our actions. This seems to have some basis in the fact that the most prevalant metaphor for dignity addresses just this issue:

DIGNITY IS AN OBJECT
He *cast off* his dignity.
He *preserved* his dignity.
She *lost* all her dignity.
His grey hair and solemn manner *lent him* dignity.
He *set aside* his dignity and accepted a menial job.
She *discarded* her dignity.
She *kept* her dignity in the face of all adversities.
He *disposed of* his dignity.

Similarly to a portion of the PRIDE IS AN OBJECT metaphor, dignity is seen here as something which, if S has it, prevents S from doing certain things and if he does not, then S does things he would not do otherwise. As can be seen, we have quite a few expressions at our disposal to denote loss of pride, and hence giving up the controlling effect of pride (i.e., dignity). These expressions in the metaphor are: *lose, set aside, cast off, discard* and *dispose of* dignity.

What has been said about self-esteem yields the following prototypical model:

1. S is directly involved in many X's.
   S sees the X's as having high value.
2. As a result, S values himself highly.
   S's self-esteem is high; S is proud (of himself or herself).
   The value and the pride scales are even.
   S has dignity: It determines what S should not do.

Conceit

So far we have only considered cases where the value scale and the pride scale are balanced. Now I will turn to cases where the pride scale is higher than the corresponding value scale. First I will discuss CONCEIT, and then VANITY.

Some of the behavioral reactions and physiological effects that are assumed to accompany conceit seem to form the basis for some of the major metaphors for conceit. In particular, the behavioral reaction HEAD HELD UNNATURALLY HIGH seems to provide the motivation for the CONCEITED PERSON IS UP/HIGH metaphor.

A CONCEITED PERSON IS UP/HIGH
He's *been on his high horse* ever since he was elected captain.
You don't have to be so *stuck-up*.
Don't you think he's a little bit *uppish?*
She became *high and mighty* when she won the prize.
It was another *lofty* speech.
Look at that *uppity* bastard.
It's time you *got off your high horse*.

And also, historically, *superior* and *haughty*.

And the behavioral reaction CHEST UNNATURALLY THRUST OUT seems to motivate a related metaphor for conceit:

A CONCEITED PERSON IS BIG
When the teacher made John the monitor, he became *too big for his boots*.
He's *big as you please*.
He *got a big head* after winning the race.
She has a *swollen* opinion of herself.
She's had a *swelled head* ever since she got her Ph.D.

Both of these metaphors are concerned with greater than normal physical size: Greater than normal height and greater than normal bigness, respectively. This defines a scale with two points on it: A point indicating normal size and a point indicating greater than normal size. There seems to be an obvious link between this scale and the pride scale I have mentioned before. The point indicating normal size would seem to correspond to an appropriate amount of pride and the point indicating greater than normal size to more than an appropriate amount of pride. An appropriate amount of pride is here defined as a point of the pride scale that is on the same level as the corresponding point on the value scale.

We have seen how the folk model of behavioral reactions captures the increase of pride to a level that is inappropriate (cf. as pride increases, its behavioral reactions increase). Thus, ERECT POSTURE becomes HEAD HELD UNNATURALLY HIGH and CHEST OUT becomes CHEST UNNATURALLY THRUST OUT. This same aspect of pride is also captured by the metaphors we use. Thus, cases of pride with an appropriate amount of pride seem to be expressed by the FLUID IN A CONTAINER and HEART metaphors that confine pride to a level *within* the body as a CONTAINER, while cases of inappropriate amount of pride (greater than normal HEIGHT and BIGNESS) are captured by metaphors that define a level of pride as being, as it were, outside the normal body.

The metaphor A CONCEITED PERSON IS UP/HIGH indicates more than just "a person with an inappropriate amount of pride." It also indicates that this person considers himself as superior to other people. It is important to note, however, that it is often only in the judgement of an outside observer that S considers himself superior. This attribution of superiority goes hand in hand with the attribution, also by an outside observer, of more pride than is appropriate.

The concept of superiority may arise as a result of the way our emotion concepts (and some related concepts) are structured metaphorically. Since in this system THE OBJECT OF CONTEMPT IS DOWN/LOW, it is easy for the metaphor A CONCEITED PERSON IS UP/HIGH to have the implication of superiority. Superiority is thus an inherent concept of conceit. People displaying this attitude to others are called *haughty*. As has been mentioned at the beginning, the principal causes associated with haughtiness are SOCIAL CLASS/STATUS/POSITION. This is not surprising in view of the fact that these are concepts that are all oriented UP, just like CONCEIT. Thus the UP orientation of CONCEIT is maximally coherent with other parts of the metaphorical system.

There is another metaphor in our metaphorical system that is relevant to our understanding of PRIDE. This metaphor is SIGNIFICANT IS BIG (taken from Lakoff and Johnson 1980):

SIGNIFICANT IS BIG
He's a *big* man in the garment industry.
He's a *giant* among writers.
It's no *big* deal.
I was astounded by the *enormity* of the crime.

His accomplishments *tower over* those of *lesser* men.
He's *head and shoulders above* everyone in the industry.

Whereas with other forms of pride the proud person attaches importance to the cause of his pride, in the case of conceit he attaches importance to his own person. This makes self-importance inherent in conceit. THE CONCEITED PERSON IS BIG metaphor can be viewed as a special case of the SIGNIFICANT IS BIG metaphor. Thus, we have a case where a metaphor is doubly motivated. Part of its motivation comes from the behavioral reaction CHEST UNNATURALLY THRUST OUT and another part from a more general metaphor in the system: SIGNIFICANT IS BIG.

A third concept inherent in conceit is self-love. This is suggested by the following expressions that can mean either conceit or self-love or both, depending on the context:

He is *full of himself.*
She is *entirely wrapped up in herself.*
He *is stuck on himself.*

In the physiological reactions of conceit, we have seen that there is INTERFERENCE WITH ACCURATE PERCEPTION and INTERFERENCE WITH NORMAL FUNCTIONING that are assumed to accompany CONCEIT. That is, these physiological effects emphasize inability to function normally. The same idea is brought into focus by the following two metaphors.

CONCEIT IS AN OPPONENT/SUPERIOR
He was completely *overcome* by conceit.
Conceit *robbed him of* the ability to judge things properly.
Conceit *did not allow her* to see things as they are.

The metaphor CONCEIT IS A DANGEROUS ANIMAL can be regarded as a special case of the OPPONENT metaphor:

CONCEIT IS A DANGEROUS ANIMAL
She *was swallowed up by* conceit.
He *was devoured by* conceit.

These metaphors make us see conceited people as being unable to function normally.

This discussion yields the following prototypical model for CONCEIT:

1. S is directly involved in X (or several X's)
   S perceives X as having high value on the value scale.

2. S is proud of X (or of himself or herself).
   S's pride scale is high.

In the opinion of an outside observer, the pride scale is higher than the value scale.
S is unable to function normally.
S experiences physiological effects: Interference with accurate perception, interference with normal mental functioning.
S exhibits behavioral reactions: Head held unnaturally high, chest unnaturally thrust out, forms of walking, ostentatious behavior, thinking one is unique, boasting.
Inherent concepts: Superiority, self-importance, self-love.

As has been noted, the word *pride* is also applicable to the concept represented by the above cognitive model. This is why, traditionally, it was possible to rank pride among the "seven deadly sins."

Vanity

Let us now turn to vanity. The central (i.e., the most productive) metaphor for this concept appears to be the metaphor VANITY IS A (SENSUAL or INDULGENT) PERSON.

VANITY IS A (SENSUAL or INDULGENT) PERSON
He is really *wallowing* in the praises of this new book.
What you said *wounded* his vanity.
Her vanity is just *insatiable*.
Her praises *soothed* his vanity.
They *tickled* his vanity by praising his work to the skies.
It only *fed* her vanity.
Your words of appreciation *pandered* to his vanity.
Her vanity was eventually *gratified*.
His vanity was *offended* by your critical comments.
He tried desperately *to cater to* her vanity, but nothing *satisfied her*.
She *indulged* her vanity by looking at her hair in the mirror for hours.

We noted at the beginning that the typical causes for vanity have to do with appearances. Achievements, possessions, moral qualities, belonging to a group, and social position/status/class are not proper causes for vanity. However, as some of the examples suggest, intellectual capability can also be a cause for vanity. These (unfortunately unexplained) facts would then explain why some of the sentences below are acceptable and why some of them are not:

She is vain about her long dark hair.
He is vain about his cleverness.
*He is vain about winning the race.
*He is vain about being an aristocrat.

In addition to this feature of vanity, there are some other important aspects of it that are focused on by this metaphor. Perhaps the most important of these is the aspect which is captured by the expression *insatiable vanity*. Here the question is what it is that vanity has an appetite for. Let us call this aspect the purposive aspect of the concept. The related aspect of vanity is captured by such expressions as *feed, cater to,* and to some extent, also *pander to*. The expressions suggest that it is mostly some food that can satisfy the person's vanity. More generally, it can be claimed that there is a desire in vanity that needs to be satisfied. The satisfaction of vanity's desire can take various forms, of which feeding is one. Some other forms are *soothing* and *tickling,* and the general forms *gratify* and *satisfy*. But what, in turn, corresponds to the food in *feed* or *cater to,* the cool(ing) fluid or air in *soothe,* and the gentle touch in *tickle* in the concept of vanity? As the examples suggest, the corresponding entity is praise or flattery.

An obvious question to ask at this point is: Why does the vain person need praises or flattery? One might say that he needs it because appearance, the typical cause for vanity, and maybe also abilities we are born with, are things that we are not responsible for, cannot take credit for and thus need confirmation of. These things are the opposites of achievements that are the typical things a person can take credit for, and thus be proud of.

A further aspect of vanity is that the vain person enjoys the praises and flattery (as in *wallow* in praises). And not only does he enjoy them but actually invites them. This would seem to follow from the use of such expressions as *He's always fishing for compliments*. And since the vain person is out for compliments and praises, it is only natural that he does not tolerate criticism.

The expression *fish for compliments* deserves some attention, for it reveals a still further aspect of vanity. Fishing implies trying to catch fish. Catching is an act the target of which (the fish) does not readily lend itself to the act. Correspondingly, the person whose praises must be sought is not a natural and/or sincere source of praise. Praises and flattery are forms of public acknowledgement. *Fishing for* compliments can then be seen as seeking unwillingly given public acknowledgement.

So far we have not seen any explicit indication of the presence of pride in vanity. However, there is a minor but important metaphor whose instances clearly indicate that pride is present in vanity.

VANITY IS AN INFLATED OBJECT
His sarcastic remarks *pricked* her vanity.
His vanity has been *punctured*.

Here the inflated object can only correspond to bigness in the CONCEITED PERSON IS BIG metaphor, which in turn is motivated by the CHEST UNNATURALLY THRUST OUT behavioral reaction.

We have seen in the VANITY IS A (SENSUAL or INDULGENT) PERSON metaphor that vanity has a desire. The same aspect of vanity can be found in the OPPONENT metaphor.

VANITY IS AN OPPONENT
She *yielded to* her vanity.
Her vanity *has been appeased.*
She *overcame* her vanity.
He *gave in to* his pride.

In this metaphor it is the expression *appease* that shows that vanity has a desire. *Appease* presupposes that the person (the opponent) has demands that have to be met.

Similarly to conceit, self-love is inherent in vanity. This is indicated by such expressions as the following:

He *loves the sound of his own voice.*
She is completely *wrapped up in* her own beauty.

Self-love brings with it undue preoccupation with oneself. The cause of vanity becomes the center of the vain person's attention. This attitude can be exemplified by:

She is always looking at herself in the mirror.

We can conceive of this type of behavior as a behavioral reaction that is assumed to accompany vanity.

Our treatment of vanity gives rise to the following prototypical model for the concept:

1. S has/is X (where X has to do with appearances).
   S perceives X as having high value.
2. S is proud of X.
   The pride scale is higher than the value scale.
   Behavioral reaction: Undue preoccupation with oneself.
   Inherent concept: Self-love.
   S wants more public recognition than is due to him or her.

Conclusion

In this chapter several issues have been dealt with. One major issue was to show that "enhancement"—one of the key experiences and ideas characterizing pride—is inherently metaphorical. Indeed, it would be virtually impossible to think of "enhancement" in other than metaphorical terms. This can be taken to support the more general claim that many of the key aspects of the emotions are, both regarding our concepts and experiences, metaphorical in nature.

Next, an informal analysis of the causes of pride was also given. The analysis made use of the notion of prototype. The prototype approach to the causes of pride allowed us to capture some of the subtleties that go into the connection between the causes and the self (who is proud).

Moreover, we have seen that "balanced pride as immediate response" can be regarded as a cognitive reference point in the system of concepts that we ordinarily designate with the term *pride*. Pride of this kind can serve as a prototype with respect to which other closely related emotion concepts, as characterized by their own respective prototypes, can be defined. The term *pride* can be used of this prototypical pride as well as of self-esteem, dignity, conceit, and maybe even some cases of vanity. However, the terms *self-esteem, dignity, conceit,* and *vanity* could not be used to refer to what has been called prototypical pride. This is because these forms of pride derive from "balanced pride as an immediate response," and not the other way around. (Storm and Storm [1987] make a similar argument.) There is also some non-linguistic evidence that points to the same conclusion. As Lakoff (1987) suggested, prototypes often take the form of ideals. In the case of two related scales, such as the pride and value scales, we tend to take the state of balance between the two as the ideal. This phenomenon is not limited to pride but is pervasive in our thinking (see, Johnson 1987). "Balanced pride" is thus a more ideal form of pride than such "non-balanced" forms as conceit and vanity.

But, we have also seen that the differences between the concepts are not limited to the workings of the two scales. Significant differences can be revealed if we examine the metaphors and metonymies characterizing each concept. Without taking these into account, our understanding of the generic category of pride would be greatly diminished.

7
Respect

The notion of worth or value plays an important role in the conceptualization of many of our emotions. We saw this in the case of self-esteem in the previous chapter and, as we shall see, it is especially true of respect. It will be shown that a large part of our conception of respect is based on the metaphorical notion of a person's having a certain worth, or value.

What are the causes of respect? One might expect that people respect each other for, at least roughly, the same things that they are proud of. However, this commonsensical expectation will be shown not to be the case at all. Instead, it seems that the notion of respect is intimately linked to that of power—either in its metaphorical or nonmetaphorical forms.

In studies that try to find out which specific emotional concepts are representative, which ones are less so, and which ones are not of the general category of emotion, respect always ends up in the latter group. Most people find respect a poor member of the emotion category. In the light of the analysis that follows, some reasons for this can be provided.

Finally, the prototype of respect will be given, together with a number of nonprototypical cases. This will make the structure of the discussion very similar to that of anger. This is not so by accident. The general purpose of the chapter is to prove that the lexical approach employed in this study is not limited to the passions (like anger and love), but can be applied with good results to such nonprototypical emotional concepts as respect.

The Major Metaphors of Respect

We have seen in the case of pride that the proud person is conceptualized as being UP/HIGH. In the same way, we also conceptualize the respected person (the object of respect) as being UP/HIGH. The OBJECT OF RESPECT IS UP/HIGH metaphor receives partial motivation from the behavioral reactions TAKING THE HAT OFF, BOW, and KNEELING (all to be discussed later), where the respecter's lowering results in the respected person's relative gain in height.

THE OBJECT OF RESPECT IS UP/HIGH;
THE RESPECTER IS DOWN
Young children *look up to* older ones.
People *regard him highly*.
He *puts all his girlfriends on a pedestal,* and then gets frustrated every time.
He is a very *highly* regarded artist.
He ranks *high* among the world's statesmen.
She *stands high* in the opinion of her colleagues.
I think very *highly* of her.

The question arises: Why should we metaphorize the object of respect as being oriented UP? This is, I suggest, because the respecter considers the object of respect superior to or better than himself in a given domain (what these domains are will be discussed later). And being superior, or better, is also conceptualized as being oriented UP in our conceptual system:

BETTER IS UP;
WORSE IS DOWN
They are all bright, but she *stands out* among them.
He's *head and shoulders above* the others.
He's *tops*.
She's an *outstanding* performer.
He's *top* dog.
His accomplishments *tower over* those of *lesser* men.
Ali was the *greatest*.
She'll become a *star* one day.
He can *top/cap* any story you tell.

The experiential basis for this metaphor in part is that physical size typically correlates with physical strength, and the victor in a fight is typically on top. Another, and maybe more important, motivation is that good in general is UP. There is another way in which we metaphorize the object of respect: THE OBJECT OF RESPECT IS A DEITY. And this also involves an UP orientation.

Notice that the expression *put one on a pedestal* indicates more than just the existence of respect. It also carries the disapproval of an outside observer concerning the respect. What enables expressions like *put one on a pedestal* to carry this element of meaning?

To see this, consider the DEITY metaphor for respect:

THE OBJECT OF RESPECT IS A DEITY
He *idolizes* his father.
She *puts her husband on a pedestal.*

John *adores* his elder brother.
His admirers *worshipped* at his feet.
Don't make an *idol* of wealth.
She *deifies* money.

Most of these examples carry a sense of disapproval. This is possible because the metaphor is based on the ontological correspondence according to which the deity is the person who is the object of respect. In this culture, we endorse only the worship of (one) God. Consequently, when the expressions are used to designate the worship of people and not that of a deity, they indicate disapproval. Another and related source for the particular status of the expressions may be the belief that the greatest amount of respect is due only to deities. Consequently, it is wrong to regard human beings with the same amount of respect as deities.

In the case of many forms of respect, the object of respect has power over the respecter (by virtue of physical strength, social position, etc.). Thus, for the object of respect to have power is another feature of respect. This can in part explain the existence of the DEITY metaphor since in our (religious) folk models deities are the most powerful beings (cf. the expression: God *almighty*). We have noted that deities are oriented UP. In general, power and control are also conceptualized as having an UP orientation, as can be seen from the following metaphor:

POWER/CONTROL IS UP;
THE PERSON WITH POWER IS UP
I have control *over* her.
I am *on top of* the situation.
Everything's *under control*.
He *fell* from power.
She has the *upper hand*.

This metaphor, and consequently also the DEITY metaphor, seems to have the same experiential basis as BETTER IS UP, and consequently as the metaphor THE OBJECT OF RESPECT IS UP. That is, physical strength, which gives one power, correlates with physical size (especially height), and the victor in a fight, who has power over the defeated, is typically on top. The link between THE OBJECT OF RESPECT IS UP and the BETTER IS UP metaphors is provided by a characteristic feature of respect: the respecter considers the object of respect superior to or better than himself. The link between THE OBJECT OF RESPECT IS A DEITY and THE POWER IS UP metaphors is provided by the feature: the object of respect has power over the respecter (at least in some forms of respect).

We have mentioned the idea of an appropriate amount of respect. Deities would seem to deserve more respect than human beings. In general, different entities (causes of respect) would be associated with differing amounts of respect. But where does the idea of an appropriate amount of respect come from? We have seen the same idea in the case of pride. I suggest that the idea of an appropriate amount of pride, respect, and so forth arises from one of the major ways we see the world in this culture; namely, in terms of an economic model. According to this model, people and their actions are commodities, and thus have a value. Different people and actions have different values, and therefore deserve more or less respect. We have already seen the ACTIONS ARE COMMODITIES metaphor at pride. Now let us see the PEOPLE ARE COMMODITIES metaphor:

PEOPLE ARE COMMODITIES
He proved *his worth* to everyone.
She *values him highly*.
She felt an *appreciation for* her parents.
He's *good for nothing*.
His new position *added to his worth*.
This paper *lowered his value* as a scholar.
He *deserves* a good beating/spanking.
He is a *valuable* person.
She *considered him to be worthy of* trust.
The *value* of computer scientists keeps *going up*.
The Giants *traded* Jones *for* Smith.

It is worth looking at the correspondences of this metaphor in some detail.

Ontological correspondences:

- the commodities are people
- the economic value of a commodity is the intellectual/moral/emotional worth of a person
- for the commodity's value to go up and down is for the person's worth to go up and down
- a commodity with an economic value is a person with worth
- the trading of commodities is the trading of people
- the estimation of the commodity's value is the estimation of the person's worth

Epistemic correspondences:

Source: Commodities have a given value.
Target: People have a given worth.

Source: The value of commodities varies.
Target: The worth of people varies.

Source: Certain factors may raise/lower the value of a commodity.
Target: Certain factors may raise/lower the worth of a person.

Source: The value of a commodity predisposes it to certain things.
Target: The worth of a person predisposes him to certain things.

The correspondences of this metaphor reveal how human beings can be viewed in non-human terms, that is, as commodities that have a value, that can be traded, and so forth. A large part of our understanding of human emotions comes from this metaphor. THE OBJECT OF RESPECT, in addition to being viewed as UP/HIGH and a DEITY, is also conceptualized as a (VALUABLE) COMMODITY. Esteem and self-esteem are further examples. Esteem can be described in the following way: ESTEEM IS A(N ECONOMIC) VALUE (A PERSON IS ESTIMATED TO HAVE) and, as we saw in the previous chapter, SELF-ESTEEM IS A(N ECONOMIC) VALUE (A PERSON ESTIMATES HIMSELF TO HAVE). Notice that these (metaphorical) definitions all follow from the ontological and epistemic correspondences of the PEOPLE ARE COMMODITIES metaphor.

Now let us take a look at THE OBJECT OF RESPECT IS A (VALUABLE) COMMODITY metaphor:

THE OBJECT OF RESPECT IS A (VALUABLE) COMMODITY
He *lowered* himself *in our esteem* by his foolish behavior.
He *sets a great store* by his sister's abilities.
She *values* him highly.
She felt *an appreciation for* her parents.
Some people *do not hold* life *dear*.
He's *held in high esteem* by the whole village.
The bicycle was the boy's *most prized* possession.
I *rate* him highly as a poet.
He *puts a high price on* human relations.

The correspondences of this metaphor parallel those of the PEOPLE ARE COMMODITIES metaphor.

Once we conceptualize THE OBJECT OF RESPECT as a (VALUABLE) COMMODITY, it is only a short step to metaphorically view respect itself as a COMMODITY (or MONEY) that has the same value as THE OBJECT OF RESPECT. In all probability, it was this idea that led to the metaphor RESPECT IS A COMMODITY (MONEY).

RESPECT IS A COMMODITY (MONEY)
We *owe* our parents respect.
Newspapers must *pay* respect *to* the needs of the general reader.
Children should show *due* respect *to* their teachers.

He *won* honor *for* his courage.
She *earned* my respect.
They *paid* last tribute *to* the President.
His deeds *deserve* our respect.
The Ambassador *paid* respects *to* the Queen.
After what he'd done, I *lost* all my respect for him.
I think that professor receives *undue* respect.
That's only *fake* respect—he disdains his professor.

The instances of the metaphor indicate that RESPECT has its causes (parents, needs, courage, president, etc.), that there are different ways of causing respect in the respecter (*owe, win, earn, deserve*), that there is an appropriate amount of it (*due* respect, *undue* respect), that it can be genuine or false (*fake* respect), and that it can be expressed by such behavioral reactions as VISITING (*pay* respect to) and CEREMONIES (*pay* tribute to).

The metaphor is constituted by the following ontological correspondences:

- the commodity (money) is respect
- a due amount of the commodity (money) is a due amount of respect
- obtaining the commodity is getting respect
- giving (paying) the commodity (the money) is giving respect
- the genuineness of the commodity is the genuineness of respect
- the causes for giving the commodity are the causes for giving respect

We have seen that people and their actions, properties, and so forth are understood metaphorically as COMMODITIES, and that a person's WORTH is determined by the VALUE of his or her actions, properties, and so on (See the chapter on pride). The OBJECT OF RESPECT is also conceived of as a (VALUABLE) COMMODITY whose WORTH is dependent upon the VALUE of the actions, properties, and so forth of the OBJECT OF RESPECT. Furthermore, respect is conceptualized as a COMMODITY. The amount of respect one gives to the OBJECT OF RESPECT seems to depend on the WORTH of the OBJECT OF RESPECT whose WORTH in turn depends on the VALUE of his or her actions, properties, and so on. The more WORTH one estimates the OBJECT OF RESPECT to have, the more RESPECT one gives to him or her. However, a person's actions, properties, and so forth (the ultimate causes for respect) have different VALUES resulting in different WORTHS (either within the same person or across people), which requires the RESPECTER to give corresponding amounts of respect to the OBJECT OF RESPECT. Consider the following sentences:

He gets more respect than he deserves. (*undue* respect)
He gets no more and no less respect than he deserves. (*due* respect)

He gets less respect than he deserves. (we don't seem to have a special name for this)

That is, similarly to pride, we have two scales: a value scale and a respect scale. When the two scales are even we have an appropriate amount of respect (*due* respect).

The Causal Structure of Respect

As some of the examples show (*owe, earn, deserve*) there is a variety of causal relationships between the cause of respect and respect. We can think of these relationships as different ways of causing respect to come about. *Owing* respect is different from *earning* respect, which is in turn different from *deserving* respect. Consider the following sentences employing these words:

We *owe* our parents respect.
His achievements *earned* him respect.
Her self-sacrifice *deserves* respect.

It seems that the words *owe, earn,* and *deserve* in these sentences are not interchangeable to the same degree. Although they all indicate various ways of causing respect, they seem to co-occur more naturally with some causes of respect than with others. Thus, *owe* appears to go together primarily with causes that emphasize such relative social roles as child-parent, pupil-teacher, young-old, and man-woman. *Earn* seems to prefer achievements. *Deserve* is perhaps best used when some positive moral quality is present.

There are several other words (instantiating other less productive conceptual metaphors) that express further ways of causing respect: for instance, *command, compel, awaken.* Consider:

Great men *command* our respect.
His cleverness and skill *compelled* our respect.
The patience with which she took care of her ill husband *awakened* respect in everyone.

Again, *command* seems most appropriate with causes like intellectual (physical) abilities and positive moral qualities. *Compel* most frequently takes intellectual/physical abilities/skills as causes. *Awaken* is perhaps most appropriately used when it co-occurs with actions requiring the exercise of some positive moral quality.

Insofar as these verbs denote the most typical ways of causing respect and insofar as the causes can be taken to be their typical collocations, we get a set of the most typical causes for respect: social roles, achievements, moral qualities, intellectual capabilities, physical capabilities. Although I have not done a statistical survey of the causes of respect, the information obtained from dictionaries I have consulted suggests that there is some ordering between these causes in terms of frequency. The example sentences of dictionaries and the comments dictionaries make on what the possible causes of respect are seem to indicate that it is positive moral qualities that figure as the most typical causes for respect. They are closely followed by intellectual/physical capabilities. Social roles and achievements are less typical causes.

There are a number of additional causes for respect that seem to be less appropriate collocations for the verbs in question. They include feelings, opinions, wishes, needs, rights, laws, customs, and traditions. Although we cannot say things like

I owe respect to your feelings.
Our traditions awakened respect.
His rights earned him respect.

We can use the following instead:

Why don't you respect my feelings?
We should respect our traditions.
We should respect his rights.

The verb *respect* appears to cover all the possible causes of respect. Consider:

We should respect our parents. (Social role: Parent)
I respect you for your honesty. (Moral quality: Honesty)
I respect you for your skills. (Physical capability: Skill)
I respect you for your knowledge. (Intellectual capability: Knowledge)

So far a variety of causes for respect have been mentioned: moral qualities, intellectual capabilities, physical abilities, social roles, laws, rights, customs, feelings, and so on. Is there an infinite number of causes for respect? Or can we delimit their number by characterizing the causes in terms of some broad categories? I believe that the list of causes for respect is not infinite because it seems that, on the whole, the concpet of respect is linked to two notions in this culture: self-overcoming and power (cf. Solomon, 1976). That is to say, the various causes of respect must, and typically will, have to do with these notions.

Let us begin with self-overcoming. If we look at the moral qualities that co-occur most typically with respect as causes of respect, we find such causes as courage, self-sacrifice, patience, sincerity, honesty, self-denial, fairness, and perseverance. These are all cases where the self does something that hurts his own interests, narrowly conceived. Thus, in an act of courage, I risk my life; in patience, I tolerate something that I don't like; in honesty, I do not do or accept something that would give me certain benefits; and in fairness, I do something that helps someone else at my own expense. Notice that I can't respect a person even for such an obvious positive moral quality as goodness as such unless it is of the kind that some form of self-overcoming is implied. It seems generally true then that in a large number of cases we respect people for something that involves self-overcoming.

In the same way as positive moral qualities imply self-overcoming, what we have called intellectual and physical properties imply power. We can make this claim for the following reason. Some of the most salient intellectual and physical properties appear to be closely associated with the notion of power in our belief system. In particular, the physical property of strength and the accompanying features of large physical size like height (cf. the metaphor SIGNIFICANT IS BIG) are commonly held to involve power, and hence respect. It is a psychological commonplace that in children and adolescents physical strength and size are the properties that lend power to certain members of the group and thus make these individuals the most respected ones within a group. The simple reason is that if you are stronger than I am you have power over me, and if I am not stupid I'd better acknowledge this. Thus, the belief STRENGTH IS POWER has a very real basis in our experience. Maybe it is not a far-fetched idea to suggest that we should look for the origin of respect in physical strength and the power that goes together with it, and also in natural and supernatural forces—for instance, deities— and the accompanying power. Other physical abilities may be thought of as further, subtler, and more removed ways of coping with the physical environment.

In a sense, the positive intellectual properties can also be conceived of as still subtler and more removed means of man's effort to cope with his environment. The most salient of these properties is knowledge, and, not surprisingly, we have the metaphorical belief KNOWLEDGE IS POWER.

However, at this point we run into a difficulty. It can be formulated in the following way: How is it that the concept of respect applies equally easily to such widely different notions as self-overcoming and power? How can we talk about the same emotion? My answer is that the notions of self-overcoming and power are not as different as they might appear at first sight. The very idea of self-overcoming suggests that the self has a part that is to be overcome. And overcoming this part of the self often requires what we call "moral strength." This concpet is an obvious metaphor, the metaphor being MORALITY IS PHYSICAL STRENGTH. The part of the self that is overcome is constituted by things that we consider evil or wrong. Examples of such things are the following: I steal your gold watch just because I like it, in the hope of getting a promotion I tell you something favorable about you although I think you are a jerk, and I don't take care of my children just because I have more pleasant things to do. These are all things in which the self gives priority to himself at someone else's expense. This presupposes the existence of a more basic maxim: THE OTHER IS FIRST; THE SELF IS SECOND; or THE OTHER SHOULD HAVE

PRIORITY OVER THE SELF. All the wrong things can be thought of as violations of this maxim. Our (perhaps Christian) folk model of man also maintains that man is born with a predisposition to give priority to himself, and that we therefore need something to counter this and adjust it to the maxim. This something is moral strength. And that is power, too; not power over the other but power over the self.

This gives us a clue to understand why such widely different notions as physical strength, knowledge, and morality can function as proper causes of respect. This is possible because we have the (metaphorical) beliefs: STRENGTH IS POWER, KNOWLEDGE IS POWER, and MORALITY IS POWER in our belief system.

The presence of the notion of power in our folk model of respect helps us understand why things like the law, customs, traditions, rights, and needs can also function as causes of respect. We think of them as causes of respect in the following sense. For a person who recognizes the law, customs, traditions, people's rights and wishes, *respecting the law, customs, people's rights* and *wishes* will mean "acting in accordance with them." That is, he will obey the law, observe customs and traditions, pay attention to people's rights, and comply with people's wishes. And perhaps the same applies to opinions and feelings. Once recognized, all these things represent power over the person who recognizes them.

The concept of authority is a particularly instructive example in that it serves to illustrate some of the points that have been made above. Consider the three distinct uses of the word in the following sentences:

He respects authority. (a)
He respects the authorities. (b)
He respects her authority on the subject. (c)

In (a) the word *authority* is used in the sense of 'sheer power,' in (b) in the sense of 'power that belongs to an individual or group,' and in (c) in the sense of "power that belongs to an individual via the KNOWLEDGE IS POWER metaphorical belief." Furthermore, *authority* corresponds to the CAUSE OF RESPECT in (a) and the CAUSE OF RESPECT and OBJECT OF RESPECT that are conflated into a single word in (b) and (c).

"Required" Respect

The example of authority leads us to cases that include such social positions as the president, the queen, the king, the minister, the ambassador, the governor, the manager, the Pope, the director, the general, and so forth.

In these cases, power arises from the relative position of the individual occupying the position. This individual will be the OBJECT OF RESPECT and the social position that lends power to the individual will be the CAUSE OF RESPECT. It should be noted that in these cases the respect given is required, rather than optional. This means that I *have to show* respect even if I *don't* actually *feel* respect. One can, and often must, show respect in a variety of ways.

The folk model of the behavioral reactions of respect maintains that the behavioral reactions of respect are: TAKING HAT OFF, BOW, KNEELING, DISTANCE, VISITING, WAYS OF LOOKING, DOING HONOR/CEREMONY, and FORMS OF POLITENESS. Given the general metonymic principle THE BEHAVIORAL REACTIONS OF AN EMOTION STAND FOR THE EMOTION, we get the following system of metonymies for respect:

TAKING HAT OFF
He is my enemy, but I *take off my hat to* him for his courage.
Hats off to you for this fantastic meal!
He *took off his hat* as he entered the Minister's office.

BOW
Everyone *bowed* as the Queen walked into the room.
He *bowed out*.
I *raised my hat* and she *bowed*.

KNEELING
He *brought his enemies to their knees*.
When the Pope appeared people *threw themselves on their knees*.
He *fell down* before the King.

DISTANCE
They stood *at a respectful distance from* the President.

WAYS OF LOOKING
They *looked at* the statue *with great reverence*.
She *gave* the old professor an *admiring look*.

DOING HONOR/CEREMONY
There was *a ceremony in honor of* those killed in battle.
Twenty heads of state *attended the Queen's coronation to do her honor*.
You *should honor* your parents.

VISITING
The Ambassador *paid respects to* the Queen.

FORMS OF POLITENESS
He *deferred* to the professor, asking him to speak first.
She waited *in respectful silence* for the great man to speak.

He *greeted* the director *with a loud "Good morning."*
May I leave, *sir?*

It should be noticed that most of these behavioral reactions are limited to situations involving individuals with a high social position. Furthermore, most of them seem to be required and are "prescribed" for the occasion by some code of behavior. It is interesting, and somewhat surprising, that there seem to be no behavioral reactions that accompany the kind of respect that results from the (proto)typical cause of respect: moral properties. The only possible candidates for the behavioral reactions accompanying this kind of respect are FORMS OF POLITENESS. But even here, the behavioral reactions mentioned do not seem to be very closely linked to the respect one feels for another's moral properties. On the whole, these reactions somehow seem to be irrelevant to this particular kind of respect (maybe also to the respect caused by intellectual and physical properties). In general, it seems true that the behavioral reactions listed above primarily have to do with the kind of respect that arises from high social position.

The apparent counter-examples in TAKING HAT OFF ("I *take off my hat to him* for his courage" and *"Hats off to you* for this fantastic meal!") do not turn out to be counter-examples at all on closer examination. In order for the idiomatic expressions *take off one's hat to* and *hats off to* to mean what they do (i.e., some kind of general recognition or acknowledgement) they must have originated from the non-idiomatic expression *take off one's hat* as in "He took off his hat as he entered the Minister's office." Taking off one's hat is an expression, or behavioral reaction of respect (in the situation), and the linguistic expression *take off one's hat* is a description of the behavioral reaction that accompanies respect that has to do with social position. The metaphorical idiomatic expressions *take off one's hat to* and *hats off to* are not descriptions of this behavioral reaction, but they are partially motivated by it. Their meaning has been generalized to include cases other than those that have to do with social power. They have been included here because the understanding of their meaning requires us to know that taking off one's hat is a behavioral reaction or expression of respect of the stated kind.

Some Differences Between Respect and Other Emotions

We have seen that the above behavioral reactions are typically found in situations that involve respect for an individual who has social power over the respecter, and both the object and the cause of respect are simultaneously present. However, in more typical cases of respect this is not the case. Typically, for someone to have respect for another person does not require the actual presence of the object and cause of respect. Perhaps this is why it is more common to encounter sentences like "I respect him for his courage" than sentences like "I respect you for your courage." In other words, respect seems to be an emotion where the respecter and the respect on the one hand and the object and cause of respect on the other typically seem to be removed from each other. This may be one reason why respect is not considered to be a prototypical emotion. The difference I have in mind between respect and other more prototypical emotions, like love, can be illustrated in the following way. In a given situation, one can easily say: "Oh, how much I love you!" but one rarely hears people exclaim: "Oh, how much I respect you!" The normalcy of the former results from the nature of the typical love situation. Characteristically, love involves situations in which, in addition to the emotion itself, the self and the object of love are simultaneously present; that is, the situation is not removed, as is characteristically the case with respect. (Some further differences and similarities between respect and love are discussed in chapter 11).

However, there are certain forms of respect that, characteristically, do seem to require the immediateness of the object and cause of respect. These include such intense forms of respect as admiration and awe (when they contain an element of respect). Consider the following examples:

I really admire you for what you did.
The boy stood in awe of his father.

In both, the self and the self's respect on the one hand and the object and cause of respect on the other are simultaneously found in the same situation.

This way of looking at things helps us explain (or at least to begin to understand) a remarkable feature of respect. It may have been noticed that respect, unlike other emotions like anger, fear, and love, is not assumed to be accompanied by physiological effects. We do not seem to tremble or to have an increase in blood pressure when we respect someone. However, in the case of such intense forms of respect as admiration and adoration we may experience some physiological effects. Compare:

?He was breathless with respect.
?She was speechless with respect.
He was breathless with admiration.
She looked at them with breathless adoration.
She was speechless with admiration.

On a conceptual level at least, the first two sentences sound less natural than the others. The physiological effects of being breathless and speechless seem to be more closely linked with admiration and adoration than with respect. The most likely explanation for this phenomenon seems to be that, characteristically, admiration and adoration require the presence of all of its constituent entities in the same situation, whereas, typically, respect does not. In less fancy terms, it is easier and more natural for us to respond to something physiologically when that something is present than when it is not.

Another possible consequence of the difference between typical situations of love, anger, admiration, and so on and the typical respect situation concerns the way particular emotions are metaphorized. It appears that with emotions where the physiology is involved (i.e., there are physiological effects), the general metaphor THE BODY IS A CONTAINER FOR THE EMOTIONS applies more naturally than with emotions where the physiology is not involved. As we have just seen, admiration and adoration seem to involve our physiology whereas the prototypical forms of respect do not. Compare:

She was *filled with* admiration for his courage.
His courage *filled* her *with* admiration.
She was *full of* admiration for him.
?She was *filled with* respect for his courage.
?His courage *filled* her *with* respect.
?She was *full of* respect for him.

The sentences with *admiration* seem to be more natural than the ones with *respect* (but there is no claim that these latter are unacceptable). As has been suggested, the reason may be that the general metaphor THE BODY IS A CONTAINER FOR THE EMOTIONS applies more naturally to emotions like love, anger, admiration than to emotions like respect.

The Prototype of Respect

Now we are in a position to take an inventory of the ontology of respect. Let us begin with the entities. There is a person (P_1) who, by virtue of respecting another person (P_2) or thing (T), becomes the respecter. We will call the respecter S, short for the self. By virtue of being respected, P_2 or T becomes the object of respect (*OR*). There are certain properties PR (those involving self-overcoming and power) that have value (V) for people. These include positive moral, intellectual, and physical properties, social roles, and social positions. These properties become the causes of respect (CR). What the self feels toward the object of respect as a result of the above causes is respect (R). Furthermore, respect seems to involve a particular kind of situation (SIT). Since respect has a quantitative dimension, we need two scales of intensity (or amount): a scale of respect (SR) and a scale of value (SV) for measuring the value of the causes of respect.

The concept of respect is also characterized by a number of predicates. We have seen that a cause of respect causes (C) respect to exist (E). The moral property (the cause of respect in general) has (H) value for the self. The amount on the respect scale must, at least in the prototypical case, correspond (COR) to the amount on the value scale. The self values the object of respect highly (VH). S considers the object of respect superior (SUP) to himself as regards the cause of respect. Also, S recognizes (REC) the object of respect as regards the cause of respect. Respect, in the prototypical case, must exist for the right reason (RR) and must be truly felt (TF). In some forms of respect, the object of respect has power (PO) over the self.

Some forms of respect (the ones that involve real—non-metaphorical—power over the self) are assumed to be accompanied by a set of behavioral reactions (BR).

Finally, respect involves a situation where the self and the respect on the one hand and the object and cause of respect on the other are removed (REM) from each other.

SUMMARY OF THE ONTOLOGY OF RESPECT

Entities:

- Person$_1$: P_1
- Self: S
- Respect: R
- Person$_2$: P_2
- Thing: T
- Object of respect: OR
- Properties: PR
- Cause of respect: CR
- Value: V
- Situation: SIT
- Scale of respect: SR
- Scale of value: SV

Predicates:

- Cause: C
- Exist: E
- Have: H
- Correspond: COR
- Value highly: VH
- Consider superior: SUP
- Recognize: REC
- Exist for the right reason: RR
- Truly felt: TF
- Have power: PO
- Behavioral reactions: BR
- Removed: REM

Given these parts, the following can be presented as the prototypical cognitive model of respect:

There is a $person_1$ (the Self).
For $person_1$ a moral quality (Property) has value.
There is another $person_2$ (Object of respect).
$Person_2$ has a moral quality (Property—Cause of respect).
Cause of respect (Property) causes respect to come into existence.

Respect exists.
The value scale and the respect scale correspond to each other.
Self values object of respect highly.
Self recognizes object of respect as regards the cause of respect.
Self considers object of respect superior to himself as regards the cause of respect.
Respect exists for the right reason.
Respect is truly felt by Self.
Respect involves situations in which the Self and the respect on the one hand and the object and the cause of respect on the other are removed from each other.

The part in parentheses represents the causal aspect of respect; they are used to indicate that the respect situation is removed in the sense discussed above.

The various propositions in the respect prototype seem trivial and self-evident at first. Their significance will become clear only when some of the nonprototypical cases are taken into account. Before we turn to these, it might be useful to restate the model above using the notation that has been introduced. The notation will help us see the deviations from the prototype at first glance.

$E(P_1)$
For P_1, H(PR,V)
$E(P_2)$
$H(P_2,PR)$
C(CR,E[R])
E(R)
COR(SV,SR)
VH(S,OR)
REC(S,OR)
SUP(S,OR)
RP(R)
TF(S,R)
REM(SIT)

Nonprototypical Cases of Respect

This section will be devoted to cases that deviate in some way from the prototype. I will not be describing entire models here, but only indicating acceptable changes in the propositions making up the prototype. Each such change yields a nonprototypical case of respect. The list of these cases is not intended to be complete.

Cause of respect is not a moral quality: CR $\neq$ Moral PR

Other properties that are appropriate causes of respect include intellectual and physical properties, social positions and social roles involving these properties, social positions and social roles involving power, and power itself. What further structuring there is between these causes of respect in terms of their degree of prototypicality remains to be seen.

Cause of respect is social position: BR(S), PO(OR,S)

This case adds the behavioral reactions assumed to accompany respect to the features of the prototypical model, together with the feature PO(OR,S). This latter means that, due to his social position, the object of respect has power over the self.

Object of respect is not a person: OR $\neq$ P, OR = T

These cases include deities and money (cf. the expression: *a respectable income*).

Undue respect: NOT COR(SV,SR), OW(SR,SV)

Here OW is a new symbol. It stands for "outweigh." The formula says that the two scales are not even (do not correspond to each other), the scale of respect outweighing the scale of value.

Less respect than one deserves: NOT COR(SV,SR), OW(SV,SR)

In this case it is the scale of value that outweighs the scale of respect.

Equal status: NOT SUP(OR,S), EQ(OR,S)

Here EQ is a new symbol, standing for "equal." The formulas say that S does not consider OR superior to himself, though he respects OR. Instead, S considers OR as his equal. Consider the following example:

> Jim respects John but he does not consider him superior to himself.

The fact that the sentence is acceptable indicates that one can respect a person without considering him superior. In fact, for some people (like Solomon, 1976) this is prototypical respect. However, we can show that this cannot be right. If the prototypical relationship between S and OR were equal status, then the following sentence would be acceptable and would indicate a deviation (Jim considering John superior) from the supposed prototype (Jim not considering John superior = equality):

> *Jim respects John but he considers John superior to himself.

But the sentence is unacceptable. This is because the word *but* is used inappropriately. In its appropriate use, *but* marks a situation counter to expectation. Consequently, if *but* is followed by something expected, the result is an unacceptable sentence. The fact that "Jim's considering John superior to himself" is what is expected is an indication that it must be a feature of the prototype since it is the prototype that defines what is to be expected.

Respect for the wrong reason: NOT RR(R), WR(R)

Here WR(R) stands for "respect exists for the wrong reason." We can demonstrate this with the following example:

You shouldn't respect him because he is strong, you should respect him because he is courageous.

Incidentally, this example can be used to show that "courageous" is a more prototypical cause of respect than "strong" is. While the previous example is perfectly normal, the following would be odd:

?You shouldn't respect him because he is honest, you should respect him because is is strong.

Feigned/fake respect: NOT TF (S,R), F (R)

Here the respect is feigned (F), rather than truly felt.
Example:

That's only fake respect—he disdains his professor.

Required respect: NOT C(CR,E[R]), REQ(R)

In the prototypical case, there is a moral property that automatically causes respect to come into existence in S (in our notation: C(CR,E[R])). In the present case, however, respect is required (REQ). This is characteristic of situations involving high social positions.

Self-respect: $P_1 \neq S$, $P_1 = OR$

Here $person_1$ does not become the self who respects another person. Instead, $person_1$ becomes the object of respect.

Mutual respect: NOT ONLY R(S,OR) BUT ALSO R(OR,S)

In this case, $person_1$ respects $person_2$ and $person_2$ also respects $person_1$.

Admiration: NOT REM(SIT), HI(I[R]), PE(S)

The situation is not removed as in the prototypical case of respect. In addition, the intensity of respect I(R) is high (HI) and the self experiences physiological effects (PE), which he does not experience with less intense and more prototypical forms of respect.

Worship: HI(I[R]), PE(OR,S)

Perhaps this form of respect is best defined *not* as a deviation from the prototype but with regard to the form of respect that involves high social position. It was suggested that respect for a person in a high social position typically goes together with that person's having power over the self. In worshipping someone, the person is not necessarily in a high social position, yet there is power over the self. A linguistic example could be the sentence "She worships the ground he walks on".

These are then some of the nonprototypical cases of respect. It seems that most of the propositions that make up the prototype can be negated, yielding existing, though not central, forms of respect. Perhaps one proposition that could not be negated (without losing the possibility of calling the situation that of respect) is "recognizing another person." Propositions like this will be the major theme of the next chapter.

Conclusions

In the light of the analysis of the conventionalized language we most commonly use of respect, the following points need to be given special emphasis.

First, it seems that to a large degree the concept of respect is comprehended in terms of the VALUE metaphor, which applies to both the object of respect and respect itself. This metaphor comes from the way we conceptualize human beings and their actions, which are regarded as VALUABLE COMMODITIES. The importance of this is that a part of the way we conceive of our emotions seems to be determined by, or at least based on, how concepts which, strictly speaking, lie "outside" of the emotion domain but are nevertheless related to the emotions are understood. (This issue will be further discussed in the last chapter.)

Second, contrary to our expectations, the most typical causes associated with respect are not quite the same as those that are assumed to produce pride. Linguistic evidence suggests that the most prototypical cause of respect is "positive moral qualities." In general, as Solomon (1976) observed, the main characteristics of causes of respect are self-overcoming and power. I have tried to show that self-overcoming and power are closely related.

Third, the account I have given of respect provides us with a possible explanation or with a part of the explanation of why respect is considered a peripheral category of emotion. These are: the "removed" nature of the respect situation, the lack of physiological involvement, and the large-scale cognitive evaluation of the object of respect in terms of the VALUE metaphor.

8
Romantic Love

The main focus of the present chapter will be on what have been called "related concepts." It was suggested in chapter 3 that the structure of many emotion concepts is composed of four parts. These include a system of conceptual metonymies, a system of conceptual metaphors, a set of related concepts, and a category of cognitive models. So far we have seen several examples for the metonymies, metaphors, and cognitive models, but related concepts have not been explicitly discussed. They have been only briefly mentioned in connection with some emotions; in particular, it was said that anger has a "displeasure" element and that "joy" seems to be an integral part of pride. But related concepts associated with the emotions are not confined to concepts that correspond to particular emotions like joy. They can be of a variety of kinds. The idea of "recognition" and "superiority" in the case of respect are good examples, and the discussion of the concepts related to romantic love will provide further instances when related concepts are not "pure" emotions but also emotional attitudes, dispositions, and the like.

By related concepts are meant concepts that are implied or presupposed by another concept. The concept of romantic love is an especially useful one to demonstrate the notion of related concepts because it implies and/or presupposes a large number of other concepts. (In what follows where it is not explicitly indicated, by love will be meant romantic love—a concept subordinate to the basic level concept of love.) This does not mean, however, that the concept of love can or could be exhaustively described in terms of these other concepts. In chapter 3, we saw the variety of other constituents that go into the making of the concept of romantic love. Nevertheless, one aim of this chapter is to show that related concepts are also important ingredients of concepts.

Thus, the view that I endorse is that a more or less complete description of a concept requires both related concepts and the other ingredients. It is, however, more important to argue that the description of concepts in terms of related concepts alone is not satisfactory than it is to argue that the description of concepts in terms of scenarios and models consisting of entities and predicates alone is not satisfactory because the dominant tendency seems to be to propose that emotion concepts can be adequately described in terms of related concepts, which, as will be seen, correspond at least in part to the necessary and sufficient conditions often cited by philosophers writing on emotion.

Philosopher Gabriele Taylor, for example, describes love in the following way:

> If x loves y we have on the one hand x's wants to benefit and cherish y, on the other his wants to be with y, to communicate with y, to have y take an interest in him, to be benefited and cherished by y. (Taylor 1979, p. 171)

Clearly, emphasis here falls on such concepts as mutual sacrifice (benefit), affection (cherish), longing (be with), and interest. These are all concepts that are seen as being implied and/or presupposed by love. What is not clear, however, are the following: Are these the only concepts that are related to love? Is there a methodology that can help us find the concepts related to love? Are these concepts related to love with the same degree of strength? Is the nature of the relationship between related concepts and love the same for each concept? Is there any linguistic evidence to show that love and the other concepts are indeed related in our conceptual system? These are the issues which need to be addressed now.

The Object of Love and Related Concepts

The object of romantic love is conceptualized by means of a variety of conceptual metaphors. The study of these metaphors is important because the various metaphors bring to light other emotions and attitudes that, in the idealized version of romantic love, we find inseparable from it.

Let us begin with the metaphor that seems to be maximally coherent with the idea that love is a need. One of our most important needs is food. And so it is not surprising that we see the object of love in terms of appetizing food.

THE OBJECT OF LOVE IS (APPETIZING) FOOD
Hi, *sweetheart.*
She's my *sweet and sugar.*
Hi, *sugar!*
Honey, you look great today!
She's the *cream in my coffee.*
Hello, *sweetie-pie.*

The fact that we conceptualize the OBJECT OF LOVE as APPETIZING FOOD does not only link love with needs but also with liking and sexual desire. How is this possible? Let us take the concept of liking first. We do not eat appetizing food, especially sweet things, only to satisfy hunger, that is, to satisfy a need. We eat it because we enjoy it, like it. For something to be pleasant to the taste is only one kind of liking. Another kind of liking is when something is pleasant to the sight. And what is pleasant to the sight is usually something that we find beautiful. This gives us perhaps the most pervasive belief about love:

THE OBJECT OF LOVE IS BEAUTIFUL
Let's go, *beautiful*.
Hi, *cutie!*
Well, *gorgeous?*
Shall we go, *angel-face?*

It is important to note that the object of love is always considered beautiful. For it is always the lover who defines who is beautiful for him or her.

The concept of beauty plays a very important role in the conceptualization of love. It is important because it helps us understand more about the nature of the concept of liking. Consider the following metaphor for beauty:

BEAUTY IS A FORCE (PHYSICAL and PSYCHOLOGICAL);
LIKING IS A REACTION TO THAT FORCE
She *bowled me over*.
Who's that *attractive* man over there?
She's a *dazzling* beauty.
I was *hypnotized* by her beauty.
What a *bombshell!*
I was *knocked off my feet*.
She's *enchanting*.
Look at all these *glamour* girls here!
She's dressed *to kill*.

In this metaphor the force takes a variety of forms. It can be magnetic force (*attractive*), a mechanical force (*bowl over, bombshell, knock off*), a strong light (*dazzling, glamour*), and a magical force (*hypnotize, enchanting*). What is common to them is that beauty is viewed as a force that produces some effect on the self (the person who observes it). This effect, or reaction, corresponds, in this metaphor, to liking. There are two things to note about this particular way of conceptualizing liking. The first is that our reaction to beauty, as portrayed by the metaphor, is essentially passive. That is, according to the metaphor beauty is something that we experience in such a way that it is happening to us, that it affects us, without the self being actively involved as an agent in the process. The second observation is that our reaction to the force is such that as a result the self loses control (cf. *bowl over, knock off, hypnotize, enchant, kill*). Not only beauty but also love is conceptualized in these two ways.

However, liking does not necessarily involve the liking of such physical attributes as beauty. If we ask someone, *"How did you like her?,"* there can be an acceptable answer other than just *"She's beautiful."* The answer may legitimately refer to some non-physical characteristic: her personality, her nature, and so forth. Thus, the concept of LIKING which is present in love is broader in focus than the concept of LIKING as merely indicating physical appearance. But since we use the same concept (LIKING) to refer to or focus on several human characteristics, it can perhaps be assumed that we have to do, in this case also, with a mechanism that seems to pervade our entire conceptual system: The mechanism on the basis of which we try to understand, or indeed construct, the nonphysical aspects of human beings (like love) in terms of certain aspects of the physical world (like taste and vision).

But what does sexual desire have to do with the APPETIZING FOOD metaphor? What establishes a connection between the two is the fact that the object of sexual desire is also conceptualized as (APPETIZING) FOOD. And at the same time we come to view sexual desire as HUNGER for (APPETIZING) FOOD. Let us see some examples (taken from Lakoff 1987):

THE OBJECT OF SEXUAL DESIRE IS (APPETIZING) FOOD;
SEXUAL DESIRE IS HUNGER
She had him *drooling*.
He's *sex-starved*.
You have a remarkable *sexual appetite*.
You look *luscious*.
She's quite a *dish*.
She had kisses *sweeter than wine*.
Let's see some *cheesecake*.
Look at those *buns!*
What a piece of *meat!*
I *hunger* for your touch.
He's a real *hunk*.
I *thirst* for your kisses.

Only some of these examples indicate more or less clearly that love and sexual desire are related concepts in our conceptual system. *"She had kisses sweeter than wine", "I hunger for your touch,"* and *"I thirst for your kisses"* may be used to indicate the presence of love in addition to sexual desire. The user of *"She's quite a dish"* or *"He's a real hunk"* does not necessarily want to say that he or she is in love with the person referred to. The person using these sentences is more likely to imply a liking of the other person and a willingness to have sexual intercourse with him or her.

This would seem to mean then that there is only a remote and indirect conceptual relationship between LOVE and SEXUAL DESIRE that is mediated by the concept of LIKING. However, as I will show later, there is a clear and direct relationship between love and sexual desire.

The best indicators of the conceptual link between the two concepts in the SEXUALITY IS HUNGER metaphor are perhaps those that have to do with kissing and touching. I believe that this is not so by accident. The reference to love in these examples is possible in a more straightforward way because the examples draw heavily on a concept that is closely associated with love: INTIMATE SEXUAL BEHAVIOR. The relationship between LOVE and INTIMATE SEXUAL BEHAVIOR is metonymical:

INTIMATE SEXUAL BEHAVIOR STANDS FOR LOVE
She showered him with *kisses*.
It was a fond *embrace*.
He *caressed her gently*.
She *held him to her bosom*.
He *embraced her tenderly*.

The above linguistic expressions may represent various forms of intimate sexual behavior. Thus, we find instances of kissing, touching, and embracing. The expressions corresponding to them also indicate the presence of romantic love. That is, INTIMATE SEXUAL BEHAVIOR is metonymically related to LOVE. In other words, INTIMATE SEXUAL BEHAVIOR is one of the behavioral reactions associated with LOVE. But the concept of INTIMATE SEXUAL BEHAVIOR does not coincide with the concept SEX. The relationship between intimate sexual behavior and love is established by the concept of INTIMACY that figures importantly in LOVE. Intimate sexual behavior is a manifestation of intimacy in the same way as physical closeness is a manifestation of intimacy. Sex as sexual intercourse does not presuppose intimacy; as a matter of fact, it does not even presuppose the presence of intimate sexual behavior. This can explain that a sentence like *"Sally went to bed with John"* does not imply that Sally is in love with John. However, this does not undercut the reverse relationship between sex and love: the concept of LOVE, at least in the ideal cases, presupposes the concept of SEX. However, this link between romantic love and sex is by no means independent of space and time. More than two thousand years ago Plato separated love and sex. Today this nonsexual version of love is known as "platonic love."

But the metonymy INTIMATE SEXUAL BEHAVIOR STANDS FOR LOVE gives us occasion to mention some additional emotions accompanying love. It would be wrong to claim that one can only kiss, caress, or embrace someone that one loves romantically. We can also kiss, caress, and embrace our children, our parents, or our friends. In these cases, we would think of what we do as expressions of our affection or fondness. Thus, the additional emotional concept that this metonymy brings to light is affection/fondness. If we love someone romantically, the chances are that we also feel affection for or are fond of that person. And this is in turn the reason why sentences like *"She's fond of him"* can be used as euphemisms to indicate or talk about romantic love.

Romantic love also presupposes kindness. And kindness is also presupposed by affection or fondness. As some of the examples indicate (*gently, tenderly*), the attitude of the lover to the beloved involves gentleness, tenderness. Tenderness is one of the major ways in which kindness is conceptualized (cf. *soft*-hearted, *tender*-hearted, etc.). Thus kindness seems to be a concept closely associated with both romantic love and affection. It is for this reason that the sentence *"You are not kind to me anymore"* can be uttered to convey a complaint that one is no longer loved romantically.

A metaphor in terms of which we understand the lovers is the LOVERS ARE BIRDS (especially DOVES) metaphor. Consider the following examples:

THE LOVERS ARE BIRDS (DOVES)
They sat there *billing and cooing* until after midnight.
It was all *lovey-dovey*.
Look at those two *lovebirds* on the bench over there!
Here come the love *doves* again.
Their love *nest* has been discovered.

This metaphor also emphasizes the presence of affection and kindness in the conceptual network of (romantic) love. Doves are viewed as symbols of peace, love, and gentleness. The gentleness of the doves is the gentleness of the lovers. Gentleness invites care, or caring. This gives us the further related concept: care. If we love each other, we want to take care of each other. The link between (romantic) love and care/caring enables us to use expressions from the domain of care/caring to indicate romantic love: *"Sally cares a lot about John."*

A very different view of the object of love is portrayed by the metaphor that makes us see the beloved as some kind of deity. Let us see some examples:

THE OBJECT OF LOVE IS A DEITY
I *adore* you.
She *loves the air he breathes*.
He *worships the ground she walks on*.
He *put her on a pedestal*.
She *devoted* herself *to* him entirely.
He *fell on his knees before* her.

She *prayed him* not to leave her.
She *idolizes* him.
He is forever *singing her praises*.
She has *sacrificed* her whole life for the love of her husband.

The special significance of the DEITY metaphor lies in the fact that it brings to light several of the emotional concepts associated with love; in particular, the concepts of respect, admiration, devotion, sacrifice, and enthusiasm.

There is an obvious link between the concepts of deity and respect. (Note such expressions as *the praise of God*). It seems very likely that the original form of respect was the cultic worship of some deity. The conceptualization of the object of love as a deity allies respect with love by virtue of the fact that the object of respect is also conceptualized as a deity. A clear indication of this is that in the appropriate context some of the expressions in the above metaphor can be used to denote respect. Such expressions are *worship* and *idolize*. To be sure, the meaning of these words contains an element of undeserved or undue respect. And this also applies to love. When applied to love, these expressions indicate that the object of love receives more love than he or she deserves. It is important to note that the words *worship* and *idolize* are not used by the lovers to describe their own experiences but carry the judgement of an outside observer.

Respect, maybe undue respect, is then an integral part of our conception of love. But what is undue respect for an outsider is admiration for those on the inside, the admiration of the beloved. The outsider says that the lover is "singing the beloved's praises," while the lover whispers that he or she adores the other and thinks that he or she is the *"most wonderful person"* in the world. What is condemned by the outsider is the most natural thing for the lover to do. Admiration and worship are just two faces of the same coin. What is important here is that admiration is a part of love.

If we look up the etymology of the word *devote,* we find that it goes back to a form that meant something like "from a vow." The reference is possibly to the vow that one makes when one dedicates or devotes oneself to the service of God. The conceptual link between love and devotion is that the lovers see themselves as being devoted to each other in much the same way as a priest sees himself as being dedicated to the service of God. Thus, the notion of devotion in the domain of love seems to enrich our idea of love with two elements. First, in our everyday conception of romantic love we tend to think of love as an emotion that can be directed at only one person (just as a priest can only serve one God). Second, people in love see themselves as "servants" to the beloved. Most of us are familiar with phrases like *"I'll be your slave forever."* The concepts of devotion and sacrifice are difficult to distinguish. But whatever the similarities or differences between them, the important issue for our purposes is that our idea of love seems to incorporate the idea of (self-)sacrifice. If you are not willing to make sacrifices for your love, you are not considered to be really in love either.

Admiration, worship and devotion all presuppose the idea of enthusiasm. If I admire you, adore you, and am devoted to you, I am also enthusiastic about you. What makes it especially appropriate to mention enthusiasm in connection with the DEITY metaphor is that the word can be traced back to Greek and Latin words meaning "possessed by the God." Current usage of the concept suggests that there is indeed a close link between love and enthusiasm. If I have occasion to say that *"He enthuses over that pretty girl in his class,"* you would feel justified to conclude from my statement that he may be in love with her.

Finally, I must mention yet another metaphor that we use for conceptualizing the object of love. THE OBJECT OF LOVE IS A VALUABLE OBJECT metaphor enriches with two emotion concepts the network of concepts related to love.

THE OBJECT OF LOVE IS A VALUABLE OBJECT
Hello, my *precious!*
We have to leave now, my *dear*.
You're my *treasure!*

and on etymological grounds:

Darling, give me a kiss!

In the same way we treasure and want to keep possession of a valuable object, we are attached to the person we love. Thus, the related concept this metaphor brings into focus is attachment. That attachment is really a concept related to love is shown by the fact that we can use sentences like *"She's deeply attached to him"* to indicate love.

The VALUABLE OBJECT metaphor makes it appropriate to mention another related concept. This is pride. If I am in love, I am not only attached to the object of love but I am also proud of her because I value her highly. One of the typical sources of pride, as we have seen, is the possession of a valuable object. The concept of pride plays a distinguished role in the conceptualization of love. Its special status is shown by the fact that it also forms the basis of some scientific accounts of love (see, for example, Branden 1983, 1986; Solomon 1981, 1988). Solomon, for example, sees pride, and its cognate self-esteem, as forming the psychological foundation of love. He suggests that the main psychological function of love is the successful satisfaction of pride and self-esteem. He asks: "What is so good about love?" (Solomon 1981, p. 301). The answer he gives is that love maximizes self-esteem for both parties, and, as a matter of fact, love is something that is in the interest of both parties. If I love you, this will increase your self-esteem, but at the same time this will also increase the chances that you will love me, and thus maximize my own.

Further Related Concepts and Degrees of Relatedness

As we have seen so far, liking, sex, sexual desire, respect, devotion, self-sacrifice, admiration, enthusiasm, kindness, affection, attachment, caring are all concepts that in the ideal case are closely related to the concept of romantic love. In this section what I would like to do is to complete the list of emotions and emotional attitudes associated with love. Moreover, I will try to show that these related concepts are not a part of the conceptual network constituting love to the same degree. Finally, in this section I also wish to provide further linguistic evidence for the claim that the above concepts are indeed related to the concept love. I have noted that physical closeness, intimate sexual behavior, and sex are behavioral reactions associated with love. Both the concepts of INTIMATE SEXUAL BEHAVIOR and SEX involve the concept of physical closeness. Both intimate sexual behavior and sex presuppose the physical closeness of the participants. The behavioral reaction of physical closeness plays a very significant role in the conceptualization of love. It appears to be the case that one of the most important concepts related to love, intimacy, is nothing but a metaphorical counterpart of physical closeness. When we say things like *"They are very close"* or (on etymological grounds) *"They are very intimate"* we in fact talk about this metaphorically understood notion of physical closeness. That is, the claim is that intimacy is a concept that was metaphorically created on the analogy of the concept of physical closeness. Such synonyms of the word *intimacy* as *psychological* or *spiritual closeness* suggest that there must be a conceptual metaphor according to which psychological/spiritual closeness is indeed understood, or perhaps has been created, on the analogy of physical closeness. But so far, I have only been concerned with the nature of the relationship between the concepts of physical closeness and intimacy and have not produced any linguistic evidence to show the relationship between love and intimacy. The following may be considered such evidence. In certain contexts the sentence *"They are close to each other"* may also mean that the two people are in love. But perhaps more convincing examples are those that have to do with the lessening of love in a romantic relationship: *"The distance has grown between them"* or *"We have drifted apart lately."*

The behavioral reaction of physical closeness associated with love can be linguistically exemplified with sentences like *"I want to be with you all my life"*, *"Don't ever let me go,"* and *"You're so far away, I wish you were here."* What is common to these examples is that, in a more or less straightforward way, they all contain the idea that lovers desire to be physically close to each other, they want to be together. Let us call this feeling of desiring to be together "longing." This gives us longing as another concept related to love.

Physical closeness serves as a model not only for intimacy. There is at least one other concept that is also understood in terms of physical closeness. This is the concept friendship. We also say of our friends that they are *close,* and people we do not know very well are often referred to as *distant* acquaintances. Of course, the reason why I bother to mention these linguistic trivia is that friendship also belongs to the conceptual repertory of love. Perhaps the clearest indicators of this conceptual relatedness are the words *girlfriend* and *boyfriend* when they are used to refer to one's sweetheart. It might be objected that these words only represent some euphemistic usage. I would argue, however, that what makes this euphemistic usage possible at all is that there exists a conceptual link between love and friendship.

Finally, mention must be made of a concept that is undoubtedly a part of the rich conceptual network associated with love. This is the concept of interest. The presence of interest among the concepts related to love is shown by such examples as *"She is not interested in him anymore,"* which is almost equal to saying *"She is not in love with him anymore."* The relatedness of love to interest could also be shown through the concept of enthusiasm, which is a more intense form of interest and thus presupposes its presence.

So far I have treated the concepts associated with love, such as liking, sexual desire, respect, admiration, enthusiasm, intimacy, and friendship as if the relationship between love and these other concepts were equally strong for each of the related concepts. But this is not so. The relationship between romantic love on the one hand and the various emotions and emotional attitudes on the other is strong in some cases and weak in others. However, the question is how we can decide in which case it is strong and in which case it is weaker. We can employ the following procedure. As an illustration, let us take two concepts: poor and unhappy. In our everyday conceptual system, these are related in such a way that we think of a poor man also as an unhappy man. What evidence is there to show this? Well, evidence can again be found in the use of the word *but*. As has been noted several times previously, the word *but* is used appropriately (at least in one of its major uses) when it is followed by something contrary to our expectations. That is, if we say *"Peter is poor, but . . ."* then the appropriate continuation of the sentence can only be *"he is happy."* This is because in this case it is being happy that is contrary to our expectations. The sentence *"Peter is poor, but unhappy"* sounds odd because *but* is followed by a state of affairs which is *not* contrary to our expectations set up by 'being poor'; so the word *but* is not used appropriately. Of course, there may be people for whom being poor is not associated with being unhappy but with being happy. For these people, the sentence *"Peter is poor but unhappy"* would be perfectly acceptable. At this point, the link between being poor and being unhappy or being poor and being happy becomes an empirical issue. Although I have not carried out any sociological investigations into this conceptual link, I would say that we would find more people who associate being poor with being unhappy than people who associated being poor with being happy. And consequently, I would expect to come across more people who find *"Peter is poor but happy"* more acceptable than *"Peter is poor but unhappy."*

Thus, we could say on the basis of such (probable) majority opinion that such concepts as enthusiasm, affection, sacrifice, sexual desire, and intimacy are related to our idea of romantic love. Linguistic evidence seems to bear this out. Sentences like *"I am in love with her but I feel affection toward her," "I am in love with her but I admire her," "I am in love with her but I would make any sacrifice for her," "We are in love but we are close to each other,"* and *"I am in love with her but I feel sexual desire for her,"* are not really acceptable sentences.

If, however, we negate the emotion that follows *but,* we should get acceptable sentences in each case. This in fact obtains in some cases like *"I am in love with her, but I don't feel sexual desire for her," "We are in love with each other, but we are not really friends," "I am in love with her, but I don't respect her,"* and *"I am in love with her, but I am not kind to her."* In the case of some other emotions, we would hesitate to consider the sentence as clearly acceptable (the question marks before the sentences indicate this uncertainty of judgement): *?"I am in love with her, but I don't admire her," ?"I am in love with her, but I would not make any sacrifice for her," ?"I am in love with her, but I am not devoted to her,"* and *?"I am in love with her, but I don't care about her."* And again there are negated versions where one would judge the sentences the least acceptable: *"I am in love with her, but I don't feel affection for her," "I am in love with her, but I do not long for her," "I am in love with her, but I am not interested in her,"* and *"We are in love with each other, but we are not close to each other."*

Maybe in some of these cases other people's judgement would differ from mine. But this is not at issue now. What is really significant is that the sensitivity of these concepts to the *but*-test seems to show at least three degrees of variation. As the above tentative results indicate, we can imagine nonideal cases of love that lack, say, respect or sexual desire or kindness or friendship. Second, I believe that my examples show that people tend to think that romantic love is somewhat less likely to occur without admiration or sacrifice, for example. Finally, the chances are that we would consider someone a fool if he said that he was in love with a girl but at the same time he did not feel affection for her or was not interested in her or did not long for her. What all of this suggests is that some emotion concepts are indeed related to love in stronger ways (like affection, longing) than others (like kindness, sexual desire). Furthermore, there seem to be cases between the two (like devotion, sacrifice), which is an indication that the "strong-weak link" is to be conceived of as a gradient rather than a rigid dichotomy.

Of course, this does not mean that the emotion concepts linked with love in only looser ways do not form an integral part of our everyday idea of romantic love. Our conceptual network associated with the ideal cases of romantic love incorporates respect, kindness, sexual desire, caring, and so forth just as it does affection, longing, enthusiasm, emotional closeness. In addition to the linguistic evidence cited so far, this is what the *but*-test also seems to suggest.

Inherent Concepts

Insofar as the *but*-test reveals anything real about the relationship of two concepts and the strength of the link betwen them, and insofar as I am in agreement with other people (or at least with a significantly large number of people) concerning the acceptability of the above sentences, we can say that the conceptual core of romantic love is constituted by affection, enthusiasm, interest, intimacy, and longing. These are concepts that are most closely related to love. Another way of putting this is to say that these concepts are *inherent* to love. A definition of romantic love along these lines would be something like this: Romantic love is a feeling that is characterized by affection, enthusiasm, interest, longing, and intimacy. This is the kind of definition that resembles definitions as given by dictionaries. Dictionaries try to give the necessary and sufficient conditions for the correct application of a word. For example, the *American Heritage Dictionary* defines love in the following way: "An intense affectionate concern for another person." That is, this dictionary emphasizes, among other things, affection and concern. As we have seen, affection is also present in the definition that I have come up with. However, I have not found concern an inherent part of love. Perhaps concern can be equated with what I have termed caring, and in that case it would be a concept that is related to, though not inherent in, love. But all this creates a problem. Why doesn't the dictionary define the concept of love with the other concepts that I have found inherent in it (except for affection)? Several answers are possible. One is that my linguistic intuitions do not coincide with the intuitions of the editors of the dictionary. Another answer is that the *but*-test does not reveal what my examples would seem to indicate, since concern, or caring, has received a status in the dictionary different from the one I have given to it. And, thirdly, we should not exclude the possibility that the dictionary may be wrong in that it does not faithfully represent the conceptual organization of love.

However, our problems do not end here. If we look up the word *love* in other dictionaries, we find that the dictionaries are not in agreement as to which concepts can be used to define love. The *Random House College Dictionary* finds tenderness and affection important. Their definition is: "A profoundly tender, passionate affection for a person of the opposite sex." But *Funk and Wagnalls Standard College Dictionary* puts the stress on devotion and affection. Its version goes like this: "A deep devotion or affection for another person." Now, what are we to make of all this? It seems that I am not in agreement with Heritage as to the necessary ingredients of love and Heritage is not in agreement with Random House, and Random House is not in agreement with Funk and Wagnalls. The only concept that we perhaps all take as relevant is affection. But of course no one would want to say that romantic love is exclusively constituted by affection, since this would amount to saying that the two are the same. Perhaps the best thing we can do is to admit that love is a concept that it is difficult to define in terms of inherent features, and whose definition might depend on such factors as one's general view of the world or one's sub-culture or method of definition. In other words, we may not have defining features of love or, as a matter of fact, for the majority of our categories, which have the same validity forever and for everyone. If the *but*-test is a reliable method of arriving at what the defining features of a category are, then it can provide us with these features insofar as people agree in their acceptability judgments.

In addition to the studies mentioned so far in this chapter, there is at least one other ("scientific") study in which an attempt is made to define love by means of what I have called related concepts (Newton-Smith 1973). In this study, the following concepts, or "love-comprising relations" as the author calls them, are found to comprise the concept of love:

1. A knows B (or at least knows something of B)
2. A cares (is concerned) about B
A likes B
3. A respects B
A is attracted to B
A feels affection for B
4. A is committed to B
A wishes to see B's welfare promoted (Newton-Smith 1973: 118–119)

With the exception of 1 and 4, I have mentioned all of the other concepts in the prototypical cognitive model of romantic love. The first is intended to be a precondition for love, and I have also incorporated it in the characterization of the everyday model of love in the form "A comes along." The fourth can perhaps be accomodated by claiming that it roughly corresponds to what I have termed self-sacrifice. In the light of what has been done in this and the previous chapters, we can see two weaknesses in this approach. First, the conceptual features given appear to be a fairly randomly selected choice of concepts. For example, one wonders where are concepts like interest, intimacy, and longing? And if respect is included, why not include friendship, admiration, and devotion?

The second weakness that needs to be pointed out has to do with the inadequacy of any approach that tries to define a concept in terms of necessary and sufficient conditions alone. We have seen that different dictionaries find different concepts important in their definitions of love. This is an indication of the difficulty involved in the task of coming up with the necessary and sufficient conditions for the application of the concept love. But let us suppose for a moment that this is possible. The concept defined only in terms of these features would be extremely impoverished, given what we know and can reveal about love on the basis of everyday language use. Elsewhere (Kövecses 1988) I have discussed in detail the extent to which the various metonymical and metaphorical conceptualizations of love contribute to the concept of romantic love. Without these metaphors and metonymies our understanding of the various aspects of the concept would be considerably reduced. What is needed is a balanced view that recognizes the importance of both related concepts (especially the inherent ones) and the various other items we saw in chapter 3.

Love and Happiness

So far we have looked at emotions and attitudes that are related to love: liking, longing, intimacy, sexual desire, admiration, and so forth. Another emotion concept that is also related to love is happiness. But the relationship between love and happiness is different from the relationship between love and the above emotions. As we have seen, the concept of love presupposes, or takes for granted, the presence of liking, longing, intimacy, sexual desire, admiration, and so on. Another way to express the same idea is to say that if I like, long for, am emotionally close to, feel sexual desire for, or admire someone, then I am in love with that person. (Obviously, in the everyday ideal model of love some other conditions will also have to be met: For example, the lovers would have to be of different sexes.) However, the relationship between love and happiness seems to be different. Instead of saying that romantic love presupposes or takes for granted happiness we should rather say that if I am in love (and my love is returned), then I am happy. That is, in this case love results in happiness. (cf. *"This love has made me happy"*). To put the difference briefly: If I like, long for, and am emotionally close to someone, then I an in love, and if I am in love (and of course my love is reciprocated), then I am happy. But, this way of putting things blurs important differences in the meanings of the two constructions (the constructions being: "If liking, longing for, etc. someone, then love" on the one hand and "if love, then happiness" on the other). The presence of liking, longing, admiration, and so forth allows us to describe someone (including ourselves) as being in love, whereas in the case of happiness being in love leads to or brings about happiness. All this seems to suggest that while there is a causal relationship between the concepts of love and happiness, there does not seem to be a similar relationship between love on the one hand and liking, longing, admiration, and so on on the other. Perhaps the relationship between love and these emotions can be best put by saying that in order for me to describe someone as being in love, these emotions must be present in the situation. It seems then that such feelings as liking, longing, and admiration specify and/or constitute in part the rules of the applicability of the concept of romantic love. If they are present, I can appropriately say of a person that he or she is in love.

However, this should not be understood as implying that *all* of the concepts we have discussed so far must be present in order for me to correctly describe someone as being in love. We have already seen in the discussion of the *but*-test that the majority of the concepts associated with love need not each be present. I can be truly in love with someone even if I don't feel sexual desire for the person, provided that enough of the other concepts are present. That is, almost any one of these related emotions can be absent (except maybe affection, intimacy, etc., which yielded unacceptable sentences on the *but*-test. But even this is an open empirical issue). Of course, I would still want to maintain that the ideal model of romantic love in our everyday thinking is very much characterized by the complete repertory of emotions I have mentioned in this chapter.

The fact that the relationship between love and happiness differs from that between love and the other concepts raises a further issue. It concerns the possibility that the various related concepts enter the prototypical cognitive model of love at various stages. In the same way as happiness can be said to result from love, it can be suggested that, for example, liking precedes love. It was this idea that was intended to be captured in Stage 1 of the cognitive model of romantic love (see chapter 3), where we have the notion of attraction that roughly corresponds to liking. A similar proposal is made by Steck, Levitan, McLane and Kelley (1982), who suggest that "romantic relationships probably go through attraction, liking, or friendliness phases before love is ever reached" (p. 490). These are observations that are supported by our everyday experiences. Yet, at this time, it is difficult to determine how they can be utilized in the construction of prototypical cognitive models in any principled ways.

Conclusion

The analysis showed that the term "related concepts" covers a broad range of cases. Concepts can be associated with the concept of romantic love with various degrees of strength. The cases where the link is strongest have been called "inherent concepts." It is these ingredients of concepts that come closest to the status of necessary and sufficient conditions. It has been pointed out, however, that these concepts taken together do not fully exhaust what is meant by romantic love. In other words, inherent concepts can be regarded as necessary though not sufficient elements of concepts.

9 The Concept of Emotion: The Container Metaphor

We have discussed the CONTAINER metaphor in connection with anger, fear, and pride in some detail. The purpose of the present chapter is twofold: First, it is to examine how this metaphor applies to a large number of emotions and, second, to show how a single conceptual metaphor can give considerable structure to the diffuse and vague notion of emotion. Thus in the analysis to follow both major senses of the word *emotion* are taken into account: the sense in which the word designates a number of specific emotions and one in which it is a mass noun, referring to a diffuse entity.

In the course of this analysis an effort will be made to uncover most of the major implications of the CONTAINER image-schema as it relates to the concept of emotion. As will be seen, this takes us a long way in understanding the ways we conceptualize the workings of emotion. Furthermore, the CONTAINER metaphor will also enable us to see how some of the language we use to talk about the emotions has the meaning it has. In particular, it will be shown that we can make sense of large portions of the spatial language about emotion (like *deep feelings*) by evoking the container image.

But there is more, it will be claimed, to the CONTAINER metaphor than just making sense of certain linguistic expressions. The detailed study of this metaphor will also give us some insight into the nature of our folk understanding of what it means to be a person. Moreover, the examination of the metaphor will put us in a position to see how certain "scientific" theories of emotion are simply variants of the folk model represented by the CONTAINER metaphor. To illustrate this point, we will use Freud's theory of emotion.

We will proceed as follows. First, the concept of the CONTAINER metaphor is introduced and we will also briefly look at an influential CONTAINER metaphor that is used in the conceptualization of communication: the "conduit" metaphor. Second, the CONTAINER metaphor of emotion will be presented, along with the most important consequences that the metaphor entails. Third, the question of relevance of the metaphor to emotion language will be taken up. Fourth, we will examine how the notion of person is partially based on the CONTAINER metaphor. Fifth, a detailed example of how the CONTAINER image is made use of in theorizing about emotion will be presented; this is the point where we will look at Freud's theory of emotion.

The Container Metaphor in Language and Thought

Before we turn to the CONTAINER metaphor of emotion, it is important to get a more precise idea of what is meant by this metaphor in general. Lakoff and Johnson (1980) claim that our conceptual system imposes container structure on a variety of things that are not in fact containers. This is because there are certain directly emergent concepts, like containers, with a clear structure that can be utilized in understanding concepts that have no such clear structure. Consider the sentence

We are *in* the room.

The room is a clear physical container and the preposition *in* indicates that people are inside that container. In general, the typical use of the preposition *in* is to locate certain objects within the (three-dimensional) boundaries of a container. However, there are many cases where the preposition *in* is used in connection with events, social groups, time, and states of various kinds that are obviously not containers in the same sense as, for example, a room is. These cases can be illustrated with the following examples:

He is *in* the race.
We live *in* society.
I'll be there *in* five minutes.
I'm *in* love.

These examples are specific instances of more general conceptual metaphors: namely, EVENTS ARE CONTAINERS, SOCIETY IS A CONTAINER, TIME IS A CONTAINER, and EMOTIONAL STATES ARE CONTAINERS, respectively. That is, events, social groups, time, and emotional states are all conceptualized as containers. In the case of emotional states, when we are inside the container, we are in the given emotional state.

But, not all CONTAINER metaphors work like this. We also have CONTAINER metaphors in which the container corresponds to the human body, or parts of it that have entities or substances in it. We seem to operate with two major conceptual metaphors of this latter kind. Both of them are used to conceptualize some aspects of human beings. They are: THE MIND IS A CONTAINER and THE BODY IS A CONTAINER. I will say more about the BODY IS A CONTAINER metaphor in the next section. Let me now briefly comment on the MIND IS A CONTAINER metaphor.

The MIND IS A CONTAINER metaphor is assumed, for example, by the IDEAS ARE FOOD metaphor, as discussed by Lakoff and Johnson (1980), which can be illustrated by linguistic examples like "I just can't *swallow* that claim." "That's *food for thought,*" and "We don't need to *spoon-feed* our students" (Lakoff and Johnson, 1980, 46–47). Reddy (1979) describes our language about communication in terms of what he calls the "conduit" metaphor, which has the following parts: IDEAS (MEANINGS) ARE OBJECTS, LINGUISTIC EXPRESSIONS ARE CONTAINERS, and COMMUNICATION IS SENDING. Given that IDEAS ARE FOOD and THE MIND IS A CONTAINER and given the "conduit" metaphor, communication between people will be seen as sending meaning from one container to another.

The MIND IS A CONTAINER and the BODY IS A CONTAINER metaphors appear to be major ways in which we view ourselves. At this point of the analysis, it is difficult to tell how the two container metaphors are related to each other in our folk understanding of ourselves. We will get a clearer idea of the nature of this relationship after a discussion of the CONTAINER metaphor as it applies to the concept of emotion.

The Two Container Images of Emotion

Perhaps the most general metaphor for the domain of emotion is the metaphor according to which the emotions are FLUIDS IN A CONTAINER. It appears to be the most general in the sense that it applies to the largest number of emotions. However, this does not mean that each and every example of the metaphor is applicable to each and every emotion. Which examples fit which emotions seems to depend on the kinds of specific image and knowledge we have of containers with fluids in them.

The examination of the conventionalized language about emotion shows that the CONTAINER metaphor comes in two versions. We can begin with the version which is less interesting in the sense that it produces fewer metaphorical consequences.

THE EMOTIONS ARE FLUIDS IN A CONTAINER
She was *filled* with emotion.
Emotion *welled up inside* her.
He was *full of* emotion.
Her emotions *rose*.
There is a lot of passion *in* her.

It seems that this portion of the CONTAINER metaphor applies to any specific emotion, like anger, pride, love, admiration, sadness, shame, respect, joy, and many more. The examples above portray the emotions as a fluid in a container. There can be more or less fluid in the container. The container defines an intensity scale for the emotions, which has two endpoints (a threshold and a limit). The lower endpoint corresponds to the bottom of the container and the upper endpoint to the brim of the container. More of the fluid indicates more emotional intensity. This is a special case of the general orientational metaphor MORE IS UP. The rise of the fluid indicates an increase in emotional intensity. It might be interesting to note here that the emotion goes into the container "from below." This may be a consequence of the way we conceptualize the source of the emotions: emotions, in our folk understanding, come from the viscera, that is, the lower part of the container.

Given the CONTAINER metaphor, it is natural for us to talk about the lack of emotion in the following ways:

I feel *empty*.
I feel emotionally *drained*.

The lack of fluid in the container corresponds to the lack of emotion in the person.

As more and more fluid goes into the container and the fluid reaches the limit (the brim), two things can happen. One is that the fluid exerts pressure on the side of the container which, as a result, swells. Given that more of the fluid corresponds to more intensity, we get the following metaphorical consequence:

AS THE EMOTION GETS MORE INTENSE, THE CONTAINER GETS BIGGER
He got a *swelled head*.
I was *swelling* with emotion.

This portion of the CONTAINER metaphor applies to such emotions as pride and admiration.

Another thing that can happen is that the container cannot take any more of the fluid and, as a result, the fluid goes out of the container. Thus we get:

AS THE EMOTION GETS MORE INTENSE, THE FLUID GOES OUT OF THE CONTAINER
He *poured out* his feelings to her.
She *overflowed* with emotion.

This version is applicable to emotions like affection, love, sadness, and happiness. The general implication of this part of the CONTAINER metaphor is that the self, corresponding to the container, loses control over his or her emotions. In the terms of the metaphor, this means that the container (the person) has become dysfunctional (because it cannot hold the fluid). Of course, this does not apply to cases where the self intentionally causes the fluid to go out of the container, which is one of the interpretations of the expression *pour out*.

Once we conceptualize the emotions as fluids that can go out of a container, we can use this as a way of conceptualizing what is involved in controlling them. Given the container image, there appear to be several ways to understand the control aspect of emotion. These ways, as we saw in the case of anger (in the chapter on fear), have to do with controlling the outflow of the fluid from the container. The first is when we keep the fluid inside the container. Here the focus is on the container. For example:

He *bottled up* his emotions.
He *kept* it all *in*.
She *didn't let* her emotions *overflow*.

The second is when we press the fluid down. In this case we are concerned with the fluid itself. This is exemplified with

He *suppressed* his emotions.

A third way involves the reversal of the direction of the outpouring fluid. That is, the emphasis falls on the direction of the outflow. For example:

He *turned* his emotions *inward*.

The idea here is that we reverse the *outward* flow of the fluid.

The cases we have discussed so far all involved emotion as a fluid, without any further qualifications as to the temperature of the fluid. The following examples, however, indicate that the emotions are often conceptualized as hot fluids, or as the heat of a fluid, in a contaienr.

THE EMOTIONS ARE THE HEAT OF A FLUID IN A CONTAINER
I was *seething* with emotion.
She was *bubbling* with emotion.
His passion for her *simmered* for years.
She was *seething* with contrary emotions.

The main theme of this part of the CONTAINER metaphor seems to be that there is a great deal of physical agitation inside the container. Due to the heat, the fluid is in constant motion. Corresponding to this is the emotional agitation of the self. Thus, we make use of this portion of the CONTAINER metaphor in the conceptualization of those emotions that are characterized by increased body heat and a large amount of physical agitation. These include primarily the emotions that we typically consider as "passions" such as: anger, romantic love, desire, hatred, and jealousy.

It is interesting at this point to compare the way we talk about the lack of emotion in the case of the HOT FLUID IN A CONTAINER and the

FLUID IN A CONTAINER metaphors. Consider the following sentences, referring to anger and love, respectively:

Keep *cool!*
Why are you so *cold* to me?

In the case of the hot-fluid metaphor, lack of emotion seems to correspond to lack of heat, whereas in the case of the FLUID IN A CONTAINER metaphor lack of emotion was conceptualized as a lack of fluid in the container. This would seem to suggest that emotion corresponds to two different things in the two CONTAINER metaphors: to heat in one case and to the fluid in the other.

The image of the container with a boiling fluid inside is elaborated further. Since the hot fluid generates steam, we get

AS THE EMOTION GETS MORE INTENSE, IT GENERATES STEAM
He's just *letting off steam*.
He was *steaming* with passion.
She's all *steamed up*.
They had a *steamy* relationship.

Due to the cause-effect type of relationship between heat and steam, this part of the CONTAINER metaphor metonymically indicates great emotional intensity. It also suggests the idea that there is pressure inside the container.

This issue is explicitly taken up by another metaphorical entailment of the CONTAINER metaphor. The heat of the fluid produces steam and this creates pressure on the container. So we have linguistic expressions like the following:

AS THE EMOTION GETS MORE INTENSE, IT CREATES PRESSURE ON THE CONTAINER
Her feelings were *pent up inside* her.
I could feel the *pressure building up inside* me.
She was just about to *burst*.

The implication of these examples is that, if the emotion gets too intense, the container may explode and the fluid may come out of the container. The explosion is dangerous both for the self (corresponding to the container) and other people around it (especially the object of emotion).

When the emotion gets too intense (i.e., it exerts too much pressure on the container) and the self is unable to control it (i.e., cannot apply any more counterforce), the container explodes, the top of the container comes off, and what was inside comes out. This would seem to be the logic that can be called upon to account for the following examples:

WHEN THE EMOTION GETS TOO INTENSE, THE CONTAINER EXPLODES
There was an *outburst* of passion.
All her pent up feelings *burst out*.
He *flipped his lid*.

The main issue here is the loss of control over the emotion. The example *flip one's lid* is particularly interesting because it points to another difference between the two kinds of CONTAINER metaphor we have seen in this section (absence of heat versus presence of heat inside the container). This example suggests that the container for the hot fluid does have a top, or cover, whereas this does not seem to be the case when the container simply has fluid in it. As we shall see in the discussion of the relationship between the language-based CONTAINER metaphor and Freud's emotion theory, this seemingly insignificant fact will take on some significance.

However, the fluid does not necessarily have to go out of the container as a result of an explosion. It can also be let out under control. Thus, we get linguistic examples like the following:

EMOTION CAN BE LET OUT UNDER CONTROL
He *let out* his emotions slowly.
The teacher *vented* all her passions *at* us.
She *gave vent to* her emotions.

In these cases, the self retains control and consciously lets out the fluid (possibly but not necessarily at the object of the emotion). This was called "controlled response" in the chapter on fear. Controlled response is a way of controlling (or rather, not losing control over) our emotions. What makes it interesting from the viewpoint of how we conceptualize emotional control is that the self appears to retain control despite the fluid's going out of the container, which is typically understood as indicating loss of control.

But controlled response is not the only way in the conceptualization of control as it relates to the HOT FLUID IN A CONTAINER metaphor. As we have seen in the discussion of the FLUID IN A CONTAINER metaphor, there are several ways in which the outflow of the fluids can be prevented. These also apply to the emotions that are conceptualized as hot fluids, but there is an important difference. Consider the following examples:

He managed to *bottle up* his emotions.
He could hardly *contain* his emotions.
I could barely *keep it in* anymore.

What is perhaps most noticeable about these examples is that they emphasize the difficulty involved in controlling some of our emotions. This is suggested by the expressions *manage, could hardly,* and *could barely.* And maybe *suppress,* which was mentioned in the FLUID IN A CONTAINER metaphor, also belongs here, since it also implies the use of considerable force. In any case, the general implication of these examples seems to be that it requires a great deal of energy to control the emotions that are conceptualized as hot fluids in a container.

In sum, the CONTAINER metaphor highlights several important aspects of emotion. It tells us that emotion is a mass entity that is capable of independent existence from a person. Furthermore, according to the CONTAINER metaphor emotion is something that can exert considerable force on the self, it is dangerous, it has to be controlled, and a great deal of energy is required to control it. These aspects of emotion all seem to emerge from the way emotion is conceptualized. Given this picture, we can now move on to consider some of the issues that can be better understood in the light of what has been done so far in this chapter.

Emotion Language and the Container Metaphor

The first issue has to do with why we use a certain kind of spatial language when we talk about emotion. This language includes spatial expressions such as *deep, inner, innermost, central, superficial, core, shallow, peripheral, inside,* and *outside*. We can partly make sense of this language with the help of the CONTAINER metaphor. Let us begin with the word *deep,* when it refers to emotion. Most dictionaries give the following definitions for the emotional meaning of this word: (a) "strong," "intense," "extreme," and (b) "sincere," "heartfelt." How can *deep* have acquired these senses? Let us consider such examples as *deeply moved, deeply emotional,* and *deeply felt,* which for the most part exemplify the first sense. We have already seen that the notions of quantity and intensity are closely related. More of something can indicate greater intensity. Now, since the body is seen as a container, this abstract metaphor (more of quantity is greater intensity) can lead to the following inference: The deeper the container, the more fluid it can hold, and therefore the emotion is of greater intensity. It is this metaphorical inference that seems to account for the first sense of *deep* when it is used of emotional phenomena. We can account for the second emotional sense, "sincere" or "heartfelt," if we consider the following. The CONTAINER metaphor defines a three-dimensional space surrounded by the bounding surfaces of the container. The points farther away from these surrounding bounding surfaces are seen as being *deep* in the container. Furthermore, we have the metaphor SINCERE IS DEEP DOWN in our conceptual system. This metaphor arises as a result of the fact that truth is conceptualized as DEEP DOWN (cf. expressions like "You have to *dig deeper* to find the truth"). And, since truth is a concept inherent to sincerity, what is sincere will be seen as deep down as well. Given the CONTAINER metaphor for emotion that defines a depth, the SINCERE IS DEEP DOWN metaphor will be applicable to the emotions as well. The result is that certain emotional experiences (which are located deep in the container) will be considered sincere. Hence, *deeply felt emotions* will be ones that are sincere and one's *innermost feelings* are one's true feelings, and *deep inside* means "in reality." In general, what goes on *inside* the container is referred to as one's emotional life. Hence, the expression *inner life*. As a consequence of the equation of inner life with emotional or spiritual life, the expression *deep inside* appears to be restricted to emotional characteristics. Thus, while we can say of someone that "Deep inside he is a loving person," we could not say that "Deep inside he is an intelligent person."

Although the BODY AS A CONTAINER FOR THE EMOTIONS metaphor takes us some way in making sense of some of the spatial language used of emotion, it does not take us all the way. For example, it helps us account for expressions like *deeply moved,* or *deeply hurt,* or *deeply disappointed,* but it does not seem to motivate expressions such as *deeply in love*. As we noted at the beginning of this chapter, the images seem to be different in the two cases. In the former examples, the image is that of a person (container) with emotion (fluid) inside him, whereas in the latter the image is that of emotion (possibly some fluid) with the person in it. That is, in the latter case it is the emotion that functions as a container; more specifically, as a container substance.

Another kind of difficulty that is not easy to solve by relying on the CONTAINER metaphor alone is the following. Anger is conceptualized metaphorically both as a FLUID IN A CONTAINER and as a NATURAL FORCE (e.g., "He *stormed* out of the room") and yet expressions like *deeply angry* or *in deep anger* do not seem to be acceptable. To complicate matters further, it is perfectly good English to talk about being *deeply indignant* about something, although indignation is a concept closely related to anger. It seems obvious then that factors other than how a given concept is conceived metaphorically play a role in an account of the spatial language we use of the emotions.

Some Folk Theories of Personhood

But, the CONTAINER metaphor allows us to do more than just make sense of certain linguistic expressions. It also helps us understand why we have some of the folk theories of persons that we do. One such folk theory is what is known as the "onion peel" theory. This view of personhood maintains that a person is composed of several layers of emotions (feelings), thoughts, and actions. The outermost layers represent those aspects of the self that we are conscious of, that are under our control, and that we want to present to others. In other words, according to our folk wisdom these are the most misleading and least true aspects of persons. In contrast, the innermost layers, that is, the ones that are or come from the deepest parts of the self, are our real and true feelings, thoughts, and actions. It seems to be clear that the "onion peel" theory owes a great deal to the container metaphor, both of the mind and the body. In the BODY AS A CONTAINER FOR THE EMOTIONS metaphor, depth is defined relative to the top or sides of the container. And as we have seen, we have the conceptual metaphor TRUTH IS DEEP (DOWN), which renders the emotions in the deepest parts of the container our "true" emotions (feelings) and the ones that appear on the surface layers as superficial and deceptive. Accordingly, people who readily reveal their true emotions are said to *wear their hearts on their sleeves,* someone who *spills his guts* is revealing his true feelings, and a person who *has come out of his or her shell* is someone who does not feel inhibited anymore to be his or her real self.

Another aspect of the language-based folk model of the self is that the self is composed of distinct and identifiable parts. It is this division of the self that makes possible such expressions about emotion as "He was *beside himself*", and "She almost *jumped out of her skin.*" The prototypical person is composed in such a way that one of the selves is inside his or her container self (defined by the skin in the second example). As a result of some extreme emotional experience the self that was inside the container self may come out of the container and thus be beside it or outside it.

Leonard Talmy (1985) observes that in our "naive psychology" the self is divided into two components as exemplified by sentences like the following:

I served myself some dessert from the kitchen.
He held himself back from responding.

The personal pronouns *I* and *he* on the one hand and the reflexive pronouns *myself* and *himself* on the other represent distinct components of the self. In the first example, the distinct components *I* and *myself* arise from projecting onto a situation involving one person ("I served myself some dessert from the kitchen") a dyadic situation (like "I served Mary some dessert from the kitchen"), involving two persons—a host and a guest. Thus, the components of the self as characterized by the first sentence function as a host and a guest.

Talmy's discussion of the second example is more relevant to our subject matter. Talmy notes that the pronouns *he* and *himself* fulfill the semantic roles of what he calls *agonist* and *antagonist, he* corresponding to the antagonist and *himself* to the agonist. The agonist is identified with the self's desires and the antagonist with our sense of responsibility. The agonist is considered the central part of the self, while the antagonist the peripheral one.

A rough correspondence can be observed between the roles of agonist and antagonist on the one hand and the metaphors THE EMOTIONS ARE FLUIDS INSIDE A CONTAINER and THE MIND IS A CONTAINER

(FOR IDEAS) on the other. The role of the agonist in Talmy's system seems to correspond to the emotions as fluids in the body container and that of the antagonist to the mind that serves as a container for ideas. However, as we shall see below, this is only a rough and imprecise correspondence.

Despite its imprecise nature, the correspondence tells us that the mind and the emotions are in conflict, in the same way as the agonist and the antagonist are. Talmy explains this opposition between the agonist and the antagonist by claiming, following Freud, that the agonist represents psychological desires ("id") and the antagonist is an "internalization of external social values" ("superego") (p. 20). Furthermore, he conceives of the opposition as an introjection into a unitary self of the opposition between the self and the external world. We can perhaps supplement this by saying that the opposition between the agonist and the antagonist can be also captured in terms of the CONTAINER metaphors: The upper container (mind) functions as a lid, or cover to prevent the dangerous contents of the lower container (the passions in the body container) from coming out. Talmy notes that the Freudian concepts of id and superego may have in part arisen because these concepts were already built into the language in the form of latent semantic concepts like the agonist and the antagonist as exemplified in the second sentence above. Perhaps it can be added that the CONTAINER image, with its hot fluid bursting out and a strong cover to prevent this, may be another source for both the Freudian concepts and the semantic roles of the agonist and the antagonist.

Another aspect of Talmy's work as it relates to the CONTAINER metaphor is his characterization of the emotion container as central and the idea container as a peripheral part of the self. Talmy appears to base this characterization on the assumption that the self is more central than the external world. (Note that in his system the agonist-antagonist opposition is a metaphoric projection onto a unitary self of the "self versus the external world" opposition!) Here, again, we can supplement this by observing that in our folk model of the self the emotions are the deepest part of the self, thoughts being less deep, and actions as the most outward manifestations of the self. If the deepest part of the self is the emotional and since what is central is typically deep (as in an onion), it is natural for us to conceive of the emotional self as central and the thinking part of the self as peripheral. Moreover, since the concept of *important* is conceptualized as central (cf. the expression *central issue*), the emotional self will be seen as more important. But this seems to be a matter of the philosophical climate of the times. Cathy Lutz (1986) observes that there exist conflicting views about what is emphasized and preferred in our naive psychology: the emotional or the cognitive. The two metaphorical CONTAINERS of the self on top of each other can also motivate the priority of the cognitive part. Since the mind container is on top of the body container with emotion in it and since good is typically viewed as oriented upwards, it is also natural that the cognitive self can be seen as having priority over the emotional self.

The Container Metaphor and Scientific Theories of Emotion

The image of the emotions as fluids inside a container is a language-based folk model of the emotions. This folk understanding of the emotions helps us give structure to and make sense of a wide variety of unstructured and undelineated experiences. It creates order out of the apparently diffuse and chaotic experience that we call emotion. In fact, to a large extent it makes it possible for us to refer to this experience with the word *emotion*. It is difficult to imagine what our conception of emotion would be like without the CONTAINER metaphor (but see Lutz 1988).

The image of the container with fluid in it can be found outside the realm of the ordinary as well. The romantic poet, Wordsworth, defined poetry in the following way: "Poetry is the spontaneous overflow of powerful feelings." It is perhaps of some interest to note that what we seem to have here is the open container associated with sadness, melancholy, affection, love, and similar emotions. Clearly, the romantic poets experienced the emotional world more in terms of the open container that can overflow than in terms of the container that can lead to an explosion. Their general mood seems to have been more of gentle (though powerful) feelings than that of explosive passions.

The container image also had its impact on the scientific community. A large number of emotion theories have built into them parts or the whole of the idea that the emotions are best viewed as (the heat of) a fluid in a container. Part of the appeal of the metaphor lies in its capacity to account, via its entailments, for a large number and wide variety of emotional experiences. Another part of the success of the metaphor is that it makes a lot of sense intuitively. It looks natural because, after all, the body does appear to be a container, the blood *is* a fluid in the body, the body does produce heat during some emotional states, and so on.

If we examine various scientific emotion theories, it turns out that many of them incorporate, knowingly or unknowingly, these and other elements of the folk model. When a theory views emotion as something confined to a container (the body), as energy or force, as energy that flows, as heat, as a matter of quantity, as something that we can have to excess, we can at least guess that we have to do with the CONTAINER metaphor. And when all of these things appear in a theory all at the same time, we can be reasonably certain that it is this folk model that underlies the theory. If we look at the comprehensive survey of emotion theories until 1960 by Hillman (1962), we find that quite a few theories make use of some or most of these elements.

But the theory that has been the most influential of the views that build on the CONTAINER metaphor in large measure is Freud's. (To be sure, Freud held some other views on emotion as well, but that is not relevant here.) It has already been noted that there is a correspondence between the EMOTIONS AS FLUIDS IN A CONTAINER metaphor and the notion of id on the one hand, and THE MIND AS A CONTAINER FOR IDEAS metaphor and the notion of superego on the other. In addition, I have emphasized that the correspondence is only an approximate one. We can now see why. There are several reasons and they all seem to relate to the subtle ways in which Freud manipulated the CONTAINER metaphor. A schematic drawing might help us to see the changes that Freud made.

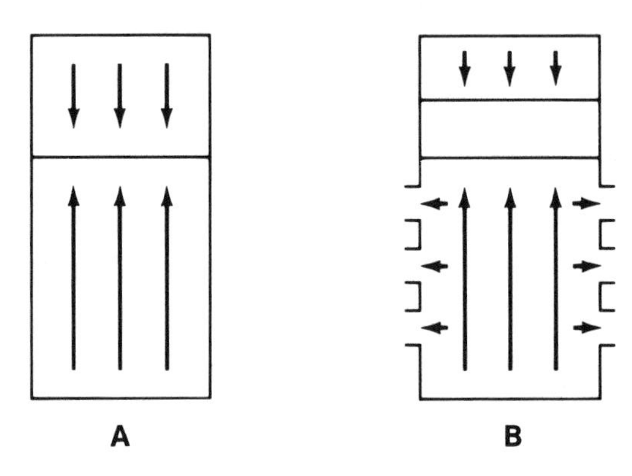

Freud's model, represented by container B, is basically a version of the EMOTIONS AS HOT FLUIDS IN A CONTAINER metaphor, represented in the figure by container A. This latter CONTAINER metaphor has been discussed in detail in this chapter. One can think of the Freudian model in two ways. First, we can interpret Freud as placing the id not in the mind container but in the body container. This interpretation would yield a mind container with only two parts (the ego and the superego) in it. This is the less likely interpretation. Second, we can also interpret Freud as placing the id in the mind container as well (thus having the ego, superego and the id in the same container). This is the more likely interpretation. I am not concerned here with the issue of which interpretation is correct. The important point that I wish to make is the following. Regardless of which interpretation is correct, Freud's system shows a close analogy to the CONTAINER metaphor of emotion implicit in language. Given the first interpretation, the analogy can be demonstrated in a straightforward way. Given the second, the analogy remains, but an additional general metaphor has to be posited as being assumed by Freud. In the remainder of the chapter both interpretations will be taken into account. For the clarity of exposition, it makes sense to suppose the possibility of the first interpretation, even though it might not be the correct one. As has been pointed out, correctness is not the issue here.

Let us begin with the first interpretation. One change introduced by Freud relates to the MIND AS A CONTAINER metaphor is that Freud conceived of the mind container as consisting of two parts: the ego and the superego. On this interpretation the id would be in the body container. The superego is the social self, the id is the biological self, and the ego is the part of the self that is "torn" between the two. The idea of the ego being torn between the superego and the id is captured in the figure by the set of upward-pointing arrows, the set of downward-pointing arrows, and the ego lying between them in container B. This is not a completely arbitrary visual representation of Freud's ideas; he talks about suppression and repression that are actions that are typically directed downward and that assume a strong upward-moving force.

More importantly, however, Freud reconceptualized and renamed the upward-moving hot fluid of container A. He thought of this fluid as somehow representing basic, primitive instincts and desires. Thus, what in the folk model represents emotion came to represent instincts and basic desires. The new name given to them was id. But the id kept most of the features that emotion as a hot fluid in a closed container had. It remained upward-moving, it retained the heat component, and it was seen as a force.

Perhaps the most significant aspect of the id was that it remained a strong force that must be kept under control. The notion of strong force in the form of the heat of a fluid presupposes the idea that the fluid must be in a closed container. By virtue of this, the hot fluid can be viewed as moving upwards, pressure can be seen as building up, and as a result the walls, especially the top, of the container can be understood as being under tremendous pressure. At the same time a counterforce can be seen to be operating, which by pressing down the upward-moving force can keep it under control.

But where did Freud place emotion in his version of the container model? Perhaps the greatest innovation Freud made to make the folk model a more complex theory of emotion was that he allowed some outlets for the basic, primitive instincts and desires in the sides of the container. With some malice and disrespect for Freud, one could say that Freud simply bored holes in the sides of the container. Thus, the emotions came to be seen by Freud as the holes, or outlets through which the dangerous, difficult-to-control instincts and desires could safely leave the container. This equation of the outlets with the emotions seems to emerge also from Rapaport (1967), a follower of Freud. Consider the following passage by Rapaport quoted in Lyons (1980, p. 27):

> The [psychoanalytic] theory of affects, the bare outlines of which seem to emerge, integrates three components: *inborn affect-discharge channels* and discharge threshold of drive cathexes; the use of these inborn channels as safety valves and indicators of drive tension, the modification of their thresholds by drives and derivative motivations prevented from drive action, and the formation thereby of *the drive representation termed affect charge;* and the progressive taming and advancing ego control, in the course of psychic structure formation, of the affects

which are thereby turned into *affect signals* released by the ego. [Rapaport, 1950, p. 508]

By way of some interpretation, it is worthwhile looking at Lyon's comments on this difficult passage:

In less tortured langauge, this theory can be expounded in the following way. When the energies of instinctual strivings or drives, which reside in the unconscious, are unable to be discharged in the normal way into appropriate instinctual behavior, because of some inhibition, repression or other block, they are discharged via a safety valve. This safety valve is emotional occurrences or affects, and they release the pent-up psychic energy through the physiological disturbances or discharges of the central nervous system which form their core. [Lyons, 1980, p. 27]

There are three things to note about these passages. The first is that the outlets in the sides of the container are not simply holes; they are safety valves. Second, the passages make it clear that in the Freudian theory (including later variations of it, like Rapaport's theory) the emotions were identified with the functioning of the safety valves in the sides of the container.

Third, and this leads us to the second and more likely interpretation, in "translating" the passage by Rapaport, Lyons observes that the energies of instinctual strivings or drives reside in the unconscious. However, the unconscious would be a part of the mind container and not a part of the body container, where we have so far assumed instincts to reside. If Lyons's interpretation is correct, this would mean that Freud and his followers moved the body container up into the mind. In other words, in addition to all the other changes in the BODY IS A CONTAINER FOR THE EMOTIONS metaphor, Freud and the Freudians seem to have made a very significant further change: They created an idea of the *mind* that incorporates and is based on the folk model of the emotions as hot fluids in the body as a container. Put in a more general way, the Freudian theories assume the very general metaphor: THE MIND IS THE BODY. That is, aspects of the body are used to understand aspects of the mind. We have already seen an example for this in the case of the IDEAS ARE FOOD metaphor, where the functioning of the mind is imagined on the analogy of the way the digestive tract works. (It may be noted in this connection that the THE MIND IS THE BODY metaphor has begun to receive some attention in recent years (see Johnson, 1987, and Sweetser, 1984).

Conclusion

The major goal of this chapter was to show that the CONTAINER metaphor pervades our thinking about personhood and emotion and that this is the metaphor that we evoke to make sense of a large number of emotional experiences. The analysis of language suggested that this metaphor for emotion exists in two versions: EMOTION IS A FLUID IN A CONTAINER and EMOTION IS A HOT FLUID IN A CONTAINER. It was pointed out that it is the latter that seems to underlie Freud's theory of emotion.

10
The Concept of Emotion: Further Metaphors

The last chapter was devoted to a detailed examination of one of the major metaphors of emotion, namely, EMOTION IS A FLUID IN A CONTAINER, and we saw how that metaphor has its theoretical counterpart in Freudian (psychoanalytic) theories of emotion. The present chapter proceeds along similar lines, but the aim is broader. Specifically, we illustrate how psychological theories of diverse orientation (e.g., behaviorist, psychophysiological, biological) accrue some of their intuitive appeal as extensions of common metaphorical expressions.

In assembling metaphors and metonymies for this chapter, we have focused primarily on expressions that are common to emotion in general, rather than to specific emotions. Such a restriction was not followed too rigidly, however. Metaphorical and metonymical expressions that apply to specific emotions are included if, as a group, they have implications for emotion in general. For example, many metaphors and metonymies refer to bodily parts (e.g., the heart or liver), with different emotions assigned to different organs. Together, such metaphors and metonymies form a general category linking emotions to bodily (especially visceral) activity.

Another methodological issue should also be mentioned at the outset. Most of the major metaphors of emotion have multiple and overlapping meanings. Consider again the FLUID IN A CONTAINER metaphor discussed in previous chapters. It depicts emotions as events that occur within the individual (they are "held" within the container), that exert a strong force or power (the "pressure" in the container builds up), and that are potentially very disruptive (the container "explodes" from too much pressure). Because of such multiple meanings, metaphors of emotion can be classified in an indefinite variety of ways, depending on the points to be illustrated.

Lutz (1986), for example, examined the Euroamerican concept of emotion, relying heavily (though informally and unsystematically) on metaphorical expressions. As an anthropologist, her concern was to clarify the ideological assumptions (related to individualism, mental health, femininity, and the like) that may prejudice our descriptions of the behavior of culturally different people. She organized her discussion around such topics as "emotion as the irrational," "emotion as unintended and uncontrollable act," "emotion as danger and vulnerability," "emotion as physicality," "emotion as natural fact," "emotion as subjectivity," "emotion as female," and "emotion as value." To take another example, Averill (in press) examined from an historical perspective the influence of metaphors on psychological theories of emotion. Five main traditions within psychological theory were delineated, along with their associated metaphors. These traditions were the phenomenological (emotion as feelings), the psychophysiological (emotion as bodily responses), the ethological (emotion as the animal in human nature), the psychodynamic (emotion as disease), and the drive tradition (emotion as motivating force).

The present chapter covers some of the same ground as that by Averill. The emphasis, however, is more empirical than theoretical. Specifically, we present a systematic overview of the major metaphors and metonymies of emotion as found in everyday speech. The overview is not exhaustive, but we believe it provides a representative sample of the most important metaphors and metonymies of emotion. These metaphors and metonymies are grouped into abstract categories on the basis of (a) similarities in meaning and (b) implications for psychological theory. We begin the chapter with an overview of the concept of emotion in general, as illustrated through metaphor. We then examine more restricted domains of discourse (e.g., emotion as agitation, emotion as motivation) and their analogues in psychological theory. Finally, we conclude the chapter with a brief discussion of the relation between metaphor and theory.

Some Major Metaphors of Emotion

In this first section, we examine some metaphors that seem to address the root meaning of emotion in general (in addition to the CONTAINER metaphor discussed in the previous chapter). Because of their generality, these metaphors have multiple meanings, and hence they have implications for a wide range of theoretical issues. More specifically, the metaphors discussed in this section treat emotions as NATURAL FORCES (e.g., storms, floods) and as OBJECTS distinct from the self. By way of introduction, let us first provide a little background on the concept of emotion, which itself originated from metaphor.

Until about the mid-eighteenth century, what we now call emotions were commonly referred to as "passions." The root meaning of the term passion is to suffer, or to undergo change. The person who is in a state of passion is, in this sense, passive with respect to events that are acting upon him. Stated somewhat differently, passion implies a lack of personal control over one's own behavior. The term "emotion" has similar implications, though a different etymological history. The Latin *e* + *movere* originally meant to move out or transport. The term was also applied to natural disturbances, such as stormy weather, and, by metaphorical extension, to psychological disturbance. "Emotion" and "passion" have similar connotation in that a person who is in a disturbed state is also liable to experience the disturbance as something that is happening to him (a passion) rather than as something he is doing in a deliberate, self-controlled way (an action).

Today, the connotations of both terms, "emotion" and "passion," have become restricted. Thus, emotion now refers almost exclusively to psychological as opposed to physical conditions; and passion refers mainly to a subcategory of emotion, namely, sexual desire. Nevertheless, the original connotations of these terms find frequent expression in our metaphors of emotion. A good illustration of this is the NATURAL FORCE metaphor:

THE EMOTIONS ARE NATURAL FORCES (STORMS, WAVES, FLOODS)
She opened the letter with a *rush* of emotion.
There were *stormy* emotions when the news of the disaster reached the town.
She was *engulfed* by her passion.
There was a *whirlwind* of emotion.
Emotions *overwhelmed* him.
Emotions *swept over* her.
Waves of emotion *came over* her.
A *flood* of emotion *swept over* the crowd.
There was a *groundswell* of emotion.
Emotions were *running high.*
There was a *surge* of emotion.
Emotions *subsided* when the president announced he would step down.

One of the main implications of the NATURAL FORCE metaphor is lack of personal control over the emotion; that is, the person is depicted as passive (helpless) with respect to the emotion, which is likened to an overpowering outside force. The metaphor also suggests that emotions are generally high-intensity phenomena. The intensity aspect of emotion becomes even more evident if we combine the NATURAL FORCE metaphor with some abstract metaphors discussed in previous chapters. Thus, the (MORE OF) INTENSITY IS (MORE OF) QUANTITY and the NATURAL FORCE metaphors jointly produce the idea that emotion is intense (*waves, flood, groundswell*). The conceptual outcome of the combination of the MORE IS UP and NATURAL FORCE metaphors is also high intensity (*surge, running high*). A decrease in emotional intensity can also be indicated by a combination of LESS IS DOWN and the NATURAL

FORCE metaphors (*subside*). But metaphors of the latter kind seem to be far outnumbered by expressions referring to high emotional intensity. Two further implications of the NATURAL FORCE metaphor deserve brief mention. First, beyond a certain point the increase in the intensity of emotion leads to an inability to function normally. Second, emotional experiences are episodic or relatively short-lived: They are like whirlwinds; they come in surges; they sweep over us and then subside; and so forth.

A variation on the NATURAL FORCE metaphor is the theme that EMOTION IS FIRE. In legal terminology, a person who commits a crime under the influence of emotion is said to have acted "in the heat of passion." This is a somewhat archaic way of speaking, but many everyday metaphors carry a similar connotation. Consider the following:

EMOTION IS FIRE
She was *on fire* with emotion.
The reverend *inflamed* the crowd with his passionate speech.
They were *ablaze* with emotion.
Seeing her every day *kindled* his passion for her.
She was *burning* with emotion.
There was *fire* in his voice when he spoke.
She has a *fiery* disposition.
His emotions *flare up* when you least expect it.
She *fanned the flames* of his desire.
Time *extinguishes* passion.
She was *consumed* by passion.
He was all *burned out*.

To illustrate the implications of this category of metaphors, let us consider in more detail the expression *to be consumed by passion*. The interpretation of this expression requires us to take into account the following: The person in the emotional state corresponds to the thing burning; the emotion corresponds to the heat that is applied; the increase in emotional intensity corresponds to the increase of the heat; finally, when too much heat is applied, the thing (person) becomes dysfunctional (is consumed, burned out).

The metaphors discussed thus far illustrate how we tend to conceive of emotions as outside forces that can overpower a person. It follows from this conception that, if we want to control our emotions, some countervailing force must be exerted. This implication is reflected in another major metaphor of emotion, namely:

EMOTION IS AN OPPONENT
He was *wrestling* with his emotions.
She *struggled* in vain *against* her emotions.

He was always *prey* to his emotions.
I was *seized* by emotion.
He was constantly *fighting* his emotions.
I could not *control* my emotions.
He was unable to *master* his emotions.
I was trying to *conquer* my emotions.
He did everything to *appease* her emotions.
Emotion *got the best of* him.
She *gave in* to her emotions.
He *surrendered* to his emotions.

In the OPPONENT metaphor, emotional control corresponds to physical control; that is, trying to control the emotion is understood in terms of trying to physically defeat an antagonist (e.g., a wrestler). Control over the opponent (emotion) is difficult to attain. Struggling, fighting, conquering, and so on, require a great deal of effort; and the effort is typically unsuccessful. There is an abundance of conventionalized expressions in the OPPONENT metaphor to indicate that we view emotion as a force we cannot control: emotions are overpowering, we are prey to them, they seize us, they get the best of us, and we give in and surrender to them. It should be noticed that these are expressions that we use exclusively to describe a loss of control over emotion. They could not be easily and naturally used to describe a successful attempt at controlling emotion. This fact and also the large number of these conventionalized expressions in the OPPONENT metaphor seem to suggest that built into our (prototypical) folk model of emotion is the idea of loss of control over emotion (despite the attempt at control).

Most of the metaphors we have discussed thus far depict emotions as potentially disruptive forces (inanimate or animate) that must (but usually cannot) be held in check. In part, this plethora of unfavorable metaphors reflects the fact that, in everyday English, negative emotional concepts outnumber positive emotional concepts by a ratio of about 2 to 1 (Averill, 1980a). But, needless to say, not all emotions are viewed negatively; moreover, the person who is incapable of experiencing even negative emotions (anger, fear, guilt, and the like) is often viewed with suspicion. Thus, we might expect the emotions also to be depicted in more neutral metaphors such as metaphors that do not suggest an opponent or destructive force, and yet that retain the fundamental distinction between passion and action. Consider the following:

EMOTION IS AN (INANIMATE) OBJECT:
He *lost* all *his* emotions for people.
She *gave* me a lot of emotion.
She tried to *get rid* of her emotion.
He *kept* his emotions to himself.

I tried to *get rid of* my feelings.
I am talking about *my* emotions not *yours*.

In contrast to the NATURAL FORCE metaphor, the EMOTION AS OBJECT metaphor leaves the possibility open for an emotion to be a VALUABLE and even a FRAGILE possession.

EMOTIONS ARE VALUABLE OBJECTS
He *cherished* his emotions.
She *guarded* the emotion.
His emotions are his greatest *treasure*.

EMOTIONS ARE FRAGILE OBJECTS
The events *crushed* all emotion.
His emotions were *dashed*.
My heart *broke to pieces*.
There was a great deal of emotional *damage*.
Emotional *repair* was needed.
All there was left to do was to *pick up the pieces*.

If an emotion is an object, whether good or bad, it follows that a person might on occasion try to *hide* or *disguise* his or her emotions. In other words, this class of metaphors suggests that emotion is an entity that either the self or other agents can act upon. This is possible because of the particular ontological status given to emotion by the OBJECT metaphor: an emotion is an entity separate from the self.

Earlier, we saw how emotions can be depicted as inanimate FORCES (e.g., wind, fire) or as live OPPONENTS in a struggle. An analogous distinction between the inanimate and the animate can also be found in the case of the OBJECT metaphors. The instances thus far examined all refer to inanimate objects. However, the OBJECT (emotion) can also be a LIVING ORGANISM.

EMOTION IS A LIVING ORGANISM (PLANT, ANIMAL, PERSON)
His emotions *wilted*.
Her emotions *died*.
I *hurt* her feelings.
My emotions *grew* minute by minute.
She *killed* his emotions.
She *awoke* in him emotions that had long been *dormant*.
His emotions *withered*.

Like the INANIMATE OBJECT metaphor, the LIVING ORGANISM metaphor has the implication that an emotion exists as an entity separate from the self. But according to the LIVING ORGANISM metaphor, emotions are capable of *doing* things on their own (for instance, they can wilt, die, grow, awaken, lie dormant). This becomes even clearer if we look at some further examples:

All emotions *left* him.
The emotion is *gone*.
My emotions *keep coming back*.
Her emotions *returned*.

This part of the LIVING ORGANISM metaphor suggests that not only are emotions separate entities, but that they are also capable of independent action such as leading a life independent of the self.

In addition, emotions can be conceived of as living organisms that are TO BE TENDED:

Her emotions were left *unnurtured*.
He *nourished* his feelings.
She *fostered* her feelings.

To summarize the discussion thus far, emotions are viewed (metaphorically) as objects—either inanimate or animate—separate from the self. At low intensities, and under the appropriate circumstances, the object may be valuable, in which case it is to be cherished, guarded, cared for, and nurtured. At higher intensities, however, emotions are more likely to be compared to overpowering, destructive forces.

In the remainder of this chapter we will examine congruencies between our folk concept of emotion as revealed in the above metaphors and some of the major theoretical traditions in the psychology of emotion. We will also introduce additional metaphors that are more specific to the theoretical positions under considerations.

Theories of emotion can be classified in a variety of ways. Based largely on philosophical writings, Alston (1967) distinguishes among theories that emphasize bodily upset (agitation), motivational tendencies, subjective experience (feelings, sensations), and perceptual (immediate, intuitive) evaluations. Calhoun and Solomon (1984) speak of physiological, sensation, behavioral, evaluative, and cognitive theories. (The distinction between evaluative and cognitive theories is based on the relative importance attributed to nonrational versus rational thought processes, as will be discussed in a subsequent section.) Mandler (1984) divides theories into three main varieties depending on whether they emphasize the disruption of behavior (conflict theories), innate motivational processes (instinct theories), or organic processes (sensory and physiological theories). To take a final example, de Rivera (1985) distinguishes among four major theoretical traditions: emotion as alternative to action (conflict theories), emotion as self-perception (e.g., of physiological change), emotions as functional patterns of behavior (instincts, motives), and emotion as the appraisal of value.

Obviously, there is considerable overlap among the above schemes, but also some divergence. Based on the metaphors already described, as well as those to be presented below, we will distinguish among six folk beliefs about emotion, namely, (a) emotion as agitation, (b) emotion as motivation, (c) emotion as physiological change, (d) emotion as physical sensation, (e) emotion as animal, and (f) emotion as nonrational evaluation. We will further illustrate how each of these folk concepts corresponds to one or more theoretical traditions in the psychology of emotion.

Emotion as Agitation

The view that emotion involves bodily upset or agitation is most closely related to conflict theories of emotion. The postulated conflict may arise from competing response tendencies or from some environmental impediment to action; but whatever the source, one common result of conflict is emotional upset or bodily disturbance. Psychoanalytic theories of emotion are of this variety; so, too, are many behaviorist theories (see Mandler, 1984, for a historical review). A quote from Young (1943) illustrates well the general theme of emotion as agitation:

> An emotion is an acute disturbance or upset of the individual which is revealed in behavior and in conscious experience, as well as through widespread changes in the functioning of viscera (smooth muscles, glands, heart, and lungs), and which is initiated by forces within a psychological situation. (p. 405)

We have already noted several examples of the folk belief that emotions involve agitation and disturbance. For example, in the CONTAINER metaphor discussed in the last chapter, we saw how emotions, if not properly "vented," may cause an explosion. The NATURAL FORCE metaphor also emphasizes the havoc that can be wreaked by emotion (wind, wave, flood, fire). However, there also is a class of metaphors directly related to the issue of agitation.

EMOTIONAL DISTURBANCE IS PHYSICAL DISTURBANCE
The speech *stirred* everybody's feelings.
I am all *shook up*.
She go all *worked up*.
Why are you *upset?*
The children were *disturbed*.
He was slightly *ruffled* by what he heard.
Why are you so *excited?*

One obvious basis for this metaphor is the metonymy (BODILY) AGITATION STANDS FOR EMOTION:

(BODILY) AGITATION STANDS FOR EMOTION
I stood there *trembling* with emotion.
The experience made him *shake*.
He *quivered* all over.
Shivers ran up and down her spine.
He was *quaking* in his boots.

These examples are not limited to any specific emotion; they can describe a variety of responses associated with a high level of physiological arousal. Another possible source of the AGITATION metaphor may have to do with animal behavior. For example, when some animals are "angry," they ruffle their feathers or their hair stands on end.

Given this way of conceptualizing emotional disturbance, it is not surprising that we can also conceptualize emotional calm as physical calm:

EMOTIONAL CALM IS PHYSICAL CALM
The boy was *soothed* by her mother's words.
He has an *even* temper.
There was *calmness* in his voice.
The experience gave him back his *peace of mind*.
You should *calm down*.

In these metaphors, smoothness of surface (*even*), lack of movement (*calm*), and lack of action (*peace*) correspond to emotional calm or lack of emotion, whereas uneven surface (*ruffle*), presence of movement (*shook up, upset*), and presence of action (*stir, work up*) correspond to emotional disturbance or agitation. The evenness of the surface in the metaphor seems to derive from two sources. One in all probability is the evenness of the sea, as examplified by the expresssion *a sea of emotion*. This in turn must have to do with the EMOTIONS ARE NATURAL FORCES metaphor. When the sea is calm, the surface of the water is even, in a storm it is not even.

Closely related to the notion of emotion as agitation is that of emotion as disease. Disease states represent an extreme form of bodily disturbance; they are also a rich source of emotional metaphors. This is due to the fact that, in addition to representing disturbed, disorganized states, diseases are things a person *suffers,* that is, things that happen to a person rather than things a person does. In other words, disease is a subcategory of passion. The Greek term *pathe* was used to cover both diseases in the contemporary sense and emotions. This meaning of *pathe* is evident in such contemporary medical terms as "pathology," "pathogen," "idiopathy," and (via the Latin) "patient," as well as in such emotional terms as *pathos* and *passion*.

In any case, emotions are often thought of as diseases—whether of the body or of the mind. Thus, we can be emotionally *hurt, wounded* and *tortured;* we can be *heart-broken;* an emotional experience can be *painful;* we can be *sick* from emotion; when emotional, we may be in a *fevered* state; and we can even be said to *die* from an extreme emotion.

A conception of emotion as bodily disease has some empirical basis in the fact that emotions sometimes lead to physical (psychosomatic) disorders. However, emotions are more commonly viewed as a form of mental rather than physical disease. In popular conception, "mental illness" is practically synonymous with "emotional disorder." A perusal of "self-help" books also suggests that emotional states such as anger, jealousy, envy, fear, anxiety, guilt, embarrassment, loneliness, and grief are on one "sick list" or another. Even such highly valued emotions as love have become the object of suggested "cures."

A conception of emotion as mental disease is fostered by the EMOTION IS INSANITY metaphor. Here are some examples:

EMOTION IS INSANITY
There were scenes of *frenzied* emotion.
He is *mad* with desire.
She *drove him berserk.*
I was *crazy* with emotion.
It was a *wild* emotion.
His emotions *drive him out of his wits.*
She was *crazed* with emotion.
He was *beside himself* with emotion.

As noted above, the concept of disease implies lack of control (passion) as well as disturbance. This implication is particularly evident in the INSANITY metaphor. Insanity is the ultimate lack of control. According to the metaphor, intense emotions can drive people into such a state that they may act in strange and unpredictable ways and on sudden impulse. (Parenthetically, it might be noted that a person is not usually held responsible for events that are beyond personal control. The person who acts out of emotion, like the person who is temporarily insane, may thus be held less accountable or blameworthy for any untoward consequences of his behavior.)

In sum, one of the oldest theoretical traditions in psychology is to view emotions as states of disturbance and agitation, typically caused by some conflict or interruption of activity. This view is made intuitively reasonable by many conventionalized metaphorical expressions. Unfortunately, when it comes to the emotions, neither psychological theory nor folk beliefs are notably consistent. Therefore, let us turn to a contrary point of view.

Emotion as Motivation

The view of emotion as motivation is similar to the view of emotion as agitation in that both depict emotions as states of high intensity. The implications of the two views are, however, quite different. Whereas the emotion as agitation view emphasizes the disorganizing and dysfunctional aspects of emotion, the motivational view emphasizes the organizing and functional properties of emotion.

Motivational theories of emotion come in two rather distinct varieties. The first variety conceives of emotion as a kind of force or "drive" that energizes behavior. According to this conception, for example, fear is the drive that motivates avoidance behavior, anger is the drive that motivates aggression, and so forth. In one common version of this kind of theory, the origin of emotional drives is attributed to biological evolution. Emotions—at least the so-called fundamental emotions—are thus reduced to biological instincts (e.g., Plutchik, 1980; Izard, 1977). We will have more to say about instinct theories in a subsequent section. Our present concern is with the notion of emotion as motivation, regardless of the presumed source of the motive or drive.

A second variety of motivational theory, epitomized by Leeper (1970), takes a more dispositional view of emotion. That is, an emotion is not treated as some kind of inner event (drive or force) that impels a person to respond; rather an emotion is a state of readiness to respond in characteristic ways to a certain class of environmental stimuli. For example, the person who is afraid (for several weeks, say) of a reported firebug in the neighborhood may take precautions to protect her home and family from possible danger. At no time during the period need she show the kinds of agitated responses described in the previous section. Yet, it is perfectly appropriate to say she took precautions out of fear.

In what follows, we will attempt to illustrate how the concept of emotion-as-motivation, of whichever variety, is made intuitively reasonable by the metaphors or ordinary language. Let us begin with drive theories of emotion. Consider the NATURAL FORCE metaphor. Winds, floods, and fire are all potent forms of energy that, if harnessed, can be made to do useful work. The force need not be destructive, as the following metaphor indicates:

EMOTIONAL EFFECT IS PHYSICAL MOVEMENT
I was *moved* by the speech.
He was *carried away* by his feelings.
They were *transported*.
She was *swept away*.

This metaphor is similar to the NATURAL FORCE metaphor, and it could have been discussed in that section. However, the implication here is less on the disruptive effects of the emotion than on its motion-producing (motivating) effects.

Another metaphor that expresses the idea of energy or drive in an emotional state is the following:

EMOTION IS AN ELECTRIC FORCE
I was *shocked.*
He *short-circuited* his emotions.
She was *electrified.*
It was a great emotional *charge.*
I feel *energized.*

These expressions suggest that a person is (almost literally) in an energetic state when emotional. The result could be agitation or disorganization; but under appropriate conditions, it could also be a well-organized and effective response.

The idea that emotions motivate behavior is not limited to notions of physical force or energy. We live in a social as well as a physical environment, and our behavior can be *ruled* and *dictated* by social forces just as it can be *driven* and *energized* by physical forces. This fact gives rise to a class of metaphors in which emotions are viewed as SOCIAL SUPERIORS.

EMOTIONS ARE SOCIAL SUPERIORS
She is *ruled* by her emotions.
His emotions *dominate* his reactions.
She *obeys* her heart rather than her head.
Passion *dictated* his reaction.
He is a *slave* to his emotions.
She is *governed* by her emotions.
He was *driven* by passion.
His emotions *urged* him on.
Her emotions *did not let* her do it.

As in the case of the NATURAL FORCE metaphor, the person is here depicted as much weaker than the emotion (which corresponds to the social superior). More important for our present purposes, however, is the different and more subtle concept of motivation implied by metaphors. This concept is more congruent with the dispositional account of emotion adumbrated by Leeper (1970). It also links emotion to a sociological tradition, for instance, as represented by the French sociologist Durkheim (1915). According to Durkheim, we do not mourn because of some deep inner force welling up within us (grief); mourning, rather, is a duty imposed by the group. A similar observation could be made with respect to other emotions. We would only add that, if the relevant social norms have been internalized, then duties imposed by the group (represented here by SOCIAL SUPERIORS) can be as passionately experienced and expressed as are biologically based impulses.

Emotion as Physiological Change

There can, of course, be no bodily agitation without physiological change; and motivational theories have often postulated physiological arousal as the source of emotional drives. But physiological change also has been considered important in its own right as a necessary (e.g., Schachter, 1971) or even as a sufficient condition (e.g., Wenger, 1950) for emotion.

Needless to say, all psychological phenomena ultimately depend on physiological processes. However, in the case of the emotions, this dependency has been given special status. Why should this be so? One reason, we would maintain, is the many metaphors and metonymies in which emotions are associated with physiological change. Consider the following examples:

EMOTIONS ARE PHYSIOLOGICAL REACTIONS
He felt it *in his gut*.
She had a *visceral* reaction.

Often, the emotions (or specific emotions) are associated with particular organs of the body, especially the heart.

EMOTIONS ARE IN THE HEART
Just listen *to your heart*.
Don't take it *to heart*.
There was passion *in his heart*.
He thanked her *with all his heart*.
She is *heartless*.
He is *mean-hearted*.
You *have no heart*.
The news made him *light hearted*.

Organs other than the heart are also sources for metaphor, sometimes of a highly fanciful nature. The following are a few examples:

He is *lily-livered*.
She has a lot of *gall*.
Don't be so *spineless*.

The examples we consider next function mostly as metonymies rather than as metaphors in the strict sense:

CHANGE IN HEART RATE
His heart was *pounding* with emotion.
His heart began to *beat* faster.
My heart was *throbbing*.
She asked the question *with beating heart*.
He entered the room *with his heart in his mouth*.
My heart *stood still*.

CHANGE IN RESPIRATION
She was *heaving* with emotion.
I felt his *hot breath* on my neck.
It *took my breath away*.
She was *breathless* from emotion.

CHANGE IN SKIN COLOR ON FACE
She *colored* with emotion.
I stood there, *flushed*.
He slowly turned *red*.
I was *pale*.
His brow *darkened*.
She *blushed* with emotion.

Vision, or more specifically the eyes, provide an especially rich source of metaphorical metonymies. The presence and kind of emotion is often judged by examining a person's eyes. This is consistent with the idea that the eyes are the "mirror of the soul." We can take some examples from Lakoff and Johnson (1980):

THE EYES ARE CONTAINERS FOR THE EMOTIONS
I could see the fear *in* his eyes.
His eyes were *filled* with anger.
There was passion *in* her eyes.
His eyes *displayed* his compassion.
She couldn't *get* the fear *out of* her eyes.
Love *showed in* his eyes.
Her eyes *welled* with emotion.

The above expressions are metaphors because they make us see emotions as a substance (fluid) which is in a container, corresponding to the eyes. They also serve as metonymies in that they describe how the eyes can reveal various emotions.

The eyes are closely associated with crying as well as with vision, and crying is a source of metonymies of emotion.

Her whole body was shaking as she *cried* in her mother's arms.
When he came home after the phone conversation, he found her *in tears*.
There were *tears* in her eyes when she looked at him.

Crying, it should be noted, is not specific to any particular emotion. We can cry as a result of joy, anger, love, and fear, and not just sadness or grief (although prototypically it is associated with these latter emotions).

Crying is a prime example of an expressive reaction. Theorists who believe that visceral changes are insufficient to account for the experience of emotion often emphasize feedback from facial expressions (see Izard, 1977; Ekman & Friesen, 1975). Support for such a position can be found in many metaphors and metonymies that link emotions to various expressive reactions. Frowns, smiles, grimaces, knitted brows, flaring nostrils, rosy cheeks, bared teeth, tight lips, and the like can stand for one emotion or another. These are summarized in such general expressions as:

Her emotions were *written all over her face.*
His face was *an open book.*

In sum, bodily change, especially visceral and expressive reactions, provide a rich source of metaphors and metonymies of emotion. Needless to say, bodily change is a prominent feature of many emotional episodes, such as sudden fright, nausea on smelling a putrid odor, lashing out against a painful stimulus, depression following loss of a loved one, and so forth. In such states, the body seems to act "on its own," sometimes against the person's will and desires. Such seemingly autonomous responses may appropriately be regarded as "happenings"—as passions rather than as actions. It should be emphasized, however, that noticeable bodily change is a prominent feature only of relatively intense emotional episodes; and it is not even characteristic of some emotional syndromes (e.g., hope), no matter how intense.

Still, through the use of metonymy in common speech, we often allow a part to stand for the whole (e.g., *sweaty palms* for fear, a *broken heart* for grief, being *red in the face* for anger, and so forth). The intuitive appeal of physiological and related theories of emotion is based, in part, on such everyday metonymical expressions.

Emotion as Physical Sensation

In this section we turn from the objective (physiological) to the subjective (experiential) side of emotion, and to one very common hypothesis linking the two. That hypothesis formed the basis for William James's (1890) influential psychophysiological theory of emotion; to wit, the experience of emotion arises when the perception of bodily change (proprioceptive feedback) is "added" to the cold perception of the initiating event. For an updated version of this hypothesis, see Schachter (1971).

Let us consider some metaphorical expressions that are possible sources and/or transmitters of the belief that the experience of emotion is reducible to physical sensations. Consider first the EMOTIONAL EFFECT IS PHYSICAL CONTACT metaphor, with examples borrowed, in part, from Lakoff and Johnson (1980):

EMOTIONAL EFFECT IS PHYSICAL CONTACT
It was a *slap in the face*.
His mother's death *hit* him *hard*.
The idea *bowled* me *over*.
That was a *kick in the pants*.
I was *struck* by his insincerity.
That really *made an impression on* me.
I was *staggered* by what I saw.
I was *touched*.

In the above expressions, PHYSICAL CONTACT implies a physical sensation. This arises via the image the metaphor evokes: A physical object or force (corresponding to the cause of emotion) comes into contact with the physical body (corresponding to the subject of emotion). In addition, the metaphor emphasizes that emotion is something that arises suddenly and lasts only a short time.

Many other metaphors suggest that the sensations we experience take place inside the body (e.g. the heart, the mouth) and not simply on the surface.

EMOTION IS AN INTERNAL SENSATION
I *felt* it *in my heart*.
Feelings were running high.
It caused *in me* a *sensation* between joy and fear.
It was just *sensational*.

If we can talk about the presence of emotional experience by making reference to physical sensations of various kinds, then we should also be able to talk about the lack of emotional experience in terms of the same metaphor. The following expressions can be taken as examples:

I am emotionally *numb*.
He is emotionally *paralyzed*.
He is *dead,* as far as emotions go.
Come out of your shell, and show some emotion.

All of these examples indicate a lack of emotion. If we are numb, paralyzed or dead, or if we are inside a shell, we cannot physically feel anything. This in turn corresponds to an inability to experience emotion.

In chapter 2, we saw how Ryle thought of emotional feelings as physical sensations, and we discussed Brown's criticism of the Rylean paradigm.

The main burden of the criticism was that Ryle had a very limited view of emotional feelings as merely physical sensations. Based on the metaphorical expressions we have examined, we can see how easy it was for Ryle (as it was for William James before him) to slip into this "error."

Emotion as Animal

The publication of Darwin's *The Expression of the Emotions in Man and Animals* (1872/1965), is often taken as the start of yet another prominent theoretical tradition, one in which emotions are considered remnants of biological evolution—instinctive reactions that may be observed in "lower" animals as well as in humans. Actually, the idea that emotions are common to animals and humans is quite ancient, although it traditonally has been based more on ethical than on empirical considerations.

According to the teachings of Western civilization, a civilized person is supposed to keep his emotions under control. A person who loses his temper too easily or too often is not considered civilized. One may speculate about the possible sources of this maxim. It seems likely that at least one source is that lack of personal control is considered as an undesirable state in general. Another, perhaps complementary, source may be that intense emotions are often viewed as dangerous (cf. the NATURAL FORCE, OPPONENT, and INSANITY metaphors). The following metaphor also carries this implication:

EMOTION IS AN ANIMAL
He *unleashed* his emotions.
She had a *wild* emotional experience.
The speech *aroused* a great deal of emotion.
He has some *fierce* emotions.
He is *violently* emotional.
She acted with *unbridled* passion.
He kept his emotions *on a short leash*.
Her passion was *insatiable*.
She is a creature of *untamed* emotion.
His emotions are *bestial*.
His emotions *got away* from him.
She was trying to *keep* her emotions *in check*.
His emotions *ran away* with him.

The animal depicted by the metaphor is seemingly dangerous: it is wild, fierce, violent, bestial; it tries to get away; and its appetite is insatiable. It poses danger to both the owner and to others. This implication of danger, it should be noted, does not mean that the metaphor is necessarily restricted to the so-called negative emotions. On the contrary, it also applies to such paradigmatic positive emotions as romantic love. Once an association between emotion and dangerousness is made, it is only natural for us to think of emotion as something that has to be controlled. Indeed, some expressions in the ANIMAL metaphor indicate how the emotions can be kept under control: for example, we can *tame* them, or else *keep* them *on a short leash, bridle* them, and so forth.

It may be recalled that one example of the OPPONENT metaphor discussed in an earlier section involved the notion of *appeasement*. The expression *insatiable* in the (dangerous) ANIMAL metaphor has a very similar implication. Both expressions point to the presence of the notion of desire in the concept of emotion. That is, emotion has a desire that has to be fulfilled. The desire corresponds to a "demand" in the OPPONENT metaphor and to an "appetite" in the ANIMAL metaphor. Both the demand and the appetite have to be satisfied. The desire can be satisfied if various specific actions are performed by the subject of the emotion. As we shall see in the next chapter, this part of the metaphor highlights a very important aspect of emotion.

Emotion as Nonrational Evaluation

The last set of metaphors we will consider here are related to the proposition, common to so-called "cognitive" theories of emotion, that a close (conceptual and/or empirical) link exists between emotional reactions and certain kinds of judgments. On a very general level, for example, emotions such as love, admiration, and hope imply positive value judgments; conversely, hate, fear, and disgust imply negative value judgments. To take a more specific example, anger and envy are closely related emotions. They differ in that the angry person has made a judgment that the target has done something wrong and deserves punishment. The envious person has made a different kind of judgment, namely, that the target possesses something desirable, rightfully or wrongfully, that he (the envious person) wishes to destroy.

To preserve the distinction between passions and actions, some theorists argue that bodily agitation and/or motivational tendencies must accompany any evaluative judgment associated with emotion. Other theorists, however, attribute distinguishing characteristics to the emotional judgment itself. To understand these distinguishing characteristics, we might first note that behavior based on *rational* judgment is paradigmatic of action as opposed to passion. Rational judgments are *dis*passionate; the implication is that emotional judgments are nonrational.

Emotional judgments may be nonrational in several different ways. For example, the ancient Stoics believed the emotions to be a form of *irrational* (false) judgment. Few contemporary theorists take such a negative view of the emotions in general. Rather, the argument may be made that emotional judgments are such that the norms of rationality simply do not apply. Arnold (1960), for example, argues that emotions are based on *intuitive* judgments regarding the potential benefit or harm that an object might have for the individual (or animal). Sartre (1948) speaks of emotional judgments as *magically* transforming a situation to fit our needs and values. Solomon (1976), following the lead of Sartre, regards emotions as *evaluative* judgments.

The above views (i.e., emotional judgments as irrational, intuitive, magical, and/or evaluative) all find ample expression in the metaphors of everyday speech. For example, the INSANITY metaphor, discussed earlier, emphasizes the presumed irrationality of many emotional responses. So, too, does the following metaphor, that mostly has to do with, but is not limited to, positive emotions:

EMOTION IS RAPTURE
They were *intoxicated* with passion.
He was *drunk* with emotion.
They were *high* on emotion.
It was a *delirious* feeling.
He was *heady* with emotion.

To make sure what the primary focus of a metaphor is, it is often helpful to look at the metaphorical consequences of the expression. In the EMOTION IS RAPTURE case, a metaphorical consequence is that we can talk about emotionally *sober* or *sober-minded* people. An emotionally sober person is one who is either not intellectually affected by his emotions or who can think clearly despite the strong emotions. This person would be called a rational person or one who does not lose control over his emotions.

The EMOTION IS A TRICKSTER metaphor is also concerned with the issue of irrationality. Let us see some examples:

EMOTION IS A TRICKSTER
His emotions *deceived* him.
She was *misled* by her emotions.
Emotions *led* him *astray*.
Her emotion *tricked* her.
Don't let your emotions *fool* you!

This metaphor depicts emotions as a person who can deceive, mislead, trick, and fool us. In the same way as a trickster takes advantage of a victim, emotions take advantage of the subject of emotion. The metaphor assumes that the subject of emotion (the victim) is not clever or intelligent enough to judge for himself or herself the harm that the emotion (the trickster) can do. It is perhaps at this point that mention can be made of the verb *cloud* when it refers to emotional phenomena, as in "His emotions *clouded* his judgment." Here again, the expression indicates that the subject of emotion is incapable of cognitive ("higher" mental) functioning.

Some of the metaphors discussed in previous sections extend beyond the issue of irrationality and suggest that emotions are nonrational in a broader (e.g., intuitive, evaluative) sense. For example, the conception of EMOTION AS OBJECT tends to separate the emotions from the self, and hence from the domain of deliberate, rational behavior. The identification of emotions with PHYSIOLOGICAL CHANGE has similar implications. Thus, if emotions are IN THE HEART, they are separate from reason, which is in the head. Or consider the ANIMAL metaphor. Animals lack the same capacity for reason as do humans. This reinforces the notion that emotions are based on intuitive ("instinctive") judgments.

The following metaphorical expressions also imply that emotions are nonrational, in the sense of being evaluative judgments:

She was wearing *rose-colored glasses.*
After his loss, *all the world looked dark and blue.*

Stated most generally, emotions *color* the way we perceive the world, in either a good ("light") or bad ("dark") fashion.

The power of emotions to "magically transform" the world is implied by such expressions as the following:

Love *makes the world go round.*
Fear is a *great inventor.*

In some respects, metaphors of this last type are similar to those discussed earlier under the general heading of emotions as motivation. In the present case, however, the emphasis in on the way the external world is moved or transformed, and not on the self.

A leading controversy in the psychology of emotion is whether emotions are cognitive or noncognitive (Lazarus, 1984; Zajonc, 1984). In part, this controversy is due to an ambiguity in the term "cognition" (not to mention ambiguities in the term "emotion"). As used by some psychologists, cognition is roughly equivalent to "mental" or "judgmental." In this sense, theories that treat emotions as nonrational evaluations presume that emotions involve cognitions. However, "cognition" is often used in a more narrow sense to mean, roughly, rational or "higher" thought processes. In this latter sense, emotions may be noncognitive; that is, they may be based on intuitive judgments that something is good (liked) or bad (disliked).

Conclusions

We have now illustrated how six theoretical traditions in the psychology of emotion can be viewed as extensions of our folk beliefs about emotions, as those beliefs are expressed in the metaphors and metonymies of everyday speech. To recapitulate briefly, the six traditions are (a) emotion as agitation, (b) emotion as motivation, (c) emotion as physiological change, (d) emotion as physical sensation, (e) emotion as animal, and (f) emotion as nonrational evaluation. We will conclude the chapter by considering briefly some of the broader implications of our analysis for an understanding of emotion.

At one extreme, it might be argued that congruencies between metaphor and theory provide *evidence* for the theory, in that both metaphor and theory reflect some underlying reality. At the other extreme, it might be argued that such congruencies are *misleading* in that they make certain theoretical formulations appear more reasonable than they are in fact.

Both extremes are, to a certain extent, correct. Consider for a moment the theoretical proposition that physiological arousal is a necessary condition for emotion. Many of the metaphors and metonymies that link emotions to bodily change are based on actual experience (e.g., "sweaty palms" and "cold feet" are accurate descriptions of common physiological responses during fear), and to this extent they lend support to the theoretical proposition. Other metaphorical references to bodily change are, however, clearly fanciful and hence potentially misleading. For instance, "lily livered" and "yellow bellied" do not describe actual response patterns, although they vividly convey an attitude toward, or evaluation of, the behavior to which they refer.

In the above examples, it is not difficult to distinguish fact from fancy. However, as our metaphors become more abstract, the distinction begins to blur. Are emotions really "gut reactions?" To what extent is their "animal-like" quality based on biological fact as opposed to a negative value judgment? (In a kind of reverse evolutionary theory, it might be noted, Plato postulated that humans would be reincarnated as animals according to the passion that dominated their lives.) And in what sense are emotional judgments noncognitive, that is, contrary to "higher" thought processes?

The issue of whether our metaphorical expressions (and their theoretical extensions) refer primarily to inherent properties of emotional syndromes, or whether they are meant primarily to convey attitudes is complicated by the fact that the metaphors themselves may help determine the behavior they represent. La Rochefoucauld (1665/1959) once asked: "Would anyone experience love if we did not have a word for it?" We can extend this question by asking: "Would anyone ever experience love in the way we do if we did not have so many metaphorical expressions for it?" (See Kövecses, 1988, for a detailed analysis of the metaphors of love.) The same question could be asked about anger, grief, fear, pride, and any other emotion.

Our metaphors of emotion can be considered, to an extent, as veiled instructions on how to behave when emotional. The ability of persons to follow such "instructions" is well illustrated by hysterical conversion reactions, where the individual may "suffer" from paralysis or anaesthesia for which there is no neurological deficit. In such cases, the disorder (e.g., a "glove anaesthesia") is contoured according to popular conceptions and not according to physiological reality (e.g., the actual neurological innervation of the hand). Hysterical conversion reactions are difficult to accomplish, especially since they typically lack any social support and may even cause the individual great discomfort. How much easier it must be—and how much more common—for a person to "stoke the fires of his passion," for example, in order to demonstrate the ardor of his love, the sincerity of his grief, or the seriousness of his anger.

Clearly, to disentangle myth from reality would be a difficult task in the case of metaphors of emotion. It would require, among other things, an analysis of the origins of various metaphors and of the functions they might serve within the language community—an "objective" representation of some underlying phenomenon being only one possible function. Such an analysis is beyond the scope of this chapter (but see Averill, 1974, in press). Here, we can only raise the possibility that the appeal of some of our most widely accepted theories of emotion is based, to some undetermined extent, on their metaphorical associations rather than on their scientific validity.

The converse of this last possiblity should also be considered. That is, theoretical positions that do not have corresponding metaphorical expressions in ordinary language may be uncritically discounted as contrary to common knowledge and hence unintuitive. In this connection we might note that our analysis has not touched upon several theoretical traditions in the psychology of emotion. Thus, except for a brief mention in connection with the SOCIAL SUPERIOR metaphor, we have not considered the proposition that emotions are socially constituted patterns of behavior (Harré, 1986), as opposed to biologically primitive responses. Nor have we examined the proposition that emotions are, on the individual level of analysis, "disclaimed actions" (Schafer, 1976)—products of individual choice for which the person does not wish to accept responsibility. A good deal of empirical support exists for both of these positions; however, neither finds much support in the metaphors of ordinary language. Hence, they have been relatively neglected in this chapter—and in the field of psychology in general.

11 The Concept of Emotion: A Prototype

The main focus of the previous chapter was on the relationship between groups of metaphors and metonymies on the one hand and various scientific theories of emotion on the other. What was not done, however, is the study of how the various groups of metaphors and metonymies are related to each other. They were treated as isolated classes of linguistic expressions. But we have seen in many other chapters that the metaphors and metonymies do seem to converge on cognitive models that can in turn be conceived as prototypes for the emotion in question. The same applies to the concept of emotion in general. The metaphors and metonymies will enable us to propose a language-based cognitive prototype for the category of emotion as well. Furthermore, in the light of this prototype it will be possible to see the details of why certain emotions are considered as very good examples of the category, others as not so good, and still others as poor examples. More importantly, the approach will allow us to see the subtle details of the dynamic nature of the concept of emotion.

The Prototype of Emotion

The metaphors of emotion we saw in the last two chapters can be divided into two major categories. The first category consists of the CONTAINER metaphor by itself. The second is constituted by the rest of the emotion metaphors we discussed in the previous chapter. One of the major features of both categories of metaphors is that they highlight the notion and role of force in our conception of emotion. The CONTAINER metaphor is primarily based on the notion of thermodynamic forces. The other metaphors seem to represent social, biological, natural and, to some extent, also physical forces. The most remarkable feature of the CONTAINER metaphor is that it provides us with a more or less complete picture of the concept of emotion by itself. The other metaphors taken together seem to yield a picture similar to the one privided by the CONTAINER metaphor. However, it is also important to study—as we did—these other metaphors in depth because they contribute many details to our idea of emotion that a single metaphor could not do. First I will describe the concept of emotion as given in the CONTAINER metaphor and then as given in the rest of the metaphors.

The examination of the CONTAINER metaphor yielded the following overall picture. There is a fluid in the container that is cold and calm (there is a lack of emotion). Some external event produces heat and agitation in the container (emotion exists). The fluid begins to rise and the temperature of the fluid increases. There is more and more agitation inside the container (the intensity of emotion increases). The heat produces steam. As a result, pressure is building up, which is exerted especially on the top of the container (there is a great deal of emotional pressure). The pressure is dangerous because it can lead to an explosion (emotional pressure is dangerous because it can lead to uncontrolled actions). This can cause harm both to the container and to other objects or people around it (loss of control over emotion can cause harm both to self and others). There is a limiting point beyond which the pressure cannot increase without causing an explosion (the intensity of emotion cannot increase indefinitely without leading to an uncontrolled response on the part of the self). A certain amount of counterforce is applied that can prevent or delay the explosion (attempt at controlling the emotion). It requires a great deal of counterforce to counteract the pressure (emotion is difficult to control). But the force increases and when it becomes stronger than the counterforce, there is an explosion (loss of emotional control, which results in an uncontrolled response). The container becomes dysfunctional, parts of it go up in the air, what was inside comes out (there is possible damage to the self and to others). The pressure ceases to exist (emotion ceases to exist). The fluid is cool and calm again (there is emotional calm).

The various other metaphors and metonymies taken together have yielded this picture (to facilitate the presentation of the prototype of emotion, some abbreviations will be introduced): The person (S) is emotionally calm, but then an external event happens suddenly that involves S as a patient and which disturbs S. The event exerts a sudden and strong impact on S. Emotion (E) comes into existence and S is passive with regard to this. E is a separate entity from S and it exists independently of S. S becomes agitated, his heart rate increases, there is an increase in body temperature, skin color on face changes, and respiration becomes more intense. E is intense, S's experiences of E are primarily of physical sensations inside the body. S may also cry, show his emotion through forms of visual behavior, and be in an energized state. Involved in E is a desire and it forces S to perform an action (X) that can satisfy this desire. S knows that X is dangerous and/or unacceptable to do. It can cause physical or psychological harm to himself or others. S knows that he is under obligation not to perform X required by E. He applies some counterforce to prevent X from happening. It requires a great deal of effort for S to counteract the force of the emotion. However, S is now nonrational, and the strength of the force quickly increases beyond the point that S can counteract. The force becomes much greater than the counterforce. As a result, S cannot perceive the world as it is, is unable to breathe normally, and engages in extremely agitated behavior. S is now irrational. S ceases to resist the force affecting him. S performs X, but he is not responsible for performing X since he only obeys a force larger than himself. E is now appeased and S no longer feels emotional. E ceases to exist and S is calm.

The contents of the two descriptions seem to reinforce each other. The latter description is a little more elaborate due to the fact that it represents a composite of a large number of metaphors and metonymies. What emerges from these descriptions is that the prototype of the concept of emotion has at least the following aspects: there is a cause, the cause produces the emotion, the emotion is something that we try to control, we fail to control it, and this leads to some action. This characterization suggests a sequentially arranged five-stage model for the concept. Thus, there is a temporal sequence in which the events described above unfold: the cause of emotion precedes the existence of emotion, which in turn precedes the attempt at control, which in turn precedes the loss of control, and which in turn precedes the action. In addition, the first stage is preceded by a state of calmness and the final stage is followed by a state of calmness.

But there is also a causal structure built into this, which lends the concept a dynamic character. Obviously, the cause produces the emotion. What is more interesting, however, is that the emotion has a desire component which forces S to perform an action he is not supposed to perform. Thus, S attempts to control E. But when E gets too intense, S will be unable to resist E. S loses control and performs the action that was required by E.

Given these descriptions that emerge from the metaphors and metonymies we have investigated in the previous two chapters and given that the propositions that make up the descriptions can be naturally arranged in the way suggested above, we can present the following as the prototypical cognitive model of emotion:

0. State of emotional calm

   S is calm and cool.

1. Cause

   Something happens to S.
   The event is external to S.
   The event disturbs S.
   The event exerts a sudden and strong impact on S.
   Emotion comes into existence.
   S is passive with regard to the coming into existence of emotion.

2. Emotion exists

Emotion is an entity separate from the self.
Emotion exists independently from the self.
S is disturbed.
E involves a desire which forces S to perform an action (X).
X can satisfy E's desire.
S knows that X is dangerous and/or unacceptable to do (both for himself and others).
E manifests itself for S primarily in terms of physical sensations (inside the body).
S experiences certain physiological responses: agitation, increased heart rate, body temperature and respiration, and change of skin color on face.
S exhibits certain behavioral responses: crying, emotional expressive behavior, and energetic behavior.
E is intense; it is near the limit that S can control.

3. Attempt at control

S knows that he is under obligation not to perform X required by E.
S applies counterforce to prevent X from happening.
S has to spend a great deal of energy to try to counteract the force, that is, the emotion.
S is nonrational.
E's (the force's) intensity quickly increases beyond the point that S can counteract.
The force becomes much greater than the counterforce.

4. Loss of control

S is unable to function normally: S cannot perceive the world as it is, is unable to breathe normally, and engages in extremely agitated behavior.
S is irrational.
S ceases to resist the force affecting him.
E forces S to perform X.

5. Action

S performs X.
S is not responsible for performing X since he only obeys a force larger than himself.
E is now appeased and S ceases to be emotional.
E ceases to exist.

0. Emotional calmness

S is calm again.

This then is the model that seems to emerge from the metaphors and metonymies we use to understand and create the concept of emotion. It is unlikely, however, that there is a single precise prototypical cognitive model of emotion. To the extent that the metaphors and the metonymies are vague and imprecise, the models resulting from them are also vague, imprecise, and only approximate. Let me illustrate with one example. Consider the aspect of control and a sentence like "He couldn't overcome the emotion," which describes the control aspect in terms of the OPPONENT metaphor. This sentence can be easily interpreted within the model above. We can interpret it as telling us that S was extremely emotional but was trying to keep the emotion under control and not do X, but despite the effort he lost control and did X. The understanding of the sentence involves at least four stages—existence of emotion, attempt at control, loss of control, and action—with a focus on loss of control. In other words, the OPPONENT metaphor and the attempt at control is directed at the avoidance of the last stage—the action stage. But is this the only possibility? The answer is negative. It is also possible to interpret the sentence as meaning that S made an attempt to hide some manifestation of emotion, like agitation or crying. In this case, we would have to say that control was directed at some aspect of stage 2, rather than stage 5. What these observations indicate is that the notion of control may be built into our concept of emotion in more than one place in the model, depending on what and how many interpretations the control-related expressions can be given. (The multiple applicability of control to emotion is also emphasized by Frijda, 1986, and Shaver et al., 1987.)

The fact that, according to our language-based folk model, emotion is seen as leading to a loss of control renders emotion as having less value than rationality. Lakoff and Johnson (1980) observe that in our everyday conceptual system emotion is conceptualized as being downward-oriented while rationality as being upward-oriented. As they point out, in the case of a large number of central concepts in this culture the upward orientation corresponds to things that are considered good, while the downward orientation to things that are viewed as bad or less good. Within the emotion domain, the same two classes can be noticed. Some emotions are conceptualized as up (e.g., happpiness), while others as down (e.g., sadness). This seems to correspond to the distinction between positive and negative emotions. Thus, although the larger category of emotion is viewed as downward oriented, specific emotions may be thought of as having an upward orientation, which in turn makes their conceptualization coherent with concepts outside the emotion domain that are typically considered as good or having value.

The above prototype of emotion differs from the prototypes of specific emotions in at least two important respects. The first has to do with the issue of specificity. Since emotion is a superordinate concept, certain aspects of it cannot be made more specific. These aspects primarily involve stages 1. (the causal structure) and 5. (the action structure). In our folk theory of emotion, most specific emotions have their own causes and action responses. The more general category of emotion cannot be sensitive to this.

Second, the prototypes associated with specific emotions typically contain additional information in comparison to the emotion prototype. This is especially noticeable in the case of what we have called physiological and behavioral reactions. We have seen that our category of emotion is characterized by some of these, like inability to function normally, crying and being in an energized state. However, our folk theory of particular emotions maintains that each emotion is characterized by additional responses specific to the emotion. Thus, for example, in anger there is internal pressure, in fear coldness, in pride the desire to communicate success, and in love intimate sexual behavior. In general, it is typical of basic-level prototypes to be more specific and to contain more information than superordinate-level prototypes.

Moreover, the prototype of emotion seems to contain a core that is shared by several particular emotions. This core has to do with the workings of the force used in the conceptualization of emotion in general and the effect of the force on the self (especially how the force causes the self to perform actions). Depending on the extent to which particular emotions share this core, they will be considered as more or less prototypical emotions. If it is the case that the emotion that comes closest to this core is anger, then anger is perhaps the most prototypical emotion. In fact, this would not surprise anyone; anger ranks very high in all prototypicality judgments and it is on everybody's list of basic emotions. In addition to anger, we have seen that fear also contains large portions of the force image, and, as was shown in chapter 3, love, too, is characterized to a large degree by attraction, a form of force. But love is a problematic case and it will be discussed further below.

The notion of emotional force is bound up with the notion of emotion as passion. This point was discussed and demonstrated in the previous chapter. What needs to be pointed out here is that this force component may well be one of the distinguishing characteristics of emotion. For example, it is one of the properties that seems to set emotion apart from the concept of thought. Emotion is conceptualized as a force and the force causes S to perform a certain action or type of action. The force prevails and runs its full course. The action, through its link with the force, is known before it is actually executed, although it may not be consciously known by S. But since the action is somehow wrong, the emotion will have a built-in mechanism for the control of its possible outcome, the action. In thought, on the other hand, typically we do not know the action in advance. It is the result of the process of thinking, that is, making a decision. Thought arrives at an action through taking into account all the actions that are possible in the situation. It guides us to find the appropriate action. In contrast, emotion forces us to perform the (kind of) action typically associated with it on the conceptual level, regardless of the question of appropriateness. Hence, it seems more acceptable to say sentence (1) than (2):

1. His emotions made him do that.
2. His thoughts made him do that.

Thus, given the emotion prototype in general and the built-in notion of force in particular, we can begin to understand some of the major dimensions along which emotion and thought differ from each other. A similar approach could be taken to understand the differences between the concept of emotion and concepts like illness and pain.

There is some independent evidence for this analysis. I have suggested above that the notion of desire and that of action are intimately linked. In his study of the folk model of the mind, D'Andrade (1987) also found that the link between desire and action is such that action is used to satisfy desire. For this reason, I can legitimately say a sentence like "I kissed her because I had a desire." In other words, desire is often seen as the motivation for action. But what is the relationship between emotion and desire in our folk model of emotion? Desire does not seem automatically to entail emotion, for not all desires are (parts of) emotions. For example, it would be strange to call a "craving for ice cream" an emotion in the same sense as we would call a person's longing for another love. However, most emotions seem to imply some kind of desire. This is clearly so in the case of strong emotions. (Incidentally, it might be noted that Spinoza also regarded desire as the most fundamental aspect of emotion.) D'Andrade's work provides us with further evidence in this respect as well. The interviews he conducted with people suggest that emotions are thought to lead to desires. We have seen that in the prototypical cognitive model of emotion desire is an integral part of our conception of emotion. This idea was proposed on the basis of the examination of metaphors relating to emotion. The significance of D'Andrade's work for our purposes is that despite the very different methodology he arrived at conclusions similar to the ones reached in this study. Thus, it seems that the notion of emotion presented above is very close to the folk model people actually use for their everyday purposes.

Before we begin the discussion of nonprototypical cases of emotion it might be useful to consider some examples that are usually taken to be central cases of the emotion category. It was noted above that the emotion that perhaps comes closest to the prototype as described above is anger. In the chapter on anger, we saw that anger has a five-stage model and the stages are the same as in the emotion prototype. It has a very clear force component, where the force compels the self to perform an action that leads to a cessation of anger. It is also characterized by a high level of physiological arousal experienced by the self and a variety of behavioral reactions that suggest an energized state. And a large part of our conception of anger is constituted by the idea of control. These are all aspects that the emotion prototype shares with the prototype of anger. This makes anger a very good example of the category of emotion.

Let us now look at fear, which is considered as another prototypical emotion. Although fear also has a desire-force component, it seems to be significantly different from the one in anger. The desire element in anger appeared very directly in the OPPONENT and DANGEROUS ANIMAL metaphors. Thus the following sentences are perfectly acceptable:

His anger could not be *appeased.*
His anger was *insatiable.*

However, these are not possible sentences when they are applied to fear:

*His fear could not be *appeased.*
*His fear was *insatiable.*

In the case of fear, the element of desire comes through indirectly via the FEAR IS A BURDEN metaphor. When we say

He was *relieved* when he was safe.

it is implied that the person had the desire to be safe. It should be noted, however, that the same expression is also available for anger:

He felt *relieved* after he told her off.

These observations seem to mean that we have to do with two different kinds of desire: a "desire toward" and a "desire away from," corresponding in all probability to appetitive and avoidance drives. The former is conceptualized in terms of the OPPONENT and DANGEROUS ANIMAL metaphors, whereas both seem to be expressible (although indirectly) in terms of the BURDEN metaphor. If it is the case that anger is ranked higher than fear in people's prototypicality judgments, one reason for this might be that people consider "desire toward" as somehow more prototypical of desires than "desire away from." And intuitively, this would not be surprising. The sentence "I wish I was there" sounds as a better example of desire than the sentence "I wish I wasn't here." More generally, perhaps it can be hypothesized that, if only the kind of desire distinguishes between two categories, the category with a built-in "desire for" will be considered more prototypical than a category with "desire away from." Of course, in real-world prototypicality judgments the notion of desire can be overriden by other properties of the categories involved.

A prototypical cognitive model of love was given in chapter 3. It has been noted above that love is a problematic case from the perspective of the emotion prototype we have seen in the present chapter. The problem arises because despite the fact that the prototype of love as given in chapter 3 does *not* match the prototype of emotion very closely, it is often considered as one of the best examples of emotion. The major areas where the two models differ are: fewer stages in love owing to the absence of the control aspect; the absence of a clear causal component; and the absence of a clear action component. How is this possible? Given the theoretical framework developed in this study, there can be several reasons for this.

First, one of the most characteristic features of (romantic) love is that we are entirely passive in relation to it; it is a powerful force that affects us and we, as patients, undergo the effects of the force (see for example Solomon 1981 and 1988). Indeed, according to the folk model, the force puts us in the state of love without there being any rational causes for us to get into that state. Thus, since passivity is perhaps the most characteristic feature of love and since, as we saw in the last chapter, it is a decisive element in our conception of emotion, this can provide sufficient grounds for people to view love as a central member of the emotion category.

Second, another crucial element of our conception of love is the desire for the other. This finds expression in the belief that love and the object of love are considered as a need and in what have been called inherent concepts. These concepts elaborate further the notion of desire in love; longing, enthusiasm, and interest, for instance indicate various aspects of "desire for/toward." Also, the desire of love and emotion are very strong. Furthermore, as we have seen, "desire for/toward" may well be the prototypical form of desire for emotion in general. Thus, this particular and intense form of desire characteristic of love may contribute significantly to making love a central case of emotion.

Third, people may regard love as a prototypical emotion because they may have models of love in mind other than the one given in chapter 3. It was noted there that it is not the only possible prototype of love. The model given in chapter 3 was intended to capture what can be called the *ideal* model. Another model of love is the *typical* model (see Kövecses 1988). In contrast to the ideal case, the typical version does contain a control aspect. Moreover, it is also thought to lead to a specific action—marriage, which in the folk model represents the culmination of (romantic) love. When people are asked to make prototypicality judgments, it is often not clear which of several possible prototypes for a concept they may have in mind.

We can round off this discussion of some prototypical examples of emotion by returning for a minute to Alston (1967). It will be recalled that Alston provides the following as typical features of emotion:

1. A cognition of something as in some way desirable or undesirable.
2. Feelings of certain kinds.
3. Marked bodily sensations of certain kinds.
4. Involuntary bodily processes and overt expressions of certain kinds.
5. Tendencies to act in certain ways.
6. An upset or disturbed condition of mind or body. (p. 480)

Alston arrived at these typical features of emotion through an examination of the scholarly literature on emotion. He writes: "There are a number of typical features of emotional states which most thinkers agree are connected with emotion in one way or another''. What is remarkable about these features is that each of them has its counterpart in the prototypical folk model: (1) corresponds to the cause of emotion, (2) corresponds to the experience of some emotion as given in stage 2 as a whole, (3) corresponds to the physical sensations in stage 2, (4) corresponds to the physiological and behavioral responses in stage 2, (5) corresponds to certain actions associated with the emotion, given as stage 5, and (6) corresponds to emotional disturbance and bodily agitation in stage 2. Thus, the typical features of emotion as provided by scientific models can be accomodated in three stages of the folk model: stage 1, stage 2, and stage 5. It seems then that the folk model recoverable from English is a fairly rich model of emotion, which contains most, if not all, of the features found important for the characterization of emotion by scholars. This is the same point that was made in the previous chapter.

Pride and Respect as Two Nonprototypical Emotion Concepts

However, as Alston emphasizes, not all of these features have to be present in every case of emotion. The same applies to the folk model. There are specific cases that are characterized by all or most of the features given in the prototypical cognitive model of emotion, like anger, fear and love, and there are others that are characterized by only some. Furthermore, it would seem that some of the features are more specific to emotion than others (for example, the notion of passivity). This makes these features more important in the description of emotion. When we look at some nonprototypical examples of emotion, both of these factors (number of features and importance of features) will be taken into account.

We can begin with pride. In most prototypicality judgments, pride is considered to be a ''medium-good'' emotion; it is viewed as neither a central nor a peripheral example. Given the above prototype of emotion, how can we account for this particular status of pride?

First, its prototype is not characterized by extreme intensity; it is intense but not excessively so. Intensity here is not linked with the appropriateness of a certain degree of pride in relation to a value scale. When it is said that pride is intense but not excessively so, what is meant is that on a scale that measures the intensity of various emotions the intensity of pride registers less than prototypical cases of anger, fear, or love.

Second, perhaps related to this is the observation that the prototype of pride does not seem to have a control aspect that is as natural as in the case of anger or fear. Suppose someone has won a race. It would be a little odd to say of this person that ''?He tried to overcome his pride.'' It is not that the sentence as such is not acceptable. Clearly, it is. What makes it odd nevertheless is the situation in which it is said. As was noted in the chapter on pride, the situation is one in which pride exists as an immediate response to an event. Without any extra clues, one is at a loss to understand why someone was trying to overcome his pride, which follows so naturally from winning a race. A very different situation in which the sentence would not sound odd is when I decide to borrow some money from you despite my principles. This would be a different meaning of the word *pride*, which, however, does not represent the prototype of the general category. To see the difference between pride and, say, fear in this respect, consider the sentence "He tried to overcome his fear." This sentence sounds perfectly natural without any situational clues. We would never worry about why someone tried to overcome his fear. Trying to do so is a natural part of our conception of fear, but it is not of pride.

Third, if pride is not characterized by a conceptually built-in attempt to control it, then it's not likely to lead to a loss of control either. Indeed, pride as an immediate response is perhaps never conceptualized in terms of insanity or a natural force. Sentences like "He was crazy with pride" or "He was carried away by pride" are not very likely to occur.

Fourth, pride does not seem to have an actional aspect similar to anger or fear. Although it was noted that pride is characterized by the behavioral reaction of TELLING OTHER PEOPLE, this is not as salient as an action as those associated with anger and fear are. Interestingly, however, this less salient action nevertheless assumes the existence of a desire similar to the desires motivating fight or flight. When proud of an achievement, it is perfectly acceptable for someone to say "I just could not resist telling her about it."

Fifth, pride is also nonprototypical in the following respect. In the folk model given above, emotion is caused in the self when an external event occurs and the event is such that it is directed at the self. That is, the self plays the role of patient in the event. The role of the self in the most typical cause of pride—achievement—is completely different. In an achievement the self is the agent, not the patient. In pride, the self does and achieves something, rather than something happens to a passive self. Moreover, in the prototypical case of emotion the subject of emotion is different from the agent of the initiating event. In pride, the two coincide: the achiever is the one who is also proud. These features set pride apart from more prototypical emotions, like anger and fear.

We can now continue with respect. In most prototypicality judgments respect is judged to be a very bad example of emotion. In fact, very often it is not considered an emotion at all. In short, it is a borderline case with regard to its membership in the emotion category. However, the very fact that it shows up towards the end on most lists of emotion requires an explanation. Why is respect classified in this way? Again, there are several reasons. One was already mentioned in the chapter on respect. Respect is not characterized by a set of physiological reactions. Neither does it lead to physical agitation or emotional disturbance.

Second, related to this is that respect is a disposition and not a response to a particular situation. But, one could argue at this point, love is also a disposition and yet it is one of the central examples of emotion. There is, however, an important difference between respect and love in this regard. While in the case of (at least romantic) love it is usual, normal, and expected that the lover will have certain physiological responses in the presence of the beloved and often even just at the thought of the beloved, this is not usual, normal, and expected in the case of respect. And if the respecter does have these physiological effects, we have reasonable grounds to claim that he or she not just respects the other, but also loves the respected one. And, of course, if the lover never displays any of the physiological responses associated with love, we have reasonable grounds to say that he or she does not love or is not in love with the other. The point is that perhaps a major reason why respect is viewed as a poor example of emotion is that our folk model of emotion as given above is a state rather than a dispositional model. The possibility of a dispositional prototype will be discussed in the next chapter.

Third, if respect is a disposition (or "emotional attitude" as Alston would call it), it is not likely to have a control aspect. It is this lack of a control aspect which is reflected in the prototypcial cognitive model of respect in chapter 7. As Alston writes in this connection: "When someone is said to give way to his emotions or control his emotions, it is emotional states which are in question" (Alston 1967, 480). The same idea can be found in the work of psychologists. Fehr and Russell (1984) asked people to judge the naturalness or peculiarity of sentences involving emotion terms. Subjects were given sentences like the following:

Sometimes anger is hard to control.
Sometimes respect is hard to control.

The naturalness scores obtained for anger were twice as high as those for respect. That is, the conceptual model of anger seems to have a built-in control aspect, while that of respect does not. Since, as we saw in the previous section, there is a clear control aspect in the folk conception of emotion, when people are asked to rate the prototypicality of certain emotional concepts they find concepts that do have a control aspect more prototypical than those that do not.

Fourth, similar to pride, respect in not seen as leading to a loss of control. This may in part be due to the idea in our folk theory that the intensity level of respect does not vary in the same way as in more prototypical emotions. If I respect someone for his courage and nothing calls for an increase or decrease in that level, my respect will remain on the same level. This is in contrast to certain forms of such emotions as anger, fear, and pride where the intensity level of anger, fear, and pride first goes up and then down in a natural way within a relatively short period of time. Certain forms of these and similar emotions have a course to run—they have a beginning and an end and last for a short time, as described in the prototype of emotion above. The intensity level of respect and other emotional attitudes, however, remains stable and tends to last for a long time.

Fifth, that the intensity of respect does not change of its own accord might have to do with the fact that respect is not characterized by physiological responses. In the prototypical cases of emotion, physiological arousal and intensity go together: the most salient measure of intensity seems to be the level of physiological arousal. In respect, this correlation cannot hold because the physiology is not involved. Intensity is measured on the basis of how strongly or weakly I hold certain beliefs (like he or she is superior to me) about the object of respect. Thus the separation of physiology as a measure of intensity from intensity constitutes a major divergence from what is prototypical as regards emotion.

Sixth, respect, unlike anger and fear but not quite unlike love, is not thought to lead to a specific action. In the chapter on respect, we saw several actions that can be used to express respect. But this is different from causing a person to perform some action that could somehow put an end to respect (as seems to be the case with the most prototypical emotions). Respect does not seem to have a goal component that is built into desires. Respect has no desire built into it and hence it has no goal. Thus, it would be strange to say: "I could not resist taking my hat off," unless it is intended as a joke.

Seventh, the cause component of respect is significantly different from that of the emotion prototype. Contrary to the cause in the emotion prototype, nothing happens *to* the subject of respect that would produce in him the respect. As a matter of fact, nothing *happens* at all. We saw that the most prototypical cause of respect is a positive moral quality in a person. This again is a major divergence from the prototype of emotion, where typically something happens to the self that produces the emotion. This seems to be another feature that respect shares with love. It might be that emotional attitudes in general share this feature. The feature makes sense intuitively: In the case of an event involving me as a patient, I respond immediately with an emotion, in the case of a permanent trait or disposition I simply adopt a certain emotional attitude toward it. More importantly for the present purposes, it looks as if respect has too many deficiencies in comparison to the emotion prototype and cannot compensate for them in the way love can. This makes it a very bad example of emotion.

Some Further Nonprototypical Cases

But nonprototypical members of the emotion category are not necessarily specific emotional concepts. Nonprototypical cases of emotion may also arise as a result of deviations from the above prototype on a more general (the superordinate) level. These cases may cover *several* specific emotional concepts and they often appear in the form of conceptual metaphors. Let us now consider some such cases.

We have seen above that one of the reasons why respect is judged to be a poor member of the category of emotion is that it is an emotional attitude and not an immediate response to an event. And it is likely that if the concept of love did not have certain properties that compensate for its dispositional properties it would also be regarded as a less prototypical emotion. If the above emotion prototype is valid, it would seem to follow that in general emotional concepts corresponding to cases other than immediate responses to a situation will be conceived of as less prototypical instances of emotion. (The exceptions would be cases where there is a sufficient number of properties to compensate for this.) One member of the emotion category that in all probability has this status is mood. Emotional moods are understood in terms of the following metaphor:

AN EMOTIONAL MOOD IS THE WEATHER
She is in a *sunny* mood today.
His moods are completely *unpredictable*.
He was in a *dark* mood yesterday.
She is as *unpredictable as the weather*.
He is in a *stormy* mood.
The way he says "Good morning" is the *barometer* of his mood.

The expressions *sunny, dark,* and *stormy* in this metaphor refer to weather conditions that are typically assumed to be short-termed ones. Correspondingly, the metaphor captures emotional moods, which are defined, for example, by Averill (1980b) as "a temporary state which predisposes the individual to respond in a certain way" (p. 184). The WEATHER metaphor could not be easily fitted into the system of metaphors for emotion as discussed in the previous chapter and summarized in the present one. It is a "minority" metaphor in that the other metaphors can be seen as converging on a more or less coherent cognitive model of emotion. Since the WEATHER metaphor contradicts several parts and the "spirit" of the model as a whole, this can be taken as an indication that it represents a less prototypical form of emotion.

The nonprototypicality of another member of the emotion category has to do with the control aspect. In the prototypical model, the subject of emotion loses control over an emotion that is very intense. This was suggested by major metaphors of emotion, like the CONTAINER, OPPONENT and DANGEROUS ANIMAL metaphors. It was noted in the discussion of the OPPONENT metaphor that more examples of this metaphor indicate a loss of control than a successful attempt at control. The same appears to be true of the metaphor according to which a person is an object composed of parts, and emotional control is a matter of keeping these parts together. Here are some examples:

A PERSON IS AN OBJECT WITH PARTS
EMOTIONAL CONTROL IS KEEPING THE PARTS TOGETHER
LOSS OF EMOTIONAL CONTROL IS FAILURE TO KEEP THE PARTS TOGETHER
He *lost his composure*.
Try to *get a hold of yourself*.
She remained *collected*.
He was *self-possessed*.
She *fell apart*.
You'd better *take yourself in hand*.
He eventually *pulled himself together*.

Most of these expressions suggest, either explicitly or implicitly, that there is or was a loss of control. This would be in line with the prototype as given above. However, we can also see two nonprototypical cases of emotion emerge from these examples. One is that the person remains under control in the face of very strong emotion. This version of emotional control is suggested by expressions like *collected* and *self-possessed*. According to the other version, the person who has lost control makes or can make a deliberate effort to regain control. The expressions *get a hold of oneself* and *pull oneself together* are indicative of this. This case is different from the prototype in that the prototype naturally leads to emotional calm, whereas here the person makes a conscious effort to regain control, and we do not know whether he or she is emotionally calm even if control has been regained.

A third general-level nonprototypical case of emotion is implicit in the metaphor THE EMOTIONS ARE THE FUNCTIONING OF THE STRINGS (OF A MUSICAL INSTRUMENT). It has been noted that emotion is conceptualized as an entity or object. The MUSICAL INSTRUMENT metaphor provides us with an alternative view.

THE EMOTIONS ARE THE FUNCTIONING OF THE STRINGS (OF A MUSICAL INSTRUMENT)
It *struck a chord* in my heart.
She is very *high-strung*.
The crying of children *tugged at her heartstrings*.
The speaker *played on* the feelings of the crowd.
What she said *touched a discordant chord*.
He tried to *unwind* with a glass of wine.

According to this metaphor, emotion is a physical event; more specifically, the physical event of producing sound. If the chord struck is in the heart, the emotion will be sympathy or compassion. If the player strikes a discordant chord, it will be displeasure. In general, these examples seem to have to do with how one person can affect the feelings of another. The remaining examples (*unwind, high-strung*) suggest tension. In all probability, the strings correspond to the nerves in the body. The more taut the strings are, the more tense the person is.

We have now seen some nonprototypical cases of the emotion category. These cases provide us with alternative views of emotion, views that do not seem to cohere into a unified category but rather represent various isolated deviations from the prototype. They highlight three important aspects of the concept: its episodic character, the notion of loss of control, and the ontological status of emotion. There are many additional ways in which cases that we would want to consider emotion can deviate from the prototype. Attention has been limited to those instances that appear in the form of some further conceptual metaphors of emotion.

Conclusion

In line with the thinking of many other researchers, I have also arrived at the conclusion that the category of emotion is best viewed as being organized around a cognitive prototype. However, unlike these scholars, I have found that this cognitive prototype has a great deal more content and structure than previously thought. Given this detailed content and well-delineated structure of the concept, we can see not only the constituents but also the dynamics of the category of emotion; the category emerges as a system of closely knit propositions that picture emotion as produced by certain causes, as existing in certain ways, as forces that take control of us, and as forces that make us do things. Furthermore, the details of the category of emotion as described enable us to understand the details of how other members of the category can differ from the prototype in subtle ways.

12
Conclusions and Some Implications

In this last chapter I wish to summarize the major conclusions that can be drawn on the basis of the foregoing analyses. This summary will enable us to present our new view of the structure of emotional concepts and the role that the parts of this structure (the metonymies, metaphors, and cognitive models) play in the conceptualization of emotional experience. I will also discuss the usefulness of the new conception in some issues of emotion theory in general.

The Structure of Emotional Meaning

Insofar as the analyses of emotional concepts in the foregoing chapters make intuitive sense to speakers of English, it can perhaps be claimed that something real has been discovered about the structure and content of emotional concepts. In particular, as the analyses show, the structure of at least some emotional concepts can be seen as being constituted by four parts:

1. a system of conceptual metonymies
2. a system of conceptual metaphors
3. a set of related concepts
4. a category (set) of cognitive models

Let me now comment on each of these parts in the light of what has been done.

The (conceptual) *metonymies* we have seen can be of two kinds: those that refer to internal physiological responses and those that refer to behavioral responses. Examples for the former are AGITATION in anger and fear, and DROP IN BODY TEMPERATURE in fear. The metonymies of this kind primarily denote distinct feelings associated with emotions. Thus, they describe the subjective part of emotional experience. The other metonymies capture behavior characteristic of emotions. This behavior is typically regarded as expressive of emotion. Thus, in this sense, metonymies of this kind describe what is objective about emotion. INTIMATE SEXUAL BEHAVIOR for romantic love, ANGRY VISUAL BEHAVIOR for anger, and FLIGHT for fear are examples. Sometimes it is difficult to tell whether the linguistic expression at hand refers to physiological effects or behavioral responses. In assigning these cases to either of the categories, the folk understanding of physiological and behavioral responses was used.

The (conceptual) *metaphors* cannot be classified into any such types. The metaphors may be connected with several different aspects of emotional experience. Although some metaphors focus on a single aspect (like the ones for the object of love), the majority of the metaphors are connected with a number of different aspects of emotion. Examples for (conceptual) metaphors are ANGER IS THE HEAT OF A FLUID IN A CONTAINER, FEAR IS AN OPPONENT, VANITY IS A (SENSUAL OR INDULGENT) PERSON, THE OBJECT OF LOVE IS A DEITY for specific emotions, and EMOTION IS THE HEAT OF A FLUID IN A CONTAINER, EMOTION IS FIRE, EMOTION IS A NATURAL FORCE for the general category of emotion.

The metaphors contribute varying amounts of information to the content of specific emotional concepts and the general concept of emotion. The amount of information seems to depend on the source domain employed in the metaphor. Some source domains map more knowledge onto the target domain than others. The OBJECT metaphor, for example, contributes a single piece of knowledge to the content of the concept of emotion; namely, that emotion is viewed as an entity independent of the self. In contrast, the CONTAINER metaphor for the passions incorporates a great deal of knowledge about emotion. As we have seen, this is the result of what we know about containers of a certain kind in the physical world. More generally, the more (metaphorical) implications a given source domain has and if these implications can be coherently applied to the target domain, the more the conceptual metaphor will contribute to the content of the target domain. And together with the content, a great deal of structure is also imparted. This is because the content of the source domain is already structured (i.e., it comes in schemas, or models). Often, the various metaphors of emotion reinforce each other. Perhaps the most clear case is how the NATURAL FORCE, FIRE, OPPONENT, DANGEROUS ANIMAL, SUPERIOR, and similar metaphors for the concept of emotion address the same issues that the CONTAINER metaphor by itself addresses.

The *related concepts,* as we saw in the chapter on love, can be roughly grouped into inherent concepts and associated concepts (although, as was pointed out, related concepts are better viewed as a gradable category with inherent and associated concepts at the two poles of the gradient). Related concepts are defined to be emotional concepts of some kind (emotional states, emotional attitudes, etc.). Inherent concepts constitute the minimal conceptual content of some emotional categories. For example, it is hard to imagine romantic love without some such concepts as AFFECTION, LONGING, and INTEREST, pride without JOY and SATISFACTION, and anger without DISPLEASURE and the DESIRE to retaliate. What comes closest to an inherent concept in the general category of emotion is perhaps DESIRE—the desire to perform an action. But not all emotional concepts have inherent concepts. Of the emotions dealt with in this book, fear is a case in point. It does not seem to incorporate another emotional concept in it in the same way as, for example, love does, say, affection. As the metaphors for fear indicate, fear is considered to be an extremely unpleasant emotion, but this is not another emotional concept inherent in fear. It is simply an evaluation of or a judgment on fear. Associated concepts are linked with a given emotional concept in looser ways. In some cases, as we saw, it is difficult to tell how closely a concept is related to another. For example, for some people romantic love is unimaginable without sexual desire, although (on the basis of my judgment of the *but*-test) it was assigned to the category of associated concepts. But perhaps the most important characteristic of related concepts is that they represent the conceptual domains that surround a given concept.

A category (or set) of *cognitive models* is the fourth ingredient of the structure of emotional concepts. Typically, the set of cognitive models contains one or more prototypical members and a large number of nonprototypical members. In a sense, cognitive models are the most important parts of the structure of concepts. They are the most important parts in the sense that the prototypical members of the set of cognitive models represent the concept as it typically exists for us. Thus, one can perhaps claim that, for example, the prototypical cognitive model of the concept of emotion as described in the last chapter comes very close to what speakers of English mean by the word *emotion* (even if they cannot necessarily make it explicit in the form it was presented). The prototypical cognitive models serve as culturally determined folk theories of the emotion in question. As we have seen throughout, these "theories" incorporate a fair amount of detailed knowledge. And they are also more or less complete in the sense that they contain most of the conceptual material concerning a domain that is handed down from one generation to the next by virtue of learning a language (especially the conventionalized expressions in it). The individual metaphors, metonymies, and related concepts do not usually represent detailed and complete knowledge in this sense. For example, the DANGEROUS ANIMAL metaphor captures only certain aspects of the concept of emotion; it does not provide a detailed and complete model of emotion. Or, the AGITATION metonymy for fear is only a small part of what we know of that emotion, and the related concept AFFECTION does not exhaust the concept of love. Some metaphors, however, do provide more or less complete, though not necessarily sufficiently detailed, knowledge of a specific emotion or the general category of emotion. Of these, perhaps the CONTAINER metaphor is the most significant. It is exactly this aspect (its completeness) of the CONTAINER metaphor that made it more than "just" a metaphor; that is, that made it a *model* of emotion as well.

But what then is the relationship among the four parts? This question was partially answered in chapter 3, but it is perhaps useful to answer it again more fully and in the light of the foregoing analyses. This is all the more useful since it also leads us to a survey and some discussion of the methodology.

So far in this chapter, I have only talked about related *concepts* and *conceptual* metaphors and metonymies. But, as was emphasized throughout in this study, the analysis begins with conventionalized linguistic expressions, like "one's pride and *joy,*" "*consumed* by passion," and "be *hot* and bothered." These and many other expressions are seen as forming certain clusters on the basis of similarities of meaning. The clusters correspond to either simple concepts (i.e., related concepts like AFFECTION in love, JOY in pride, and DESIRE in emotion) or complex concepts (i.e., metaphorical concepts like EMOTION IS FIRE and metonymical concepts like BODY HEAT STANDS FOR ANGER).

One central claim of the methodology is that in the case of the emotions it is these parts (the conceptual metonymies and metaphors and the related concepts) that contribute most, if not all, of the content of emotional concepts. Put differently, the three parts converge on the cognitive models. However, there are differences between them in the way they do so. While the conceptual metonymies and the related concepts map directly onto the cognitive models, most of the conceptual metaphors do so indirectly. For example, the conceptual metonymy BODY HEAT STANDS FOR ANGER appears in the cognitive model of anger as "body heat" and the related concept JOY appears in the cognitive model of pride as "joy." But the EMOTION IS FIRE conceptual metaphor was not given in the cognitive model of emotion as "fire." That would not make any sense. The FIRE metaphor establishes a set of relationships between a concrete schema (the schema associated with fire) and an abstract schema. The abstract schema consists of concepts like cause, intensity, and loss of control, which all appear in the prototypical cognitive model of emotion. These correspond to the cause and intensity of the fire, and the inability of the thing burning to function normally. The relationships are established by what were called ontological and epistemic correspondences. (These latter were also called the "implications" or "consequences" of metaphors.) Thus, the FIRE metaphor appears in the cognitive model associated with the category of emotion only via its ontological and epistemic correspondences. And the same seems to be true of a variety of other metaphors. There are, however, cases where a given conceptual metaphor contributes to a cognitive model in a fairly direct way. These cases will be discussed in a later section.

As Lakoff and Johnson (1980) point out, the various metaphors need not be, and usually are not, coherent; they can conflict with each other. However, only coherent metaphors can build (folk) theories, or models. Within a single model there cannot be conflicting propositions arising from conflicting metaphors. Metaphors with nonconflicting implications will build coherent (folk) models. In other words, it is the nonconflicting metaphors that will converge on cognitive models. This puts some constraint on the kinds of metaphors that can produce such models. As we saw in the last two chapters, the majority of the metaphors of emotion yield nonconflicting implications and can thus be placed in a coherent cognitive model. This model was called the prototypical cognitive model of emotion.

However, there are also metaphors of emotion that carry implications that conflict with the implications of the majority of the emotion metaphors. We saw some examples in the last chapter: according to the metaphor AN EMOTIONAL MOOD IS THE WEATHER, emotion is more a matter of dispositions than short-term episodes and according to the MUSICAL INSTRUMENT metaphor, emotion is not an entity but an event. These implications conflict with those of the majority of the emotion metaphors and thus the metaphors define nonprototypical (or alternative) conceptualizations of emotion. In addition, it is possible for the same conceptual metaphor to give rise to conflicting implications. To demonstrate this, we can use the third metaphor discussed in the last chapter. The PERSON IS AN OBJECT WITH PARTS metaphor suggests that the attempt at emotional control can have two outcomes: one can either gain or lose control. For various reasons discussed in the previous chapter, it was decided that the prototypical case involves a loss of control over emotion. But the importance of the fact that it is also possible to *gain* control over one's emotion should not be downplayed. It defines a culturally salient alternative in our conceptualization of emotion.

We can sum up the discussion in this section by making the following points. First, emotional concepts (including the concept of emotion) seem to be describable in terms of four parts: conceptual metonymies, conceptual metaphors, related concepts, and a set of cognitive models. This gives us an idea of the overall structure of these concepts. Second, the first three parts seem to carry over a great deal of content onto emotional concepts, thus producing a variety of cognitive models. This gives us a notion of the conceptual content of the categories. Third, the nonconflicting metaphors, metonymies, and related concepts give rise to a prototypical cognitive model (or alternative prototypes) and a variety of nonprototypical cases. This puts some limitations on what conceptual materials can and cannot be contributed to the prototype. Fourth, the cognitive models arise from a systematization of a large number of conventionalized linguistic expressions into conceptual categories (i.e., conceptual metonymies and metaphors and related concepts) and a further systematization of the conceptual categories into cognitive models. This suggests a principled methodology in the study of emotional concepts.

With these points in mind, we can now turn to some related issues.

Emotional Concepts and Emotional Experience

The discussion of the relationship between emotional concepts and emotional experience can be organized around three major issues. First, it has to be established that there is a positive correlation between concepts and experience (and action) in general. Second, we can address the issue of the extent to which emotional concepts are metaphorically constituted. Third, the issue of conceptual richness (and also of experiential richness) can be examined.

The first issue we need to get clear about is this: What is the relationship between the way we think (concepts) and the way we experience things and act? (Note that this is an issue different from, though related to, the issue discussed in chapter 3. There we dealt with the relationship between language on the one hand and thought and behavior on the other. Here the issue is the relationship between thought *and* behavior.) It has been assumed throughout this book that the former can influence the latter. This idea is, of course, not new. It has its origin in the same anthropological and philosophical traditions that were mentioned in chapter 3. The view that a particular conceptual system can determine the experience and behavior of the people who have that conceptual system was first proposed by the anthropological linguists Sapir (1949) and Whorf (1956). In philosophy, it is perhaps most clearly represented in the work of Winch (1958). He states the relationship between thought and experience succinctly: "The concepts we have settle for us the form of the experience we have of the world". (p. 15). It seems that this is especially so in the realm of human relations. For example, in her study of American marriage, Quinn (1987) found that differences in the metaphors in terms of which spouses view their marriage may be responsible for marital difficulties and may even lead to divorce. Similarly, it does not seem to be a far-fetched idea to believe that the kind of concept (including the kind of metaphors) one has of a particular emotion will have an effect on one's emotional experience and behavior associated with that emotion. We have already mentioned this issue in the discussion of love in the concluding section of chapter 10.

The issue of the metaphorical nature of emotional concepts was raised already in chapter 3, where it was suggested that the metaphors actually create (certain aspects of) our emotional concepts. And a similar idea came up in the previous section, where it was claimed that some metaphors map onto the cognitive models in a fairly direct way. Perhaps the best way to show that most emotional concepts are largely constituted by metaphor is to begin with cases where the conceptual metaphor is mapped onto cognitive models in a direct way. The WORTH or VALUE metaphor for self-esteem serves as a good example. One of the major metaphors for self-esteem is: SELF-ESTEEM IS A VALUE (A PERSON ESTIMATES HIMSELF TO HAVE). This metaphor is mapped onto the prototypical cognitive model of self-esteem in the form of the proposition: "S values himself highly." This is a fairly direct mapping from the source domain onto the target domain and onto the prototypical cognitive model associated with self-esteem. The notion of value in terms of which self-esteem is conceptualized also appears in the cognitive model characterizing self-esteem. This is one clear example that indicates that an emotional concept is in part constituted by metaphor. We can take another example from love. One of the propositions in the prototype of (romantic) love as given in chapter 3 is this: "I view myself and the other as forming a unity." This seems to be a direct carryover from one of the most central metaphors for love: LOVE IS A (PHYSICAL OR BIOLOGICAL) UNITY (OF TWO COMPLEMENTARY PARTS). In this case, it is the notion of the unity of two complementary parts in the physical or biological world that gets mapped directly onto a psychological domain via the metaphor. Thus, in both self-esteem and romantic love, a conceptual metaphor maps conceptual material directly onto the cognitive models associated with the two emotions. What is important for us about these cases here is that the metaphorical notions of value and unity could not be easily and readily replaced by nonmetaphorical equivalents. To the extent this is true, the two cases demonstrate that at least some parts of emotional concepts are, and cannot but inevitably be, metaphorical in nature. It is in this sense that I wish to claim that certain aspects of emotional concepts are actually *created* by metaphor.

The metaphorical creation of certain aspects of a concept assumes that the entities and/or predicates comprising a given aspect are not present in the target domain before the application of a given conceptual metaphor. This means that the predicates "value highly" in pride and "form a unity" in love do not exist in the concepts of pride and love independently of the VALUE and UNITY metaphors, respectively. These predicates in the two concepts are created when the metaphors are first applied. This gives the analysis an historical perspective. From this historical perspective, most, if not all, predicates characterizing emotional concepts are metaphorically created. Emotions are not really *entities* in the same way as a rock is; they are not really *forces* in the same way as the wind is; they cannot really *make* us do things in the same way as a superior can; they do not really involve a *desire* in the same way as an animal can have an appetite; and we cannot really *lose control* over them in the same way as we can lose control over our body when we slip and fall. But this is all possible in the metaphorically created world of human emotion. The various metaphors we have seen in the previous chapters seem to create these aspects of the concept. It might be suggested that from a contemporary (synchronic) perspective these aspects can nevertheless be considered literal. But can they? How could we explain or understand the above notions without recourse to metaphor? It is not likely that anyone would know the emotional meaning of such notions as "entity," "force," "desire" or "control" without also knowing, and thus having recourse to, the corresponding nonemotional meanings. More generally, could we understand the world in purely abstract terms, that is, without recourse to familiar and well-delineated concrete domains? Or, to put the same question differently, could we have a conceptual system that has no access to concrete but only of abstract domains? To the extent that this is not possible, I find these characteristics of our concept of emotion largely constituted by metaphor. And I think that the same considerations apply to the specific emotional concepts as well.

As we have seen, the metaphors contribute a great deal of content to emotional concepts. Together with what the metonymies and related concepts contribute, they make the conceptual content of emotion words extremely rich. The idea that emotional concepts have a rich conceptual content contrasts sharply with suggestions according to which emotional concepts can be captured in terms of a minimal number of sense components. In order to be able to appreciate the difference between the idea of conceptual richness for emotional categories and the suggestion that emotional categories are made up of a minimal number of sense components, let us take yet another minimal definition. Ortony, Clore and Foss (1987) define the best examples of emotion terms in the followng way: "The best examples of emotion terms appear to be those that

(a) refer to *internal, mental* conditions as opposed to physical or external ones,
(b) are clear cases of *states,*
(c) and have *affect* as opposed to behavior or cognition as a predominant (rather than incidental) referential focus" (p. 341).

Whether these components are appropriate or not is not at issue here. We should not worry about whether the component "affect as predominant referential focus" introduces circularity into the definition or not either. (The authors argue that it does not.) What is important, however, is the question of how much real world experience of emotion is captured by the concept as thus defined. It is obvious that the three components capture just a tiny fragment of the knowledge that is incorporated into the concept. In the previous chapter, we saw how much knowledge can be uncovered about emotion on the basis of the examination of ordinary language expressions. The conceptual richness of the prototypical cognitive model of emotion is completely absent from the above definition. Although minimal definitions may be undoubtedly correct as far as they go, they can only offer an impoverished view of the concept of emotion.

The conceptual richness associated with emotion has another aspect. Built into the various emotional concepts are concepts from outside the emotion domain, as strictly conceived. Most of these are brought in by way of the various metaphors and they play a significant role in our conception of emotion. One such concept is that of a person, which assumes an entire theory of personhood. According to our metaphorically based folk theory of personhood, a person is composed of several parts that interact with each other (cf. the chapter on the container metaphor of emotion). Our folk theory of emotion assumes a basic division between body and mind, where the location of the emotions is in the body. Emotion is an entity separate from the body and independent of the mind (the rational self). It involves another entity—desire. The mind responds to certain events in the outside world (and less prototypically inside the mind), which produces emotion. The emotion acts as a force on the self. It also causes the body to do certain things, which the mind is unable to control. Our folk theory of emotion involves at least this much about the notion of a person.

Another "outside" concept that we can mention here by way of illustration is that of balance. At a first glance the notion of balance has nothing to do with emotions. However, a closer look reveals that both the concept of emotion and most of the specific emotional concepts have this notion integrated in them. When we say of a person that he or she *overreacts* emotionally, we are talking about a lack of emotional balance. Balance can take a variety of forms. As we have seen, in the case of anger it takes the form of retributive justice, which is based on the principle of *an eye for an eye, a tooth for a tooth*. What makes the idea of *turning the other cheek* so cognitively salient (unless, of course, one is a sincere practicing Christian) is that it does not aim at redressing balance. Also, the prototype of pride was taken to be "balanced pride as an immediate response." "Balanced pride" meant that the amount of pride one shows has to be proportional to the value of the achievement one is proud of. And, as it was pointed out by Kövecses (1988) and many others, prototypical love involves the notion of mutuality and equal amount as regards the love given and received, which is yet another form of balance. What is particularly interesting about balance in our conception of emotion is that it is prototypical cases of emotions that typically involve balance. This should not be taken to mean that emotions cannot have unbalanced prototypes. They can, but these seem to be cases where the new (unbalanced) prototypes are defined in opposition to an already existing (balanced) prototype, as, say, for anger mentioned above. Thus, the notion of balance seems to be a crucial notion in our understanding and experience of emotion. It has to be also noted that balance in the emotional realm is a metaphorical extension of physical and/or gravitational balance (Johnson, 1987). This underscores the point that most of the emotion domain is metaphorically constituted.

We can conclude this discussion by observing that some concepts we would not normally associate with emotion play a very significant role in our conceptualization and experience of emotion and make emotional concepts all the more richer. But perhaps this should not be surprising if we view emotional concepts not as a domain rigidly distinct and separate from the rest of our conceptual system but as a domain that interacts with it in complex ways.

The Differentiation of Emotions by Metaphors and Related Concepts

As has been noted, the cognitive models are largely determined by the metonymies, metaphors, and related concepts. This means that it is largely these parts of a concept that differentiate between emotions on a conceptual level. The differentiation of emotional concepts in terms of metonymies will be dealt with separately in the next section. This section is concerned only with the metaphors and related concepts.

We can begin with the metaphors. It can be suggested that, in general, emotions are differentiated to a large degree in terms of conceptual metaphors. Anger was shown to be characterized mainly in terms of an elaborate CONTAINER metaphor. The conceptualization of anger as THE HEAT OF A FLUID IN A CONTAINER leads to all sorts of inferences. These inferences (or implications) lend anger a particular character that will differentiate it from other emotions. One aspect of that character is that anger is an "explosive" emotion that can produce sudden and uncontrolled aggressive actions.

Fear is distinguished from other emotions by virtue of a whole set of metaphors, including FEAR IS A VICIOUS ENEMY, FEAR IS A TORMENTOR, FEAR IS AN ILLNESS, and FEAR IS A SUPERNATURAL BEING. As was pointed out, these metaphors make fear an extremely unpleasant emotion. Indeed, to the extent that these metaphors are specific to fear, they will render fear the most negative and unpleasant emotion.

In the case of pride, we saw another version of the CONTAINER metaphor. According to this version, the proud person can *swell* and *burst* with pride. That is, this metaphor emphasizes an increase in the size of the container. This in turn corresponds to the notion of enhancement, which is one of the main characteristics of pride.

The metaphor that seems primarily to characterize respect is the VALUE metaphor. We saw how this metaphor pervades our thinking about respect. Not only is respect itself conceptualized as a (VALUABLE) COMMODITY, but also the object of respect. Moreover, in a related metaphor, people in general are understood as COMMODITIES.

Finally, the chapter on love showed that the object of love is seen in terms of metaphors that are likely to be unique to love (or some closely related concepts like affection or friendship). Furthermore, Kövecses (1988) points out that one of the major metaphors for love is the metaphor according to which LOVE IS A UNITY (OF TWO COMPLEMENTARY

PARTS). This metaphor is also likely to be unique to love (and some closely related emotions).

The general point I would like to make is that certain metaphors seem to be uniquely used in the conceptualization of certain emotional experiences, and consequently play a major role in differentiating among emotional concepts. However, this is not to deny that there many other metaphors that are common to many emotions (e.g., the NATURAL FORCE, INSANITY, OPPONENT, or RAPTURE metaphors).

The metaphors, at least in some cases, differentiate not only among emotional concepts but also among the main senses of a given emotional concept. The best example to illustrate this is the concept of pride. We saw that the general category of pride has at least the following major senses: "balanced pride as an immediate response," "self-esteem," "conceit," and "vanity." The first of these was analysed as the prototype of pride. Self-esteem was primarily described in terms of the OBJECT and VALUE metaphors. Characteristic of conceit are the metaphors THE CONCEITED PERSON IS UP/HIGH and THE CONCEITED PERSON IS BIG metaphors. And vanity is set apart from the other senses by means of the VANITY IS A (SENSUAL OR INDULGENT) PERSON metaphor. Thus, the various senses of an emotional concept seem to be differentiated in the same way as the various emotional concepts are. It remains to be seen how far this idea can be generalized with regard to other emotional concepts.

Related concepts seem to play a role similar to that played by conceptual metaphors. They can also be unique to particular emotions and thus set emotions apart. We can use pride and romantic love as examples. In the case of pride, joy is a concept inherent in pride. Love, on the other hand, seems to be characterized by such inherent concepts as affection, longing, interest, and intimacy (happiness, as we saw in chapter 8, plays a clearly different role in love). Thus, one of the things that distinguishes pride from love are the kinds of related concepts built into each emotion. Moreover, similarly to the metaphors, the various senses of emotional concepts can be partially distinguished in terms of related concepts. Pride can serve as an example again. Whereas pride is characterized by joy, conceit for example has self-love and superiority as its inherent concepts.

In summing up this section, it can perhaps be suggested that both metaphors and related concepts play a differentiating role in the domain of emotion. They can do this both on the inter-emotional and the inter-sense level.

The Differentiation of Emotions by Metonymies

As we have seen throughout this book, it is a major aspect of our folk theory of emotions that emotional states are viewed as being accompanied by or gaining expression through certain physiological and expressive responses (we have used the terms physiological effects and behavioral reactions, respectively, to cover the same things). Both the idea of "accompaniment" and "expression" can be thought of as effects being produced by a cause (i.e., by an emotion). Since we have in our conceptual system the very general metonymic principle EFFECT STANDS FOR CAUSE and since we see emotions (the cause) as producing certain responses (the effects), it is natural for us to have the more specific EMOTIONAL RESPONSES STAND FOR AN EMOTION metonymy.

The overall picture that has emerged as regards the metonymies is that, similarly to the metaphors and related concepts, the metonymies also differentiate among emotional concepts. However, in one respect the case of the metonymies is more important than that of the metaphors and related concepts, since it coincides with a hotly debated issue in emotion research; namely, the question of whether the emotions are characterized by specific response patterns or not. This gives special significance to our findings in this area. When we examine the issue, it seems that we should treat the metonymies denoting physiological responses separately from the metonymies denoting behavioral ones.

Let us first look at the behavioral (or expressive) responses. The analyses of the corresponding metonymies associated with the emotional concepts under study indicate that according to our folk models these emotions are characterized by differential response patterns. Thus, characteristic of anger are such expressive responses as violent frustrated behavior, insane behavior, aggressive verbal behavior, aggressive visual behavior; of fear, inability to think, inability to move, startle, flight; of love, intimate sexual behavior, physical closeness, sex, loving visual behavior (see Kövecses, 1988); of pride, erect posture, chest out, smiling, telling someone about an achievement; and of respect, various forms of politeness. These examples show a clear differentiation among these emotional concepts in terms of the metonymies referring to behavioral responses. At least in these cases, the emotions are characterized by uniquely different sets of behavioral responses.

The linguistic analysis of the metonymies relating to the physiological responses suggests a less clear picture. Anger was seen as being primarily associated with body heat, internal pressure (both blood and muscular), agitation, interference with accurate perception, and redness in the face. Fear is assumed to be accompanied by agitation, increase in heart rate, blood leaving the face, skin shrinking, and a drop in body temperature. As the prototype of romantic love as given in chapter 3 shows, romantic love is characterized by body heat, interference with accurate perception, blushing, and increase in heart rate. The prototype of pride seems to be characterized by the physiological responses redness in the face and increase in heart rate. Finally, respect was seen as lacking physiological responses altogether. Given these metonymies, we get a more complicated picture than in the case of behavioral responses. While it is true that, similarly to the behavioral responses, these responses are also differential, they are not differential in the same way. In the light of this analysis, we may hypothesize the following. First, there are several overlaps across the concepts. Anger shares with fear the physiological response agitation; common to anger and love is an increase in body heat; pride and anger share redness in the face; and so on. Thus, while at the expressive level most responses occur in only one concept (except, for example, such general responses like smiling and crying), at the physiological level it seems that most responses, like agitation, body heat, and redness in the face, occur in more than one case (except, for example, drop in body temperature, which occurs only in fear. However, it seems reasonable to suppose that this response also occurs and gets linguistically manifested in other emotional concepts that we have not investigated here.) Second, a special case of the previous point is when a physiological response occurs in not just some but in a large number of emotional concepts. An example that may have this status is increase in heart rate, which occurs in fear, love, and pride and which can perhaps be assumed to occur in several other emotional concepts (like joy). Third, some emotional concepts may lack physiological responses altogether (like respect), which does not seem to be the case for behavioral responses (where all the concepts investigated involve some forms of behavioral responses). Fourth, there seems to be a positive correlation between the prototypicality of an emotional concept and the number of physiological responses associated with emotional concepts. Thus, anger, fear, and love, which are all prototypical emotional concepts, are assumed to be accompanied by more physiological responses than pride is, and pride in turn by more than respect is. The same does not seem to hold for behavioral responses. For example, pride involves more of these than anger. In sum, our general conclusion can be that, in cases where there are physiological responses at all, these responses also differentiate among emotional concepts, but the responses in terms of which this is done are not uniquely characteristic of a particular concept (i.e., there are several overlaps) and there are more of them in the prototypical than in the less prototypical cases.

It should be emphasized, however, that these are mere hypotheses. First of all, more emotional concepts have to be examined, and second, more detailed and thorough linguistic analyses are needed. Until then, these results are hardly more than conjectures.

But let us assume for a moment that these conclusions have some validity. We can then ask: How do they compare with the results obtained by others? I believe that the analysis of the metonymies (of both kinds) provides overwhelming evidence for the view that, in general, the various emotions have their typical response patterns. However, as regards the physiological responses, it can be suggested that despite, or along with, the differentiation there is some indication for a generalized arousal as well. This is especially clear in the many and extensive overlaps in the physiological responses emphasized in the first and second points above. Thus, paradoxically, the results concerning the physiological responses support the views of both those scholars who maintain that there is differential response patterning in emotion and, to a lesser degree, those who claim that emotions are characterized by a state of generalized (physiological) arousal. These findings parallel closely those of Rimé and Giovannini (1986), obtained with a methodology based on self-report questionnaires.

It should be stressed at this point that I regard the responses that have been investigated in this study as "merely" elements of a folk theory of emotion. This follows from the methodology of using (conventionalized) language to uncover something about the structure and content of emotional concepts. However, it seems unlikely that there is nothing real about the differential physiological responses we have uncovered. As Klaus R. Scherer puts it: "It is difficult to believe that there is no such differentiation at all and that people are generally wrong in noticing what is going on inside their body" (Scherer, et al. 1986, p. 184). This idea gained some support experimentally in the results of the Ekman group that was discussed in the chapter on fear.

As with the metaphors and related concepts, the metonymies can also distinguish among various forms of the same emotion. For illustration, we can use pride again. As was observed in the chapter on pride, the prototype of this emotion ("balanced pride as an immediate response") was seen as being associated by such behavioral reactions as erect posture, chest out, and telling someone about an achievement. In contrast to this, another member of the pride category, conceit, was characterized by such reactions as head held unnaturally high, chest unnaturally thrust out, and boasting. As was pointed out, these reactions can be regarded as more intense versions of the reactions associated with "balanced pride as an immediate response." This suggests that one way in which the two forms of pride differ from each other is intensity as it is expressed by behavioral reactions. It should be stressed, of course, that this is not the only way in which these two forms of pride are different. More generally, when I said in this section that two emotional concepts or two senses of the same emotional concept can be distinguished in terms of metonymies, I meant that a class of metonymies is just one of the devices that can distinguish either among emotional concepts or among senses of the same concept. In addition to the metonymies, there can be, and usually there are, several other devices, including metaphors, that can serve this purpose.

The Folk Model of Emotion and the "State versus Disposition Paradigm" Issue

It has often been observed (for example, by Alston, 1967, and W. Lyons, 1980) that the majority of scholars consider occurrent emotional states as more paradigmatic of emotion than dispositions. But there is also a rival camp. Other scholars argue for a dispositional paradigm; that is, they regard dispositions as more representative of the emotion category than states. This gives us a problem. The question is whether the approach employed in this book can in any way contribute to the resolution of this dilemma.

The prototypic model of emotion that has emerged from the various metaphors and metonymies examined in chapters 9 and 10 is one which can be viewed both as a state and an event. Thus, it can be called a "state-event" paradigm. The state aspect of the model is manifest in stage two, where the particular feelings, cognitions, and physiological and expressive responses constitute a state a person can be "in." The event aspect is most clear in that the model is a scenario, an unfolding story with a beginning and an end. The story unfolds quickly and ends quickly. As it unfolds it produces and envelopes the state. The scenario consists of stages that make up the main chunks of the story. The stages follow a temporal and causal order. For example, stage one both precedes and brings about stage two (the emotional state).

However, the state-event prototype may be actualized very rarely. We may not often experience anger or fear in the way it is depicted in their respective prototypes. There may not be involvement of the physiology, there may not be control, and there may not be fight or flight. It may be the case that a dispositional prototype is much more frequent and that we are more often angry or afraid without being physiologically aroused, without having to control our emotions, and without fight or flight. Nevertheless, both types of anger and fear would be prototypical or paradigmatic of anger and fear. In other words, emotions may have more than one prototype. As has been noted in the chapter on fear, prototypicality is a surface phenomenon that may have a variety of sources. Members of a category can be taken to be representative of the category because they are ideal cases, they are salient, they are common, they are stereotypes, they are paragons, and so on (see Lakoff, 1987). Applying this to the emotions, it can be suggested that the state-event model may be considered prototypical because it constitutes a case that is more salient than the one based on commonness. Although it may seldom be actualized in practice, it reflects a dramatic or extreme form of emotion. By contrast, the dispositional paradigm would seem to receive its prototypicality from the fact (if indeed it is a fact) that it is very common. If a member of a category is very common, then no matter how nonsalient it is it can come to represent the category. This may be the case with the dispositional paradigm for emotion. It may be so common that it can be used as a prototype.

But I still have not tried to account for why the majority of scholars consider emotional states as more prototypic of emotion than dispositions. What has been explained so far is only that both states and dispositions can be prototypic. Why are states more prototypic of emotion than dispositions in most expert theories of emotion? I think the answer has in part to do with the state-event model of emotion sketched in the previous chapter. That model represents our folk understanding of emotion. It is a model we unconsciously learn when we internalize culture through, say, the English language. Hence it is deeply entrenched in us. The occurrent state model offered by many scholars as the paradigm of emotion is very close, or in any case closer than the dispositional paradigm, to the language-based state-event model that represents "only" a folk theory. I propose that it is this that makes the occurrent state paradigm scientific "common sense." The folk theory motivates or justifies the scientific theory. It seems, and this is not surprising, that even when we construct scientific theories we cannot "step over" our own conceptual shadow.

Incidentally, we might further ask a more general question: But then why is the state-event model more prototypic than a dispositional one in our *folk understanding* of the world? My guess is that the answer to this question has to do with sources of prototypicality mentioned above. As we have seen, the state-event model we have given is a salient example of the category and the dispositional model (which has not been made explicit) is, or may be a very common case. It seems to me that, in general, if a category has two prototypes such that one is based on salience and the other on commonness the salient example will be considered as a better example, hence more prototypic, of the category than the one based on commonness. But this again is a hypothetical claim which needs to be verified experimentally.

Core Meaning versus Cognitive Models of Emotion

The discussion so far enables us to revise our arguments for a view of meaning that rejects the "core vs. periphery" distinction. (The distinction was dealt with in chapters 2 and 3.) Perhaps the most important of these is that in most of the cases we have investigated we have not found essential properties that would define a core. This means that emotion categories are not defined in terms of necessary and sufficient conditions. If no core can be isolated in most emotion categories, then the "core versus periphery" distinction ceases to be a valid distinction in most cases. Instead of a set of necessary and sufficient conditions (i.e., the minimal definitions of core meaning), emotion categories seem to be defined by prototypes, or idealized cases. These prototypes can be represented in terms of cognitive models, which, in the main, arise from conceptual metonymies, conceptual metaphors, and related concepts. Cognitive models are composed of neither a minimal nor an infinite set of propositions. Their number is determined by our folk understandings of emotion categories as reflected in the conventionalized language people commonly use to talk about their emotional experiences. A major advantage of conceiving of emotion concepts as prototypical cognitive models is that the prototypical models capture a large number and perhaps the (culturally) most important of our emotional experiences. This is something that minimal definitions of emotion categories cannot do. Associated with each emotion category is an ontology. Ontologies provide a list of all the entities and predicates (properties and relations) out of which the propositions that make up cognitive models can be formed. The propositions occur in what we have called "stages" and the stages follow each other in some order (usually temporal and causal). These characteristics, contrary to the assumptions of the classical view, lend cognitive models (including what could traditionally be considered peripheral attributes) a great deal of structure. Moreover, cognitive models can be arrived at in a systematic way: the language we use to talk about the emotions comes in three conceptually distinct systems—the metaphors, metonymies, and related concepts. These map their contents onto the cognitive models, which appear to represent or embody our culturally defined emotion concepts.

Concluding Remarks

We began with a critique of previous approaches to emotional meaning. This criticism led us to a positive program in the study of emotional concepts. As we look back, I would like to believe that this program has been successfully realized. In particular, this means the following: First, there was a shift in perspective. Instead of trying to study the entire system of emotion categories, we studied particular emotion categories in great detail. This has given us an idea of the complexity of the *structure* of individual emotional concepts and allows us to see the many links with which these concepts function within a larger conceptual system. Second, for several reasons we decided to give up on the idea that it is possible and useful to conceive of emotional meaning as core meaning. This has had a liberating effect concerning the way we see the *contents* of emotional concepts. Emotional concepts can now be seen as elaborate and rich structures (cognitive models) that are largely the products of various cognitive processes, including metaphor and metonymy. A chief advantage of this view is that a better fit can be ensured between the way we conceptualize emotions, on the one hand, and what we experience when in some emotional state, on the other. Third, a new *method* for the study of emotion categories was worked out. This method is based on the conventionalized language people use for the purposes of everyday life. The study of this language has the advantage that it is both objective in that it is "outside" both the researcher and the individual speaker (i.e., it does not uniquely belong to particular speakers) *and* subjective in that it reflects the presumably most common and important emotional experiences (of a community of individual speakers). Because of its objective nature in the above sense, it becomes possible to study cognitively rich and complex emotional experiences in an objective way.

However, the work that has been done so far is only the beginning. There is a lot more to be done. There is a large number of other emotions that await analysis along the same lines. Furthermore, emotional concepts as analyzed here on the basis of the English language can be analyzed in similar ways in other languages (as was begun by King, 1989). The comparisons would no doubt be instructive. Finally, our entire psychological makeup, including, for example, memory, attention, and perception, could be investigated using the methodology that has been proposed. Again, the end results would be exciting, because they would reveal our folk models of the psychological functioning of human beings and because some possibly useful comparisons with the corresponding expert theories could be made. All of these investigations might be used to the benefit of both the relevant expert theories and a more profound understanding of the way we see ourselves as functioning emotionally or otherwise.

References

Alston, W.P. (1965). Expressing. In M. Black (Ed), *Philosophy in America*. London: George Allen and Unwin.

Alston, W.P. (1967). Emotion and feeling. In P. Edwards (Ed.). *The encyclopedia of philosophy* (Vol. 2). New York: Macmillan and The Free Press.

Armstrong, S.L., Gleitman, L., & Gleitman, H. (1983). What some concepts might not be. *Cognition 13*. 263–308.

Arnold, B. (1960). *Emotion and personality*. (2 vols). New York: Columbia University Press.

Austin, J.L. (1961). *Philosophical papers*. Oxford: Oxford University Press.

Averill, J.R. (1974). An analysis of psychophysiological symbolism and its influence on theories of emotion. *Journal for the Theory of Social Behavior. 4,* 147–190.

Averill, J.R. (1980 a). On the paucity of positive emotions. In K.R. Blankstein, P. Pliner, & J. Polivy (Eds.), *Assessment and modification of emotional behavior* (pp. 7–45). New York: Plenum Press.

Averill, J.R. (1980 b). The emotions. In E. Staub (Ed.), *Personality: basic aspects and current research* (pp. 133–199). Englewood Cliffs, NJ: Prentice Hall.

Averill, J.R. (in press). Inner feelings, works of the flesh, the beast within, diseases of the mind, driving force, and putting on a show: Six metaphors of emotion and their theoretical extensions. In D. Leary (Ed.), *Metaphor in the history of psychology*. (Cambridge: Cambridge Unviersity Press.

Averill, J.R., & Boothroyd, P. (1977). On falling in love in conformance with the romantic ideal. *Motivation and Emotion, 1,* 235–247.

Averill, J.R., Catlin, G., & Chon, K.K. (in press). *Rules of Hope*. New York: Springer-Verlag.

Ax, A.F. (1953). The physiological differentiation between fear and anger in humans. *Psychosomatic Medicine, 5,* 433–442.

Barcelona Sanchez, A. (1985). On the concept of depression in American English: A cognitive approach. Unpublished manuscript.

Berlin, B., & Kay, P. (1969). *Basic color terms: Their universality and evolution*. Berkeley: University of California Press.

Branden, N. (1983). *The psychology of romantic love*. New York: Bantam.

Briggs, J.L. (1970). *Never in anger: Portrait of an Eskimo family*. Cambridge: Harvard University Press.

Brown, J.F. (1982). *Affectivity: Its language and meaning*. University Press of America.

Calhoun, C., & Solomon, R. (Eds.). (1984). *What is an emotion?* New York: Oxford University Press.

D'Andrade, R. (1987). A folk model of the mind. In Holland & Quinn (eds.) *Cultural models in language and thought*. (pp. 112–148). New York: Cambridge University Press.

Darwin, C. (1965). *The expression of the emotions in man and animals*. Chicago: University of Chicago Press. (Originally published, 1872).

Davitz, J. (1969). *The language of emotion*. New York: Academic Press.

De Rivera, J. (1977). *A structural theory of the emotions*. New York: International Universities Press.

De Rivera, J. (1985). Biological necessity, emotional transformation, and personal value. In S. Koch & D.E. Leary (Eds.), *A century of psychology as science*. New York: McGraw-Hill.

De Rivera, J., & Grinkis, C. (1986). Emotions as social relationships. *Motivation and Emotion, 10,* 351–369.

De Sousa, R. (1980). The rationality of emotions. In A.O. Rorty (Ed.), *Explaining emotions* (pp. 127–151). Berkeley: University of California Press.

Dil, A. (Ed.). (1980). *Language and cultural description: Essays by Charles O. Frake*. Stanford: Stanford University Press.

Duck, S., & Pond, K. (1988). Friends Romans countrymen, lend me your introspections: Rhetoric and reality in personal relationships. In C. Hendrick (Ed.), *Review of Social Behavior and Personality, 10: Close Relationships*. SAGE: Newbury Park.

Durkheim, E. (1915). The elementary forms of religious experience (J.W. Swain, Trans.). New York: Macmillan.

Ekman, P. (1971). Universals and cultural differences in facial expressions of emotions. *Nebraska Symposium on Motivation*. Lincoln: University of Nebraska Press.

Ekman, P., & Friesen, W.V. (1975). *Unmasking the face*. Englewood Cliffs, NJ: Prentice Hall.

Ekman, P., Friesen, W.V., & Ellsworth, P.C. (1972). *Emotion in the human face*. Elmsford, NY: Pergamon Press.

Ekman, P., Levenson, R.W., & Friesen, W.V. (1983). Autonomic nervous system activity distinguishes among emotions. *Science, 221* (No. 4515), 1208–1210.

Fehr, B., & Russell, J.A. (1984). Concept of emotion viewed from a prototype perspective. *Journal of Experimental Psychology: General, 113,* 464–486.

Fehr, B., Russell, J.A., & Ward, L.M. (1982). Prototypicality of emotions: A reaction time study. *Bulletin of the Psychonomic Society, 20,* 253–254.

Fillenbaum, S., & Rapoport, A. (1970). Emotion names. In *Studies in the Subjective Lexicon* (pp. 100–124). New York: Academic Press.

Fillmore, C. (1975). An alternative to checklist theories of meaning. In *Proceedings of the First Annual Meeting of the Berkeley Linguistic Society*. Berkeley: Berkeley Linguistics Society.

Fillmore, C. (1982). Frame semantics. In Linguistic Society of Korea (Ed.), *Linguistics in the morning calm* (pp. 111–138). Seoul: Hanshin.

Frijda, N. (1986). *Emotion*. Cambridge: Cambridge University Press.

Geertz, H. (1959). The Vocabulary of emotion. *Psychiatry, 22.*

Gentner, D., & Grudin, J. (1985). The evolution of mental metaphors in psychology: A 90-year retrospective. *American Psychologist, 40,* 181–192.

Harré, R. (Ed.). (1986). *The social construction of emotion.* Oxford: Basil Blackwell.

Hillman, J. (1962). *Emotion: A comprehensive phenomenology of theories and their meanings for therapy.* London: Routledge and Kegan Paul.

Holland, D., & Quinn, N. (Eds.). (1987). *Cultural models in language and thought.* New York: Cambridge University Press.

Izard, C.E. (1977). *Human emotions.* New York: Plenum Press.

James, W. (1890). *The principles of psychology.* (2 vols.). New York: Henry Holt.

Johnson, M. (1987). *The body in the mind. The bodily basis of meaning, imagination, and reason.* Chicago: Chicago University Press.

King, B. (1989). *The conceptual structure of emotional experience in Chinese.* Unpublished Ph.D. dissertation. Ohio State University.

Kövecses, Z. (1986). *Metaphors of anger, pride and love: A lexical approach to the structure of concepts.* Amsterdam: John Benjamins.

Kövecses, Z. (1988). *The language of love. The semantics of passion in conversational English.* Lewisburg, PA: Bucknell University Press.

Kövecses, Z. (1989). Minimal and full definitions of meaning. *Symposium on Cognitive Linguistics,* Series A, No. 252. Duisburg, Germany: Linguistic Agency University of Duisburg.

Labov, W. (1973). The boundaries of words and their meanings. In J. Fishman (Ed.), *New Ways of analyzing variation in English* (pp. 340–373). Washington, DC: Georgetown University Press.

Labov, W., & Fanshell, D. (1977). *Therapeutic discourse: Psychotherapy as conversation.* New York: Academic Press.

Lacey, J.I. (1967). Somatic response patterning and stress. Some revisions of activation theory. In M.H. Appley & R. Trumball (Eds.), *Physiological stress: Issues and research.* New York: Appleton Century Crofts.

Lakoff, G. (1972). Hedges: A study in meaning criteria and the logic of fuzzy concepts. In *Papers from the Eighth Regional Meeting of the Chicago Linguistic Society* (pp. 183–228). Chicago: Chicago Linguistic Society.

Lakoff, G. (1987). *Women, fire and dangerous things. What categories reveal about the mind.* Chicago: Chicago University Press.

Lakoff, G., & Johnson, M. (1980). *Metaphors we live by.* Chicago: Chicago University Press.

Lakoff, G., & Kövecses, Z. (1983). The cognitive model of anger inherent in American English. *Berkeley Cognitive Science Report No. 10.* Berkeley: University of California. (Also appeared in a slightly different form in Kövecses 1986, Holland & Quinn (Eds.) 1987, and Lakoff 1987.)

La Rochefoucauld. (1959). *Maxims* (L. Tancock, Trans.). Hammondsworth, England: Penguin. (Original work published 1665).

Lazarus, R.S. (1984). On the primacy of cognition. *American Psychologist, 39,* 124–129.

Leech, G. (1982). *Semantics.* Hammondsworth, England: Penguin.

Leeper, R.W. (1970). The motivational and perceptual properties of emotions as indicating their fundamental character and role. In M.B. Arnold (Ed.), *Feelings and emotions: The Loyola symposium.* New York: Academic Press.

Lutz, C. (1980). Emotion words in cultural context: An Ifalukian example. Paper read at the *9th Annual Meeting of the Society for Cross-cultural Research*, Philadelphia, PA.
Lutz, C. (1986). Emotion, thought, and estrangement: Emotion as a cultural category. *Cultural Anthropology, 1,* 287–309.
Lutz, C. (1987). Goals, events, and understanding in Ifaluk emotion theory. In D. Holland & N. Quinn, *Cultural models in language and thought* (pp. 290–312). Cambridge: Cambridge University Press.
Lutz, C. (1988). *Unnatural emotions: Everyday sentiments on a Micronesian atoll and their challenge to Western theory.* University of Chicago Press.
Lyons, W. (1980). *Emotion.* Cambridge: Cambridge University Press.
Mandler, G. (1984). *Mind and body: Psychology of emotion and stress.* New York: Norton.
Newton-Smith, W. (1973). A conceptual investigation of love. In A. Montefiori (Ed.), *Philosophy and personal relations* (pp. 113–136). Montreal: McGill-Queen's University Press.
Ogden, C.K., & Richards, I.A. (1923). *The meaning of meaning.* London: Routledge and Kegan Paul.
Ortony, A. (1988). Are emotion metaphors conceptual or lexical? *Cognition and Emotion, 2,* 95–103.
Ortony, A., Clore, G.L., & Foss, M.A. (1987). The referential structure of the affective lexicon. *Cognitive Science, 11,* 341–364.
Plutchik, R. (1980). *Emotion: A psychoevolutionary synthesis.* New York: Harper & Row.
Quinn, N. (1987). Convergent evidence for a cultural model of American marriage. In D. Holland & N. Quinn (Eds.), *Cultural models in Language and Thought* (pp. 173–192). Cambridge: Cambridge University Press.
Rapaport, D. (1967). *The collected papers of David Rapaport.* Merton Gill (Ed.). New York: Basic Books.
Reddy, M. (1979). The conduit metaphor. In A. Ortony (Ed.), *Metaphor and Thought* (pp. 284–324). Cambridge: Cambridge University Press.
Rimé, B., & Giovannini, D. (1986). The physiological patterns of reported emotional states. In K.R. Scherer, H.G. Wallbott, & A.B. Summerfield (Eds.), *Experiencing Emotion: A cross-cultural study.* Cambridge: Cambridge University Press and Paris: Editions de la Masion des Sciences de l'Homme.
Roedigger III, H.L. (1980). Memory metaphors in cognitive psychology. *Memory and Cognition,* 8, 231–246.
Rosaldo, M. (1980). *Knowledge and passion: Ilongot notions of self and social life.* Cambridge: Cambridge University Press.
Rosch, E. (1973). Natural categories. *Cognitive Psychology, 4,* 328–350.
Rosch, E. (1975). Cognitive reference points. *Cognitive Psychology, 7,* 532–547.
Rosch, E. (1977). Human categorization. In N. Warren (Ed.), *Studies in cross-cultural psychology.* London: Academic Press.
Rosch, E., & Mervis, C. (1975). Family resemblances: Studies in the internal structure of categories. *Cognitive Psychology, 7,* 573–605.
Ryle, G. (1949). *The concept of mind.* London: Hutchinson.
Sapir, E. (1949). *Selected writings in language, culture, and personality* (D.G. Manderbaum, Ed.) Berkeley: University of California Press.

Sartre, J.P. (1948). *The emotions: Outline of a theory* (B. Frechtman, Trans). New York: Philosophical Library.

Schachter, S. (1971). *Emotion, obesity, and crime*. New York: Academic Press.

Schachter, S., & Singer, J. (1962). Cognitive, social and physiological determinants of emotional states. *Psychological Review, 69,* 379–399.

Schafer, R. (1976). *A new language for psychoanalysis*. New Haven: Yale University Press.

Scherer, K.R., Wallbott, H.G., & Summerfield, A.B. (1986). *Experiencing emotion: A cross-cultural study*. Cambridge: Cambridge University Press and Paris: Editions de la Maison des Sciences de l'Homme.

Shaver, P., Schwartz, J., Kirson, D., & O'Connor, C. (1987). Emotion knowledge: Further exploration of a prototype approach. *Journal of Personality and Social Psychology, 52,* 1061–1086.

Smith, C.A., & Ellsworth, P.C. (1985). Patterns of cognitive appraisal in emotion. *Journal of Personality and Social Psychology, 48,* 813–838.

Smith, E.F., & Medin, D.E. (1981). *Concepts and categories*. Cambridge: Harvard University Press.

Solomon, R. (1976). *The passions*. New York: Doubleday Anchor.

Solomon, R. (1981). *Love: Emotion, myth, and metaphor*. New York: Doubleday Anchor.

Solomon, R. (1988). *About love: Reinventing romance for our times*. New York: Simon & Schuster.

Sperling, A. (1984). *Psychology made simple*. London: Heinemann.

Steck, L., Levitan, D., McLane, D., & Kelley, H.H. (1982). Care, need and a conception of love. *Journal of Personality and Social Psychology, 43,* 481–491.

Storm, C., & Storm, T. (1987). A taxonomic study of the vocabulary of emotions. *Journal of Personality and Social Psychology, 53,* 805–816.

Sweetser, E.E. (1984). *Semantic structure and semantic change*. Unpublished doctoral dissertation, University of California, Berkeley.

Talmy, L. (1985). Force dynamics in language and thought. In *Papers from the Parasession on Causatives and Agentivity*. Chicago: Chicago Linguistic Society.

Taylor, G. (1979). Love. In T. Honderich & M. Burnyeat (Eds.), *Philosophy as it is* (pp. 165–182). Hammondsworth: Penguin.

Verschueren, J. (1985). *What people say they do with words: Prolegomena to an empirical-conceptual approach to linguistic action*. Norwood, NJ: Ablex Publishing.

Wallace, A.F.C., & Carson, M.T. (1973). Sharing and diversity in emotion terminology. *Ethos 1,* 1–29.

Wenger, M.A. (1950). Emotions as visceral action: An extension of Lange's theory. In M.L. Reymert (Ed.), *Feelings and Emotions: The Mooseheart-Chicago Symposium* (pp. 3–10). New York: McGraw-Hill.

White, G.M. (1979). "Some social uses of emotion language: A Melanesian example." Paper read at the *78th Annual Meetings of the American Anthropological Association*. Cincinnati, OH.

Whorf, B.L. (1956). *Language, thought and reality: Selected writings of Benjamin Lee Whorf* (J.B. Carroll, Ed.). New York: Wiley.

Wierzbicka, A. (1972). Emotions. In *Semantic primitives* (pp. 57–70). Frankfurt/M: Atheneum Verlag.

Winch, P. (1958). *The idea of a social science and its relation to philosophy*. London: Routledge and Kegan Paul.
Wittgenstein, L. (1953). *Philosophical investigations*. New York: Macmillan.
Wolf, S., & Wolff, H.G. (1947). *Human gastric functions*. New York: Oxford University Press.
Young, P.T. (1943). *Emotion in man and animal*. New York: Wiley.
Zajonc, R.B. (1984). On the primacy of affect. *American Psychologist, 39*, 117–123.

General Index

Index of Metaphors and Metonymies